The Dance Claimed Me

The Dance Claimed Me

A Biography of Pearl Primus

Peggy and Murray Schwartz

Yale UNIVERSITY PRESS
New Haven & London

This publication was supported, in part, by funds from the Book Publication
Subvention Program of the University of Massachusetts Amherst.

Yale University Press books may be purchased in quantity for educational,
business, or promotional use. For information, please e-mail sales.press@yale.edu
(U.S. office) or sales@yaleup.co.uk (U.K. office).

"On Leaping and Shouting," by Langston Hughes, July 3, 1943.
Courtesy of the *Chicago Defender*.

"Dreams," from *The Collected Poems of Langston Hughes,* by Langston Hughes,
edited by Arnold Rampersad with David Roessel, Associate Editor, copyright © 1994
by the Estate of Langston Hughes. Used by permission of Alfred A. Knopf,
a division of Random House, Inc.

Dunbar, Paul Laurence. Edited by Joanne M. Braxton. *The Collected Poetry of
Paul Laurence Dunbar,* page 71. © 1993 by the Rector and Visitors of the
University of Virginia. Reprinted by permission of the University of Virginia Press.

Designed by Mary Valencia.
Set in Monotype Bulmer type by Duke & Company, Devon, Pennsylvania.
Printed in the United States of America.

Library of Congress Cataloging-in-Publication Data
Schwartz, Peggy.
The dance claimed me : a biography of Pearl Primus / Peggy and Murray Schwartz.
    p.   cm.
Includes bibliographical references and index.
ISBN 978-0-300-15534-1 (hardback)
1. Primus, Pearl. 2. Dancers—United States—Biography. 3. African American dancers—Biography.
4. Choreographers—United States—Biography. 5. African American dance—History. I. Schwartz,
Murray. II. Title.
GV1785.P73S38 2011
792.802'8092—dc22
[B]
2010049533

A catalogue record for this book is available from the British Library.

This paper meets the requirements of ANSI/NISO Z39.48-1992 (Permanence of Paper).

10 9 8 7 6 5 4 3 2 1

For
Celia Renner Topf
and
Lena Baruch Schwartz
With Pearl, among the ancestors

The quest to discover another's psyche, to absorb another's motives as deeply as your own is a lover's quest. But the search for facts, for places, names, influential events, important conversations and correspondences, political circumstances—all this amount to nothing if you can't find the assumption your subject lives by.

—Ann Michaels, *Fugitive Pieces*

My career has been a quest . . . a search for roots. The journey has taken me deep into the cultures of many people in many countries of the world.

Dance has been my vehicle. Dance has been my language, my strength. In the dance I have confided my most secret thoughts and shared the inner music of all mankind. I have danced across mountains and deserts, ancient rivers and oceans and slipped through the boundaries of time and space.

Dance has been my freedom and my world. It has enabled me to go around, scale, bore through, batter down or ignore visible and invisible social and economic walls.

Dance is my medicine. It is the scream which eases for awhile the terrible frustration common to all human beings who, because of race, creed or color, are "invisible." Dance is the fist with which I fight the sickening ignorance of prejudice. It is the veiled contempt I feel for those who patronize with false smiles, handouts, empty promises, insincere compliments. Instead of growing twisted like a gnarled tree inside myself, I am able to dance out my anger and my tears.

Dance has been my teacher, ever patiently revealing to me the dignity, beauty and strength in the cultural heritage of my people as a vital part of the great heritage of *all* mankind.

I dance not to entertain but to help people better understand each other. Because through dance I have experienced the wordless joy of freedom. I seek it more fully now for my people and for *all* people everywhere.

—Pearl Primus, 1968

Contents

Photo gallery appears between page 132 and page 133

The Dance Claimed Me

Introduction

OPEN ANY MAJOR BOOK of twentieth-century American dance history and you will encounter the name Pearl Primus and, most likely, an exuberant image of a powerful, leaping body. The recipient of the National Medal of the Arts, Pearl was a dancer, anthropologist, and educator who had a significant impact on American arts and culture in the twentieth century. She danced to protest the conditions of African Americans, brought the ancient dances of Africa to America, and, controversially, carried her knowledge of dance, music, theater, anthropology, and education to Africa itself. Yet the full story of her creative life and teaching, which spanned decades, continents, and many cultures, has not been told.[1]

"In some ways Primus' career seems enigmatic," wrote dance historian John Perpener. "At the height of her concert appearances, she was considered one of the most exciting dancers of her time. Her dynamism, dramatic flair, and kinetic magnetism were incomparable."[2] Yet she did not create a continuing school or style, and her journey was as much a process of self-definition as it was a quest for cultural retrieval. Her uniqueness is elusive because Pearl Primus lived and worked among several worlds, each only partially known to the others.

Sketched in barest of outlines, indicating her meteoric career in dance, with emphasis on her early years, existing accounts only gesture toward her personal struggles and the scope of her contributions to the arts and education. A shining light in the field of dance, this stocky, strong, beautiful, and dark-skinned woman also came to represent the pride of black America and the dignity of Africa for audiences throughout the Western world. "Her transformation absorbed the dance and went beyond it as the African spirit

1

became a part of Pearl," stated dance historian Joe Nash, one of Pearl's life-long friends. Judith Jamison, herself a powerful force in American dance, said of Pearl's place in the dance pantheon:

> She was a queen on stage, absolutely a different looking kind of queen. She created a niche for anyone following her that looked like she looked, that danced like she danced . . . that lectured the way she lectured, that did anthropology the way she did. She opened a window that had been shut, and that puts her in a spotlight of dance history . . . because she was looking at it from another perspective. And, she was a brilliant dancer. My God, she was so beautiful.

How Pearl Primus "went beyond" to create "another perspective" is the subject of this biography.

Pearl Primus blazed onto the dance scene in New York in 1943 with stunning dances of social commentary and protest. Born in Trinidad in 1919 and raised in the United States, she had initially aspired to be a physician but was turned away from laboratory jobs because of her race. She found dance work in a National Youth Administration project, and, as she put it, "the dance claimed me."[3]

Pearl's immigrant, working class family was part of the first large wave of New York–bound West Indians that peaked in the 1920s. She grew up in New York but found her spiritual roots, her ancestral home, on a trip to Africa in 1948–49, supported by the last and largest fellowship awarded by the Julius Rosenwald Foundation. Before her trip, she wrote prophetically, "I shall go into the land of my forefathers. My heart will be filled with the music and drums and my soul will dance with the people." From then on, Africa formed the core of her identity.

Before her African journey, Pearl had emerged not only as a performer but also as a member of the radical group of dancers who founded the New Dance Group. She was the first black scholarship student and very quickly became a teacher. Here, among (at first, all-white) women for whom the motto was "Dance is a Weapon," she created such powerful dances of social protest that she was featured at the first Negro Freedom Rally at Madison Square Garden in 1943, at American Youth for Democracy rallies, and at other political actions calling for greater democracy and equality for black people and all workers. She absorbed the teachings of the earliest pioneers of modern dance, studying with Martha Graham and Doris Humphrey, among others. As with Paul Robeson, who became her great supporter, Pearl's political activism and travels in the Jim Crow South triggered an extensive FBI investigation, which went on for years. She nevertheless continued her constant struggle against the forces of racism in dance, theater, and society at large.

Pearl's first trip to Africa was transformative. She was adopted by many tribes, given the name "Omowale"—or "Child Returned Home," by the revered Oni of Ife, spiritual leader of the Yoruba people—and among the Watusi was declared by the Chief to be a man so that she could be taught the dances performed only by the men of the tribe. "Africans recognized her as the embodiment of a spirit that had returned to Africa. They couldn't believe that an American could capture the feeling of the authentic African. And Pearl did," Joe Nash said. She became a true link to the griot of Africa. "You become the story, your whole personality is taken over by the content to be communicated. She told the African stories with every part of her body," Joe continued.

But this is not simply the story of "Saint Pearl," for she was a complex, dynamic woman. Nor do we claim that her role in bringing African dance to the American concert stage was singular. Even before her leap onto the stage followed by her African journey, black dancers were beginning to form companies and break into the world of concert dance, resisting an attitude among some blacks as well as whites that their dances were shamefully "primitive." Eugene Von Grona, a German refugee, brought the American Negro Ballet to the Lafayette Theater in Harlem in 1937; the African dancer Asadata Dafora's African Dance Theater was performing in New York in the late 1930s; Katherine Dunham's first full-length ballet, *L'Ag'Ya*, was performed in 1938; Beryl McBurnie, performing as Belle Rosette from Trinidad, performed *Antilliana* in 1941. Indeed, Pearl performed with McBurnie in 1942 and with Dafora at Carnegie Hall in 1943. She and Dafora were great friends, and she

3

visited his people in West Africa. What she valued most was his enlivening authenticity.

In her family relationships and her work, we see her leading a transcultural life, navigating among worlds. The relations and tensions between blacks and Jews were prominent facets of her cultural landscape, reflective of her upbringing—she had a Jewish grandfather—and her world in New York culture and politics. Her first husband, Yael Woll, was the son of the principal of the Downtown Torah School on New York's Lower East Side.

In 1954, after her first trip to Africa, Pearl took a group to study in her native Trinidad, where she met Percival Borde, an acclaimed dancer and drummer. He became her second husband and life partner in dance. The complexities of Pearl's union with Percy played themselves out over the next twenty-five years in their family and professional lives. They had a son, Onwin Borde; opened a school; and formed a company, the Primus/Borde Earth Theater. They lived and worked in West Africa, primarily Liberia, during Onwin's young years and, at the request of the Liberian government, created the Konama Kende Art Center in 1960. Her teaching in Africa reached many groups in many countries but also generated controversy. On one occasion she feared for her life as she was caught between political factions. In America she received great recognition, but her motivation for transposing African dances to the concert stage was sometimes questioned.

In the academic world, Pearl earned a PhD at New York University, completing a groundbreaking dissertation on African masked dances that combined research in dance and anthropology, thus laying the foundation for a newly emerging field. She was intent on bringing ancient African traditions not only into the world of dance performance but to educational settings at all levels. She was as devoted to teaching dance as a form of life as she was to choreographing and performing. She designed lecture demonstrations as a way of organizing and presenting herself and her work, crossing yet another boundary between performance and education. These became a model for the developing field of arts and dance education, another arena in which her work was original.

Shaping her life by navigating the cultural boundaries that both joined

4

and separated her West Indian heritage, her New York upbringing, and her African sense of self, Pearl traveled widely and almost continuously, to the American South, Europe, Israel, Africa, and the Caribbean. She held numerous academic appointments, but her creative life never settled easily into the academic world, and in her last years it was in Barbados that she finally felt at one with herself, her art, her spiritual needs, and her closest people.

We first met Pearl Primus in 1980, when she applied for a position as the Master of the Cora P. Maloney College, a residential and academic black studies unit at the State University of New York at Buffalo. As the Dean of the Colleges at that time, Murray hired her. Peggy was chair of a newly created Department of Dance at the Buffalo Academy for the Visual and Performing Arts. When Dr. Primus came for an interview, the plan was that we would take her out to dinner with a small group from the university, after which we would come to our home for a visit. Peggy's big question was, "What shall I make for dessert?" She amused herself by settling on a large meringue shell laden with fresh fruit, called a Pavlova. A Pavlova for Pearl Primus, this icon of black dance in America!

We went to pick her up at the home where she was staying and waited and waited while she finished dressing, undoubtedly putting on the Phi Beta Kappa pin she was never without, and further adorning herself with the silver bracelets, rings, and beads she felt were just right for the occasion. Dinner was a lively affair at a small restaurant in downtown Buffalo, and then we returned to our home, where she met our three daughters, three cats, and dog. By this time, Dr. Primus was Pearl to each of us. Thereafter she never tired of regaling our youngest with the story of that evening. "You were lying across the whole sofa, trying to be nonchalant about the group that had come in, peeking under and over the book you appeared to be reading but which, in point of fact, was upside down!" Then they would both laugh.

Thus began a friendship that grew and deepened in the years ahead, a period that marked the last—and most challenging—stage of Dr. Primus's life. There were frequent telephone calls, either early in the morning or at dinnertime, surprise visits to Murray's office or to our house, sometimes just to sit together quietly, other times she would excitedly outline a proposal for an academic exchange, an institute, a performance. In the earliest years, every call began with, "How are daughters number one, number two, and number three? How are the cats? How is doggie?" In time we understood this as emerging from the truest of African traditions, and knew she would not proceed without asking these questions. We have learned to ask them ourselves.

Over the next fourteen years, from 1980 until her death in 1994, while Murray twice provided an academic base from which she could work, she and Peggy spent many hours together, on the phone or in studios or one kitchen or another as they traveled from here to there. This book has been evolving and taking shape since 1995 and with conscious dedication since 2003.

In her last years it was as if she was preparing us for our roles as her biographers, as she told of the many people who were important to her and whom she influenced in her myriad worlds, whether the Trinidadian community in New York, Hunter College friends and associates, southern teachers and educational leaders, or dancers from the early days of her career. We gradually understood that Pearl was truly as at home in the African bush as she was on stage at Lincoln Center, as satisfied eating taro root and peanut soup with villagers in West Africa as she was having a corned beef sandwich and cream soda at the Carnegie Deli in New York. She maintained strong connections to people in all these worlds, valuing her relationship with Alvin Ailey in New York along with her friendship with Margaret Cunningham, director of a community center in upstate New York. Maya Angelou referred to Pearl as a "play mother," an old southern expression meaning that she had the right to ask questions no one else could ask.

Our research took us to New York many times as well as to North Carolina, Los Angeles, and beyond. In Trinidad, guided by Cheryl Borde, Pearl's stepdaughter, we explored the mountains where she studied the rituals derived from Africa. In Barbados we met many times with Mary Waithe, spiritual heir to many of the dances, and with the archbishop Granville Williams of the Spiritual Baptist Church, her spiritual companion in her last years. In West Africa "Baba" Chuck Davis, her friend and one-time student, was our teacher and guide. We needed to sit by the sea in Barbados and dance on her beloved African soil. We hungered to hear about the different periods of her life, not just the public highlights we could read about in dance history books. What gifts did she give you? What did you talk about when you sat around having your hair braided? What were the early days of her first marriage like? Where did you eat and sleep on that 1946 tour as an interracial troupe traveling the country? Mary Waithe, also of West Indian heritage, said, "You need to be a griot." That is the storytelling voice we hope we have found, for in that personal voice we might catch the rhythm and cadence of Pearl's song. It is also the reason Pearl's writings are quoted, from high school poetry to excerpts from an extended African essay written in the heat of a crucial moment.

Over and over, we heard certain names. These became the people Peggy knew she needed to find to begin this book: David Hodges, Terry Baker, Louis Ramos, Margaret Cunningham, Glory Van Scott, and many others. In 1983 Pearl told Peggy she had had a Jewish husband before Percy, but it was years before we learned of his name and could finally locate him. Another time she said, "You must meet Emiko and Yasuko," which led Peggy to the Tokunaga sisters in Boston. Sadly, we missed some of the greats with whom she worked closely—Babatunde Olatunji, Chief Bey, Alphonse Cimber, and Charles Queenan, among others, as well as her companion Joyce Knight, who disappeared before Peggy could find her for an interview.

At times Peggy had the sensation of being guided in her task. There were many coincidences that seemed directed from a world beyond. Pearl believed in the spirit world and in the power of "the Ancestors." Part of her connection to us was her trust in Murray to deal with the complexity and institutional politics of the actual world, and her reliance on Peggy to share her trust in the spirit realm. Perhaps the many worlds she inhabited finally came down to these two. She knew their separateness but also needed to negotiate an interplay between these most basic realms of experience.

Pearl received myriad national awards and honors in fields as diverse as anthropology, education, and dance, but the texture of her life emerges most clearly in her personal relationships. We have told her story through a combination of memories and histories, personal testimonies, and documentary evidence of her life and career. At its center is Pearl's quest for authenticity, in dance and in the life that informed her art. After her death, Peggy interviewed more than one hundred friends, family members, dancers, choreographers, and students, including her first husband, Yael Woll; dancers Chuck Davis, Judith Jamison, Geoffrey Holder, and Donald McKayle; historians Joe Nash and Richard Long; childhood friends Frances Johnson and Sophie Charles; son, Onwin Borde; the archbishop of the Spiritual Baptist Church in Barbados, Granville Williams; Holly "B" Betaudier, renowned radio announcer and entertainment personality in Trinidad; percussionists Montego Joe and John "Tunisi" Davis; college presidents Donna Shalala and Johnetta Cole; poet Maya Angelou; and many others.[4]

In addition to finding her life's story through the people who knew her, and examining the fraught historical contexts in which she worked, we have relied extensively on the American Dance Festival Archives, where many of her letters, diaries, essays, poetry, and other papers and photographs are housed. We have also documented the early tours through concert reviews and other commentary. Much of this material has been made available for the first time in recent years and is still in private collections. The labor of interviews was Peggy's. The narrative is the work of our collaboration and dedication to this remarkable story. Our years with Pearl were intense and intimate, and the reader will find the tone shifting as our lives intertwined with hers in her later years.

Over time themes emerged—a love of words and a gift for writing; spiritual connections that people could experience as eerie at times; "queenliness," a word many used to describe her; Pearl's longing to establish a school, an institute that would transcend racial and disciplinary boundaries. She gave gifts freely and with purpose. There were always people in her life who would serve her. She had a great need to be supported in this way and an uncanny ability to have her needs met, but some cherished aspirations eluded her.

Naming is important in many cultures, intensely so in African culture. When we first met Pearl, she invited us to call her Pearl. If we were among students she referred to Peggy as Professor Schwartz, and we introduced her

8

as Dr. Primus. Murray was Murray in private, Dean Schwartz in public. Many dancers referred and still refer to her as Miss Primus. Others were invited to call her Mna, pronounced just like "ma," from the Efik language of Kalabar, Nigeria, meaning "mother who did not birth you." In Africa she was given many names. "Omowale" was her favorite, speaking directly of her African roots and the spiritual reconnection to Africa coincident with her first trip in 1949. But to us she was Pearl, and this is how we will refer to her in this book.

The stories are dramatic, ranging from Jacqueline Hairston, a black dancer on the 1946 southern tour, telling of the urine-soaked bed in the "only" hotel which had a room, to Donald McKayle's describing his head moving back and forth like a spectator at a ping-pong match as tempers flared and doors slammed at the New Dance Group studios. Eva Koonan Zirker, a lifelong friend, recalled vividly a small group of women preparing to go off into the hills of Trinidad for a Shango fete, and Pearl stomping around glistening and naked while she decided what to wear and which jewelry to put on. Holly "B" described the disarray in which he found Trinidadian dancers and drummers living when, following the Trinidad trip, she brought a group to New York in the early 1950s. Johnetta Cole talked about Pearl as one of her "sheroes," who didn't fit the traditional categories of academe, and Maya Angelou remembered weeping when she first saw Pearl perform. All of these people testify to the importance of Pearl in their lives, and the value of her work in her times, and beyond. These voices are the threads that together weave the story of a life filled with passion, drama, determination, fearlessness, and brilliance. It took years to find the communities, gain the confidence of people in those communities, and immerse ourselves in her life, to successfully cross the boundaries of the worlds which, in her lifetime, she often kept separate.

Pearl responded forcefully to but often was not in harmony with the institutions within which she lived, whether in the United States or Africa, in academia or the professional world of dance. It was this tension that enabled her impact even as it provoked recurrent crises in her life, and herein lies the drama of her story. By exploring her different worlds in their separateness and their intersections, we hope our readers will gain an understanding of this remarkable woman and the ways in which she both suffered and shaped aspects of twentieth-century cultural history.

Pearl's story is timely. In recent years there has been a renewed interest in her dances, writings, and style of teaching. Peggy documented a work of Pearl's, "Bushasche, War Dance, A Dance for Peace," for the American Dance Legacy Institute as part of their Etude Project, whose goal is to make significant modern dance studies accessible to public schools throughout the nation. The Five College Dance Department in Amherst, Massachusetts, commissioned a new work based on "Bushasche" by Jawole Willa Jo Zollar, the artistic director of the renowned company Urban Bush Women, who found a spiritual taproot in the Primus legacy and went on to create a cycle of dances called "Walking with Pearl." This work was based on Pearl's African and southern diaries and garnered brilliant reviews as well as a 2006 Bessie Award.

With the election of President Barack Obama, the celebration of ethnicities and the mixing of cultures that Pearl embodied have reached new prominence in American life, making her story even more relevant today. Dance and cultural historian Brenda Dixon Gottschild described Pearl's influence on American dance and culture as "subterranean."[5] How and why this was so came to define our search for her as a person and a public personality, as we discovered her many successes, her failures, and her broad legacy. Along the way, we also realized the depth of the claim she had made on us.

From Laventille to Camp Wo-Chi-Ca

Hold fast to dreams
For when dreams die
Life is a broken-winged bird
That cannot fly.

Hold fast to dreams
For when dreams go
Life is a barren field
Frozen with snow.

—Langston Hughes

LAVENTILLE, THE POOR NEIGHBORHOOD in Port of Spain where Pearl Primus was born, stands in the hills above the city, looking down on the commercial center and the ocean. "I was born in Trinidad, July or November, 1919."[1] Pearl was never sure which was correct. Some history books say November 29, 1919. Other sources give dates ranging from 1917 to 1923. Pearl's homeland is an island of complex colonial histories and richly intersecting ethnic identities. Her maternal grandfather, the head drummer of Trinidad, was descended from the Ashanti tribe in Ghana and the Ibo from eastern Nigeria. "I grew up in a home," she said, "where discussions about Africa were everyday occurrences. My father and uncles had been in various countries of Africa, either as merchant seamen or as soldiers."[2] Her strong identification with her African heritage became the bedrock of her work.

Along with her Ashanti heritage, there was another, converging lineage, one that Pearl rarely spoke of, yet near the end of her life she exclaimed, "I know all about Yom Kippur. I had a Jewish grandfather."[3] Her son, Onwin, said that Pearl's paternal grandfather fled Germany in the late nineteenth century to escape persecution, became an indentured servant, later escaped and became a pirate, and eventually joined the Merchant Marines. At the same time, Onwin claimed that "Herr Primus was a rabbi, a very upper-class,

Ashkenazi Jew." Onwin loved to tell stories, and the details of this genealogy may well be fictional, though Pearl did seek the support of Jewish men throughout her life.

In all likelihood, Pearl's father, Edward, was born in Bogles, Carriacou, an island in the Grenadines, and, as a young man, moved to Trinidad to get work. According to Loris Primus, Pearl's first cousin, he was probably a carpenter or tradesperson while they lived in Trinidad, but he had become a merchant seaman at the time the family moved to New York. The original family in Carriacou was a large one, and Onwin said that his grandfather had seven or eight brothers in Trinidad. Loris described a whole other set of Primus relatives from the Grenadines, particularly Carriacou. Latir Primus, a second cousin, said that there are Primuses in Granada, Trinidad, Aruba, and Carriacou, and he recounted numerous names for each family member, which makes it challenging to trace this family tree. According to voodoo belief, hiding one's real name protects one from evildoers, Loris explained. "One brother's name was General, who was also called Alfred. Uncle Darling's name is Conrad. There's Adam known as Herbert, Newton known as Tano, and Dalvon whose name is Wilpot. And then there was Royal. I believe Royal is actually the same one who is Pearl's father. There's a sister Lillian called Calla Lily," and on it goes. "You can go an entire lifetime and not know a person's real name," Loris said.

In the island cultures, voodoo beliefs coexisted with colonial styles, and Onwin remembered his grandmother as a "very Victorian lady." "I never saw my grandmother without full makeup, hair done, coiffed and everything else." Pearl's childhood friend Frances Charles said, "Mrs. Primus was the nicest person I ever met, a jewel." Pearl would later tell the dance critic Margaret Lloyd that "her mother was such a beautiful social dancer that she was called the Queen."[4] Yet, much later, speaking in an interview at the University of Michigan, Pearl said that her parents were "horrified of dance." When her mother said that "exposure of limbs would close doors," Pearl replied, "I'll knock them down!"[5]

The family moved to New York when Pearl was around two, at the peak of the first wave of emigrating West Indians, her father arriving first.

Pearl, her mother, and her younger brother, Edward, followed the father, whom another childhood friend, Sophie Johnson Charles, remembered as "cold and distant." Pearl's second brother, Carl, was born in New York, the first American Primus.

In New York, West Indians were segregated by race but integrated by ethnicity and class. Langston Hughes described them as "warm, rambunctious, sassy . . . little pockets of tropical dreams on their tongues."[6] Already in the 1920s Trinidadians in New York were celebrating Carnival, and ballroom dances were carried over from the islands. The Primus family settled in this West Indian world within a segregated black world. They lived at West Sixty-ninth Street and Broadway, where her father worked as a building superintendent. Onwin said that in New York, Pearl's father got a job shoveling coal for ninety-eight cents a week and his grandmother took in washing.[7] The family moved around a lot until they got to Hell's Kitchen in about 1930 or 1931. A few years later, they moved to 536 Madison Avenue in the Williamsburg section of Brooklyn, a building that remains in the family to this day. Onwin described a shield that used to be on the door on the second floor of the house, reflecting part of the Primus clan's heritage. It read, "No retreat, no surrender, in victory or in death." To help pay for the house, Pearl's parents had to rent out the top floor. In order to have a space for the three kids, her father sectioned off the living room to create very small bedrooms.

Racially, in America West Indians came to be considered "black." "Caribbean New Yorkers of the 1920s and 1930s might have been immigrants in a city of immigrants, but it was race that structured their life chances. Being black determined where they lived and could not live, where they could and could not go to school, what type of job they could get and the way they were treated by Americans of all color," writes historian Philip Kasinitz.[8]

For West Indians, the advantages of economic upward mobility were often ironically accompanied by downward mobility in social status, a dilemma that the second generation would strive to overcome. Of Pearl's generation, Kasinitz observes, "Their primary interests were in pushing back the limits on opportunities imposed on the entire black community, limits that chafed them more than their parents."[9] Reflecting on the community's family life, Pearl's student and lifelong friend Mary Waithe said, "You had to go to school, you had to get a good education, you didn't play in the streets all night, you were very strict. They used to call the West Indians 'the black Jews' because they could save their money." In fact, the Primus family had become Episcopalians, attending church once in a while.

Sophie Charles Johnson described life in the neighborhood and its very precise boundaries. She and Pearl met when they were six-year-old public school students at P. S. 94 on Amsterdam Avenue. On Wednesday afternoons the bus would pick them up and take them to the church on Sixty-fifth Street and Central Park West for Bible class. Their parents would give them some pennies for the church plate, but they would always hold back a few for a visit to the candy store after class, before heading over to Central Park.

Pearl and Sophie had a German friend, Gertrude Ederle, who would later become the first woman to swim across the English Channel. Once, when Pearl's brother Eddy joined them, Gertrude's father intruded and said, "Who is this black so and so? I don't want that monkey in here." Sophie and Pearl stood up to the father. "If he's not allowed in here, then we're not allowed in here. Come on Pearl, let's go." Young kids were expected to stay in their own neighborhoods. Sophie recalled ethnic concentrations, with Italians on Sixty-ninth Street between West End Avenue and the Hudson River, Irish on Sixty-eighth Street, Germans on Sixty-seventh. West End north of Seventy-second was mainly Jewish, blacks were on Sixty-third, Sixty-second, and down. "But if one of our fathers took us out it was different," Sophie said. They could eat food cooked only in their own homes, and their fathers would watch them returning from school on the corner of Sixty-eighth and Amsterdam. They sometimes had fights with kids at school, and they fought back. They could have friends in the house but couldn't go out. When it was time for Pearl to go home, her parents came for her, and Sophie's mother would drop a key out a window so they could come up and retrieve their daughter. The girls were separated when Pearl went to junior high school, but the friendship continued throughout their lives.

In a 1985 Hampshire College commencement address, Pearl reimagined a house she lived in on 117th Street in East Harlem, the last house before the East River. (She said that ultimately the house wasn't torn down, "it fell down.") She described how she sat on the curb by her house, dangling her bare feet in the rainwater that ran through the gutter. As the drainage water flowed over them, her imagination soared.

> The water brought down old pieces of crumbled paper, nasty paper, old cigarette butts, old dirt piling up on the side of her feet. . . . [T]he pages of great books were made from those dirty pieces of paper. The cigarette butts became logs, logs for great houses, for palaces, for sculpture. That dirt piling up, against her feet became paths, mountains, valleys that she could walk through, deserts that she could traverse, mountains she would climb. This little girl sat dangling, dreaming of tomorrow. The greatest books of the world . . . she studied from those pieces of paper. And the log cabins and the palaces and the sculpture, and the roads. Roads into the homes of the worlds' people. Roads to the shrines and altars. Roads to the podium for all kinds of honor . . . I knew this girl, for I am she . . . I've fallen through the cracks, bruised my knee, banged my head. I've faced prejudice, hatred, anger, defeat of all kinds, yet I made it to the top. This is my message to you.[10]

Donald McKayle, also of West Indian heritage, recalled a tight-knit community organized "along class lines and highly social." The primacy of racial discriminations was an American, not Trinidadian, adaptation. Loris confirmed that within the West Indian community, one didn't feel limited by the color of one's skin. You didn't grow up "hearing the [racial] drumbeats every day" and that "if you are black, you are inferior. You grew up with a different expectation. I was actually in my twenties before I had my first dream where I could identify people in colors. I didn't see people in color because in my upbringing you didn't have to deal with differentiating people in colors. Education was seen as the key, like a drumbeat over and over."

Pearl followed that drumbeat with a passion that characterized everything she did. With her parents' support, which sometimes evoked the envy of her brothers, she seized the opportunities presented to her and, from early on, strove to leap beyond assigned places. She excelled both athletically and intellectually. She was one of the few black students to attend Hunter College High School and Hunter College, both selective institutions. With her powerful legs, she was a winning athlete, setting records in the high jump and broad jump, and she was a star sprinter. She became an avid reader and writer. Evelyn Karlin, a friend and fellow dancer at Hunter High, remembers Pearl as "bubbly, cheerful, and with a wonderful sense of humor," but she could also be moody and introspective. Above all, she was ambitious, and determined to surmount obstacles.

In high school, Pearl began to develop her style as a writer. A teacher commented on an essay titled "A Typical Doctor," "Content good but 'ware those honeyed phrases," but this was not a criticism that Pearl took to heart. Rather, over the course of her life, she developed her natural eloquence, a gift for spontaneous, surprising phrases, and a musician's ear for the rhythms of speech. Another admonition she received—not to write in turquoise ink— was also disregarded. Long after high school she composed journals and letters in her favorite ink.

At about age fifteen, while a student at Hunter High, Pearl created for her teacher Mrs. Edna Flouton a collection of poetry dated August– November 1934. On the cover, over a drawing of a nature scene, she wrote, "By The Tree Worshiper, Pearl Eileene Primus." A dedication, "To Mrs. Edna Flouton also a Tree Lover," is followed by a prose introduction, "God's Garden," and fifteen original poems, as well as a poem by the French symbolist poet Paul Verlaine and accompanied by Pearl's "very free translation."

In her poetry she identifies strongly with nature along with her urban environment, writing about palm trees, oak trees, lime trees, weeping willows, and more, as well as about the wind, the moon, and the elements, but also about the BMT subway and the rules of the playground. She invokes God as revealed in the natural world and is not afraid to address God directly. She muses on life and on her own death, her work reflecting a familiarity with romantic poetry, which was emphasized at Hunter High in this period.[11]

The seeds of Pearl's writings on Africa, the mountains, the earth, and the sea are embedded in these poems. Much later Pearl wrote, "The earth is a magic dancer," as she describes the African soil. Here we have a palm tree described as "the dark sentinel of earth and sky" ("Palm Tree"), and the imagination as "the sunset wings of fantasy" ("O Come"). There are many invocations, Pearl's youthful prayers to God, expressed through poetry and through the natural environment, always with a bit of ironic distance. After each poem, each arc of life and death, natural cycles, Greek references, and experimentation with form, there's a note on the bottom of the page, a running commentary on her own work. Following "The Weeping Willow," she writes, "As the B.M.T. rises into the air, the traveler can see this cemetery, and though the whistles deafen him, the dead sleep on in peace." "Watch your trees defy the rain! It's very amusing," she comments on "The Rain and My Cedar Tree." Each handwritten poem has its own page, as Pearl plays with visual design and patterning.

A sample from "The Tree Worshiper" illustrates the allegorical idealizations of her adolescent writing. In "God's Garden" she wrote, "God makes His garden one of perfect beauty, and he revels in his handiwork. At morn, the mountain kings wrap themselves in the blue smoky veil of dawn, and the chirping birds rise into the air to praise their maker with song. . . . He that planteth a seed is a servant of God, and unknown generations shall rise and bless him." Pearl's evocation of nature hints at sublime experience and imbues the trees with the rhythms of dance. She imagines building her home "Among a thousand haughty trees / Their awful arms spread wide in prayer," and resting in death "beneath a weeping willow tree. . . . Beside a laughing river where the trees / Make mock'ry of their quivering dancing shapes."

Between August 1937 and January 1939, Pearl wrote many letters to a dear friend and confidant, "My Dear Miss Mage." Pearl was eighteen or nineteen, a student at Hunter College, and Lily Mage was a high school teacher with whom she had a mentor-student relationship.[12] The letters reveal her young character, almost as if she were aware that these might become part of an epistolary biography. They express her range of imagination as well as the rhythms of life of a serious, young woman supported by her home life in her educational goals and dreams. They introduce Pearl's storytelling style, her calculated use of expressive language and ever-present humor. When a girl enters the office at Hunter where Pearl is working and demands a folder for her diploma, she is "just chilled to my toe nails. . . . My words feel like icicles which clip off sharply from empty branches on cold days."

Pearl expresses devotion to her family, but also reveals the turmoil of her youthful energy. Of her temper she says, "The eruptions of Mt. Vesuvius would sound like a soft breeze compared to this. . . . I should have been christened Stubborn Primus." "You know when I receive my PhD in Biology I shall betake myself to all countries of the globe just to see the rising and setting sun. . . . After my vacation . . . I shall settle down and become a surgeon." Yet, amid many ambitions, dance emerges as a growing interest. "Did I tell you I have a double minor now? Well, I have. The new one is Physical Ed. I can hardly wait to start it in the fall. I'll be taking Dancing, apparatus, fencing, basketball and tennis next term. Swimming if I can get it. I'd love to specialize in the dancing but it is not stressed more than the others."

She asks Miss Mage about herself and then describes how she feels about studying. As in her poems, the experience of space is central to her imagination. "Why have you been so silent? Don't tell me that like me you have been sunk down into the great abyss of study—finding it at one time too small to hold you—feeling you must escape or be crushed by its firm walls—then at other times it becomes too large—making you smaller than an atom of air. Swamped in the mud of cruel tests which seem to accomplish no more than worrying us—(you know how a cat worries a helpless mouse) I am unable to think. Really sometimes I have so much to do, I just curl up on the floor, haul out an old magazine and read." She mentions gaining weight after vacations but notes that "gym is slimming."

Reading *Gone with the Wind* triggers a long letter in which she tries to sort out her passionate and conflicted response to the novel, which makes her want to "scream with rage." She loves the descriptions of the South, "hills and meadows . . . a glorified land—a perfect place," but then "fury sweeps in flaming clouds across my face—I must pause and return to reality—my room—the safest place in the world for me—I look around—at familiar ob-

18

jects—and the winds cease to blow—the waters cease to grumble." Then she reflects on the price of her own compliance with social demands. "Unconsciously and gradually I have built up a dummy to act for me—to cater to the wishes of the world . . . but ah, the real self! How it suffers." The tension remains unresolved. "*Gone with the Wind* drives me back into my shell—I hate people—I love nature—but Nature is the mother of people—O-what a grand mix up—!!!!"

Planning to become a physician, Pearl graduated from Hunter College in 1940 with a B.A. in biology and premedical sciences, but the fact that she was black made it impossible for her to find work as a lab technician. Forced to reduce her expectations, she finally took work as a vegetable picker and shipyard riveter, among other itinerant jobs. She enrolled in health education courses at New York University, and in May 1941 she transferred into the graduate psychology program at Hunter College. There is no record of her reasons for leaving this program, but by this time she was avidly taking dance classes in Manhattan and discovering the link between dance and political activism.

Pearl's first dance classes were at a school called Dance on the Moon, between Lexington and Third Avenue. She and Sophie would go on Friday or Saturday. At first Pearl was afraid to tell her parents, but when they found out she was talented, they went to see her and were supportive. Her father helped her set up her studio at 17 West Twenty-fourth Street. In the late 1930s there were also classes at the University Settlement House on Henry Street and down around Wall Street, where free classes were given by the Works Projects Administration (WPA). Later on these classes cost twenty-five cents. "We were always looking for inexpensive or free classes. We ferreted them out wherever we could and tried to get scholarships," another friend, Evelyn Karlin, recalled.

By the time Pearl leaped both literally and figuratively onto the New York stage in 1943, she had woven her experiences in childhood and adolescence into the central themes of her being. The dancing body would always be at the center of her expressive life, but she was also becoming a teacher whose medium was storytelling. Memories of her Trinidadian childhood became the imagistic sources of narrative variations that would express her relationships to herself and others and form the basis for her anthropological methods. "When I was a child I would sit on my grandmother's lap and my grandmother would beat out rhythms with her feet and that's how I got the rhythms," she recalled.[13]

"I have three pieces of memory," she told James Murray. In the first, she is being taken into the water by her father as an infant, with her hands around his neck, terrified as he dives. She said her mother didn't speak to her father for some time after that.

The second memory involved sitting under the house playing with what she thought were beads, but which turned out to be poisonous coral snakes. This became an oft-repeated family story. According to Onwin the house Pearl was born in was a "shotgun shack, which stood up in the mountains, up on stilts where, unbeknownst to my grandmother, there was a viper pit down underneath. But my mother, having the gift that she did, used to go underneath and adorn herself with these snakes and they never bit her." The family story was that Pearl's mother rescued her in time and they packed up.

The third memory was of a carnival creature leaping over the fence, "flying in the air."[14]

These three memories contain images and hints of themes that resonated throughout Pearl's life and work. The memories of the sea, the snakes, and the leapers would provide a foundation for the study of and identification with the Orishas, Yemanja and Dambala, the goddesses of the sea and of snakes. The explosive and sustained leap would become the dance movement for which she became internationally famous. Pearl's early images developed cumulative power over the course of her lifetime and became part of her dance work, anthropological study, storytelling, self-perceptions, writings, and worldview. She told stories with symbolic meanings many times, changing details here or there, embellishing when needed, to indicate where she was from and who she was.

Suggestive images of snakes appear in her writings: "You cannot play with the son of a snake however little he may be," she wrote in her Africa diary. And, later, "Do you know what Loneliness is? / It is a snake / crawling behind an antelope . . ." The poem concludes:

> It is the single cry
> of a dying bird.
> It is the hand lifted
> to strike an aged woman
> It is you
> cringing
> Naked in the moonlight . . .

Then, there is the sea. In a 1949 diary on a three-by-five note card, in tiny script, she wrote:

> I stood on the edge of a cliff last nite
> Below me the ocean tossed
> And her arms reached up
> To take me.
>
> But there was a breeze
> And that breeze got tangled in my hair
> And seeped into my brain.
>
> I could hear the voice of the ocean—
> And my limbs grew weak to obey him
> But that breeze that got tangled inside me
> Had fastened me onto the cliff wall
> And the ocean receded without me
> Last nite.

An undated draft of a poem associates the sea with return—return to Africa, return to the ancestors: "I must take myself / to the ocean / and sit silently on the shore / and when the sunlight dips behind the evening clouds, / send myself across the waters / by and by and by and / I shall take myself across the ocean / to the land of my / ancestors." References to the revered Oni of Ife, the leader of the Yoruba people, suggest that this was after her 1949 trip to Africa.

21

In another undated diary entry, most likely after a 1953 trip to Trinidad, she wrote:

> Many times in Africa I thought I knew loneliness—Once in Liberia when the ocean clutched the high rocks near the embassy, I was standing waiting in the darkness—waiting for the morning. The ocean had been roaring a fierce lullaby. Suddenly it reared up before me—up—I could see it darker than the night—then thunder!! . . . Then silence . . . I stood wet and cold—my toes extending over the new cliff created by the giant wave—then I felt drunk tottering above the invisible waters—drunk and alone—

Another entry, written around the same time, expands on this theme. At a fete in the hills, amid singing and dancing, she sees hundreds of men, women, and children "all crouched palms extended begging me for something." Resenting their demand, she feels alone. "There have been many times—but this tonight makes me feel like getting drunk," she writes. In her journal entry on loneliness, getting drunk evokes a sense of fluidity and detachment, "defying the laws of gravity," a concept that must have reached deep in her being.

Pearl also confronted danger and aggression, as in another story from her youth in New York that involves a knife. "I was not a tough creature but on the other hand I wouldn't take anything from anyone; I wasn't tough unless someone bothered me, but then I would lose my mind." In the early years, she protected her younger brother and his friends. "My mother told me to drop anyone who bothered me." After describing how rocks were thrown from windows at Pearl and her brothers, Onwin said, "My grandmother gave my mother a butcher knife and said, if ten people attack you, you must kill nine or you will not get a proper Christian burial."[15]

Both Pearl and Onwin told the butcher knife story in the context of facing discrimination outside the home in New York. "We were one of five black families on the block. Discrimination was really something, but inside the home was love and understanding. You didn't grow bitter," Pearl said. In this reflection on her earliest years in New York, Pearl assumes the stance she adopted to face down the racism within American society, from which no person of color was exempt. "Instead of growing bitter inside myself, I dance my anger and my tears," she would write.[16]

Much later, when traveling for the first time to Africa, she carried a gun along with her notebooks and camera, but she soon traded the gun for a knife, which she knew how to handle and which proved much more useful in traveling through the African bush. Like the ocean and the snake, the knife image recurs in the poetry from the Africa days. "Again— / Again the knife stabs / And again I laugh . . . / Pain spreads thru me / like slow poison . . . / I am numbed."

Clearly there were challenges in this solo travel in Africa. Some may have been personal, some from the deep identification with the peoples of Africa and the suffering they endured.

> Have you ever wanted to cry
>> From way down deep inside you
>>> And did you find Pain blocking the passage
>>>> So that only a sob could get by him . . .
>
> Have you ever wanted to laugh
>> Because Madness was standing before you . . .
>>> And laughing would break this enchantment,
>>>> And when you opened your mouth did nothing
>>>>> But breath and ashes fall from it?
>
> Have you ever wanted to sleep
>> To escape from the torment around you?
>>> And did you find with your eyes closed
>>>> Your thoughts leaped at you like daggers?
>
>>>> Like daggers thrown by some madman?
>
> Then climb up a tree and hang there
>> Let the wind beat the pain from inside you
>>> And blow out the hot breath and ashes
>>>> And harness the daggers thrown at you . . .

Then cry till your tears form an ocean
And your laugh becomes like the thunder
Then sleep will lie down beside you
And bring you rest.

In the early 1940s, Pearl became a dance counselor at Camp Wo-Chi-Ca, a rural New Jersey camp founded in 1934. A place where left-leaning New York families sent their children for overnight camping, Wo-Chi-Ca was unique in its racial and social mix and its close involvement with and ardent support from the world-famous performer Paul Robeson. In 1940, after returning to the United States from a "long self-exile," Robeson made the first of many visits to Wo-Chi-Ca and became its faithful champion and fund-raiser.[17] It is likely that this is where he first met Pearl.

Former campers June Levine and Gene Gordon remembered that farmers in the area assumed the camp with the Indian name was a place where "feather-bedecked children chanted, danced, and sat cross-legged making beaded wallets." But Wo-Chi-Ca stood for Worker's Children's Camp. "These children of workers would, in the early years, raise a red flag and sing the 'Internationale.'" Twenty percent of the campers were black, as were a fourth of the staff. The look was "slave ships and Ellis Island freighters . . . not the Mayflower," as the camp welcomed Asians, Puerto Ricans, Italians, blacks, and whites, including many Jews.[18]

The idealists and radicals who created Wo-Chi-Ca also contributed financially so that those with no money could attend. In 1935 it cost eight dollars a week to send a child to Wo-Chi-Ca, a sum that would feed a family of four for a week. On August 21, 1947, Robeson spoke to the gathered camp community about his international experiences, his admiration for the equality among people in the Soviet Union of this period, and his hesitation, even fear, about returning to the States. But when he met members of the International Workers Order and children at Wo-Chi-Ca, he said, "I knew that I could come and I could work in America." Affirming that "he wants to see a world like this where we in America can live equally as we are here today," he thanked them for the play about his life that the campers had written and performed, the faith they had in him, and the inspiration they provided. "You drive me ahead . . . I am proud to be here," he concluded.[19] According to Paul Robeson, Jr., who was a camper for two summers at Wo-Chi-Ca, his father saw Pearl perform and pretended to regret the lindy hop lessons she gave to young Paul, who was thereafter forever cutting a rug.

At Wo-Chi-Ca, Pearl entered a circle of left-wing artists who helped shape American culture in the 1940s, '50s, and beyond. Howard Fast, the author of *Spartacus,* the story of a slave revolt in ancient Rome, was a close friend of Robeson's and an important figure around camp; he worked alongside other volunteers, "hammering, hauling, scrubbing, and setting up tents."[20] At one time the artist Charles White, who illustrated the *Spartacus* book cover, was the camp art director. He also painted murals with the support of the WPA and later on developed the DuSable Museum of African American History in Chicago. Jacob Lawrence, one of the great painters of the Harlem Renaissance, and his wife, the artist Gwendolyn Knight, would paint "along with campers on sheets of brown wrapping paper."[21] Lawrence remembered meeting Augusta Savage as well as other artists of the day, such as Langston Hughes and Ben Shahn, as visitors at the camp. Vinnette Carroll was the first African American woman to direct a play on Broadway, *Don't Bother Me I Can't Cope.* An important teacher and performer and an inspiration for many minority artists, Carroll on several occasions narrated poetry for Pearl's dances.

Camp Wo-Chi-Ca also had a point of intersection with modern dance pioneers at the New Dance Group, a collective of activist teachers and performers. On January 14, 1949, New Dance Group founders Jane Dudley, Sophie Maslow, and William Bales performed a piece called "Dust Bowl Ballads," with music by Woody Guthrie, at the Hunter College Assembly Hall in the Fourth Annual Concert to Benefit Camp Wo-Chi-Ca, sponsored by the camp's Parents Association. In this concert Pearl's social, educational, artistic, and cultural worlds merged—the New Dance Group, Camp Wo-Chi-Ca, and Hunter College.

The Wo-Chi-Ca social environment supported interracial bonding. One camper, Sheila Walkov Newman, met her first boyfriend there. "We spent a lot of time touching each other's hair," she recalled. "He liked to feel my long silky strands and I enjoyed rubbing his thick wool." Interracial marriages were also an outgrowth of camp life. Through camp friends, Charles White, a black man, met and married a white woman, Frances Barrett, in 1950, the same year that Pearl married her first husband, Yael Woll. Broadway producer Robert Nemiroff married poet and playwright Lorraine Hansberry. But also in 1950, the local populace tore into Wo-Chi-Ca, accusing the camp of being Communist and thus un-American, and demanding the removal of Paul Robeson's name from the sign at the theater. Ultimately the camp was shut down.

Although Pearl did not remain directly involved at Wo-Chi-Ca once she started having meteoric success in the New York dance scene, the camp played an important role in her life, as it did for the lives of many of the artists, counselors, and campers who went there. Rena Gluck, who became a member of the Martha Graham Company and who was asked by Graham to be a founding member of the Batsheva Dance Company in Israel, was a camper at Wo-Chi-Ca from the age of nine in the 1940s, and she always associated her earliest choreographic forays with Pearl's work, even though it turns out that Pearl had not been her teacher. She studied modern dance with a disciple of Pearl's, who suggested to her a poem of Richard Wright's for a dance, "Burst of Fists." The dances that she created always were based on themes of social awareness, Richard Wright's poetry, and folk songs. She took classes with Pearl at the New Dance Group and "greatly admired her enormous power, intensity, and integrity, which I certainly was affected by in my gut."

Fred Baker, a New York filmmaker, was from a working class family and was typical of the Jewish children who attended Wo-Chi-Ca. His father, Harry Baker, a Romanian Jew, worked as a furrier and was a Communist and member of the Fur and Leather Workers Union, and was deeply involved in the Congress of Industrial Organizations (CIO) union movement. He described his family as sensitive to religious and racial persecution and remembers in 1938 hearing a new verse to "Roll Out the Barrel" which went, "Let's get the Jews on the run . . ."

Fred, who sang in an international choral group directed by Robeson, remembered the politics of the day, especially the American Lincoln Brigade in the Spanish Civil War, of which many of the counselors at Wo-Chi-Ca were veterans. Baker met Pearl in 1941 when he was nine years old and she was a college student. "She thought I was the cat's bananas because I was a funny little kid." One day Pearl grabbed him and said, "Drum for my class, I need a live drummer." She had been teaching with Folkways African Rhythm records, so she put the record on, gave him a set of Moroccan bongos, which are African red clay drums with very taut skins, and said, "Just bang on them." He did as he was instructed, and she started dancing. The affinity and the connection were immediate. "She would enhance the steps," Fred recalled. "If it was a do-si-do, she would add a bit of an African shake to it." She told him, "Keep going, keep going." "I just got into it, because I'd heard these rhythms on records that my sister had brought home like 'Zulu Warrior.' She said, 'You have to be at all my dance classes. I'll give you these drums.'

"When people ask me, 'How did you become a drummer?' I say, 'There was a dancer named Pearl Primus. She taught me how to play the drums when I was seven or eight years old.'" Pearl gave Fred the set of drums and said, "Those are yours. Take them home and never stop playing them." "That's the kind of lady she was. She said that. 'Never stop playing those drums.'"

In 1944 Pearl appeared at benefits for Wo-Chi-Ca, and on January 14, 1946, she was celebrated in return, when Howard Fast and Mrs. Paul Robeson hosted a dinner "honoring Negro and white Americans for their contribution toward a democratic America." Pearl was among a list of awardees that read like a who's who of the artistic, intellectual, and political intelligentsia of New York: Dr. Mary McLeod Bethune (education), Dr. W. E. B. DuBois (history), Duke Ellington (music), Jacob Lawrence (art), Canada Lee (theater), Dr. Alain Locke (literary criticism), Joe Louis (sports), Pearl Primus (dance), Paul Robeson (citizen), Frank Sinatra (for his courageous fight on behalf of all minorities), and Ferdinand Smith (labor leader). The evening included a theatrical presentation, "Deep Are the Roots," by Arnaud d'Usseau and James Gow, two other awardees. A table for ten cost $60.

Many of the awardees were part of the extraordinary confluence of artists who found a creative and cultural haven at Camp Wo-Chi-Ca, the spawning ground of artistic careers for children and counselors alike, and a microcosm of the radical movements of New York politics and cultural life in the late 1930s and early 1940s.

A Life in Dance

DURING HER LAST YEARS at Hunter College, in around 1940 Pearl became involved with the New Dance Group, which was founded against the background of a nation devastated by the Wall Street crash of 1929 and the Great Depression. The New Dance Group emerged in 1932 as a unit of the Worker's Dance League, when dancers in the Worker's Dance Group joined a rally and parade to protest the shooting death of a young labor organizer, Harry Simms, by police in New Jersey. The founding young women would meet to discuss social issues affecting the United States and other countries. They aimed to make dance "a viable weapon against the evils of capitalism with its deepening crises and foreboding threats of fascism and war."[1] By changing their name from the Workers Dance Group to the New Dance Group, they hoped to reach a broader, working class audience.

The curriculum included technique, improvisation on specific social themes, and lessons in Marxist theory. As time went on, the students built a repertory of dances to provoke and promote social change. New Dance Group historian William Korff describes this collective as "humanistic" and "pluralistic," with a "revolutionary character" and a "warm and encouraging atmosphere." "Lynchings still defied justice. While it may be hard to imagine the depth of racism at that time," writes Korff, "the boldest and most profound act of the New Dance Group was the decision to actively welcome all people regardless of race."[2] Deborah Friedes and Kyle Shepherd add that "the huge and simple act of opening the studio door and the democratic, creative nurturing found at the New Dance Group brought a new richness and vitality to the art form and gave the many-varied seeds of modern American dance a place to germinate and grow."[3] The New Dance Group maintained its dedication to social justice—"making dance a vital contemporary artistic experience"—even as its offerings broadened and it became professionally oriented. With its activist motto "Dance is a Weapon," the group was part of New York's cultural and political development through many eras.

Pearl had started an after-school dance club when she was a student at Hunter College between 1937 and 1941, and a fellow student, Dorothy Perron, said to her, "You ought to go to the New Dance Group and see what it's like." Dorothy urged Pearl to accompany her on the twenty-block subway ride to Thirty-ninth Street, where the studios were then located. In 1941 Pearl was one of thirty-seven students to audition. Asked by other aspiring students if she wanted to warm up before the class she replied, "Who, me? I don't need to warm up, I'm warm enough!"[4] Her strength, athleticism, and determination were recognized in the audition class, and she became the first African American dancer to receive a scholarship, though she had to earn her keep by cleaning the studio and bathrooms.[5]

Early New Dance Group members all studied or performed with the various recognized pioneers of modern dance. In this respect Pearl was no exception, but Martha Graham soon told her that she no longer needed her classes, that she already had the strength of a panther and should create her own choreography. Pearl turned to Doris Humphrey for instruction, as Humphrey was formulating a methodology for teaching choreography. In "Trio," an early dance of Pearl's that was set for herself, Jacqueline Hairston, and Joe Nash, she developed a theme and variation, created a conflict, and resolved it, utilizing classic modern dance structures, based on musical principles. At the New Dance Group Pearl learned principles of choreography in keeping with the aesthetics of these early modern dance pioneers, and encountered a philosophy of dance education that included many dance styles and embraced all people.

Pearl herself performed in works of New Dance Group member Sophie Maslow and was encouraged by Helen Tamiris and Anna Sokolow, all women who would become prominent in the modern dance world. Over the course of her career, Pearl's New Dance Group roots provided inspiration for curriculum development that derived dances from the rhythms, songs, and stories of living cultures. She never simply taught steps, but was already merging the expressive movements of modern dance with spirituals and jazz and blues rhythms she had absorbed from African American traditions.

Pearl's dancing was "so dynamic . . . she exploded!" said Muriel Manings, Korff's wife and a member of the New Dance Group. Jane Dudley, a fellow dancer, gave Pearl a costume for one of her first dances, and at one point Judith Delman, the executive secretary, let Pearl sleep on the studio floor. But, Muriel noted, "Pearl just didn't seem to fit in with the company in terms of choreography. Her body was very different than most dancers' bodies. She was chunky." Pearl started differentiating herself, working on her own dynamic choreography. Her African dance classes were very popular and physically demanding, and her teaching style was designed to build strength for powerful and controlled release. Through repetition of dance elements, she built the capacity for uniting great energy with precision of expressive movement. Muriel described Pearl's classes as "very grounded, the way she was. Your thighs would hurt. We probably did a million of these knee springs, millions of them." Pearl's classes included scholarship students, many who just wanted to dance, but also those who aspired to become professional dancers.

Even at this early stage of her teaching, she incorporated specific African uses of the body in her classes, such as the repeated use of the toes and unusual coordination of the feet, using the toes to draw the dancer across the floor, and repeated rhythmic isolations of the fingers and hands and other parts of the body. Even before her Africa travels, in her classes she was synthesizing material she gathered from books about African dance in the New York Public Library with rhythms she mastered through interaction with Nigerian students at Columbia University, and with West Indian movement from her family experience and work with Trinidadian Beryl McBurnie, also known as La Belle Rosette. She also felt a deep sense of cultural affiliation with Asadata Dafora, from Sierra Leone. She and Dafora were great friends, and her dance was the showstopper in a performance with him at Carnegie Hall in 1943, with First Lady Eleanor Roosevelt in attendance. Decades later, she would tell an interviewer:

At times movements would come to me in my dreams and I would consult with Asadata and we would share information. Asadata was also full of humor, he enjoyed living and was dedicated to the culture. You didn't find him out there bastardizing anything. I want to publish ten commandments for choreographers. To name a few, you must study the culture, the climate of the culture. We as black people are not just free to create just anything. I can't get out there and shake a feather on my backside! It's wrong within our culture.[6]

Pearl formed a deep and enduring friendship with Hadassah Spira and her husband Milton Epstein. Hadassah, as she came to be known, was born in 1909 in Jerusalem and introduced Jewish dance to the United States. Descended from a long line of rabbis, she brought deep spiritual roots to her art. In addition to Jewish mysticism that infused her dancing, she was drawn to Hindu dance forms.[7] With Pearl and Jean Erdman, Hadassah developed the Ethnic Dance Division at the New Dance Group, where students like Jacqueline Hairston studied Hawaiian and Hindu styles, as well as African dance, before joining Pearl's company.

The interweaving of dance and cultural expression in this period of Pearl's life is apparent in her relation to Jean-Leon Destine. Born in Haiti in 1925, Destine had introduced aspects of voodoo ritual in dances performed along the East Coast. Destine was introduced to Pearl at the New Dance Group in the late 1940s through the renowned Haitian drummer Alphonse Cimber, and later joined the New Dance Group faculty. They performed together on many occasions, including a 1950s television show with Maria Tallchief, to display different dance forms—classical ballet, African, and Caribbean. They performed again in "African Carnival" in 1961 at the Midtown Armory with Olatunji, Percival Borde, Mongo Santamaria (an Afro-Cuban drummer), Merle and Joan Derby, Mary Waithe, and others. The Carnival went on for three days, not a simple performance but a re-creation of a market and village that displayed everything African. They also worked together on a Fulbright fellowship committee, selecting students to go to Africa. Destine, like Pearl, was one of the artists who tilled the soil for the flowering of African and African-based cultural expression in the United States.

∽

Also of crucial personal and professional significance was Joe Nash, a dancer who left dance, had a second career with the American Council of Churches, and eventually returned to his first love as an important historian of the development of black dance in America. With his generous spirit and open-hearted nature, he became something akin to a griot for the whole black dance experience. Having danced in the early modern dance days, he knew its development from the inside. His recollections add context and texture to the narrative of Pearl's life and help define the value of her contributions.

Joe's dance story began in 1939. He was working at CBS in communications when he heard about a dance unit that was being formed under the auspices of the National Youth Administration (NYA) to introduce young people to the discipline and to offer on-the-job training. Hallie Flanagan, who would later develop the Department of Theater and become a dean at Smith College, was the director of the Theater Project of the Works Projects Administration (WPA), under which the Dance Project fell. One afternoon at the NYA headquarters, which was situated in an old tenement building on the Lower East Side, he went into an empty room during a break in a rehearsal and was stretching at the barre when he looked up to see "this short, dark-skinned girl, standing in the doorway, eyes popped open," watching him. "I'm Pearl Primus," she said. "I'm dancing with the—" He interrupted her and said, "What? You, a dancer?" "I couldn't believe that she was a dancer. She did not have the body of a dancer."

Yet Joe loved working with Pearl. "There was such joy in what she was doing. It radiated throughout the rehearsal space." The NYA Dance group rehearsed and appeared at the 1939 World's Fair in Flushing Meadows, New York, in a series of dances that enacted a history of American social forms, from a minuet through the Virginia Reel and the Cakewalk, finishing with the Lindy Hop. Pearl picked everything up quickly. This was the start of her long friendship and professional relationship with Joe.

By 1941 the NYA had disbanded and Joe was drafted. While in Europe,

33

he recalled, there was a story in the *New York Times* that described Pearl as "Dance Debutante, Number One." "That can't be the Pearl I used to dance with!" he said to himself. But in the years that Joe was away, from the World's Fair performance to 1943, Pearl had thrown herself into dance studies at the New Dance Group, choreographed her own dances, and made her solo debut at the 92nd Street Young Men's Hebrew Association (known as the 92nd Street Y). Her career had blossomed.

The changes in the professional world of dance through the New Dance Group and other venues were exciting to black students. "We all went to recitals as a little corps; it was opening up," commented Jacqueline Hairston, a dancer who had been turned away from the ballet studios. The 92nd Street Y played a central role by regularly hosting a "Choreography Workshop," which provided an opportunity for dancers of any race or ethnicity to audition to have their work produced. In the fall of 1942 Pearl applied to present solos at the Y, listing a wide variety of teachers, including Jane Dudley and Sophie Maslow for Martha Graham technique, Ann Weiner as her ballet teacher at the New Dance Group, and Belle Rosette as her teacher of "Primitive." For performance experience she cited New Dance Group performances with Josh White, "Lead Belly" [*sic*], Sophie Maslow, Bill Bales, Jane Dudley, and others. She listed herself as being on the faculty of the New Dance Group and as director of the International Worker's Organization (IWO) City Wide Children's Dance Group.

Pearl was notified in January 1943 that she was selected to appear in a concert at the Y. Soon afterward, the educational director, William Kolodney, scheduled a fifteen-minute audition for a performance in the Sunday afternoon concert on February 14, after which Pearl was asked to present "African Ceremonial," "Blues," "Lynching," "Rock Daniel," and "South American," for the artist's fee of $35. At this concert, the dance, which is now known as "Strange Fruit," was titled "A Man Has Just Been Lynched." The concert also included a potpourri of dances performed to a range of accompaniment, including poetry, Brahms, Brazilian music, Scriabin, John Cage, Josh White, Leo Smit, Conga Kongo, and jazz, as well as of dancers trained by Isadora Duncan and Martha Graham.

The *Y Bulletin* described Pearl as having received "her African dance background from a group of West Congo dancers and musicians who visited the United States in 1939," and went on to say, "She has studied West Indian dance forms with Belle Rosette, dancer and choreographer, and has appeared with her in 'Antilliana' at the Museum of Modern Art, The 'Y' Dance Theatre and the Baltimore Museum of Art."

When she made her solo debut at the 92nd Street Y in 1943, Pearl seemed to have come out of nowhere, and the world of dance was captivated. Two dances in particular, "Strange Fruit" and "Hard Time Blues," consistently brought audiences to their feet. After her debut, it was just a matter of the direction she would choose.

"Strange Fruit" was the most harrowing of the solos Pearl created. Her capacity for total immersion in her subject was at the core of her brave and unprecedented perspective in creating the dance. This very dark-skinned young woman took on the persona of a white woman at a lynching ground just as the revelers have dispersed. As the last of the mob withdraws, the woman turns to look and is caught by the horror of the scene. Pearl wanted to enter into a white woman's experience and to provoke a complex empathic identification in her audience. As a black woman, the subject matter had to fill her with terror, but the dance expands beyond its racial surface, expressing pure anguish, pain that is bone-deep, the embodiment of the recognition of an irreversible human cruelty. This psychological complexity lay at the core of one of her greatest works and attests to the universalizing intent of her artistic vision. When restaging this work Pearl was concerned that it would be impossible for more contemporary audiences to understand how radical her perspective was in 1943, when lynchings were still hideously commonplace.

The poem "Strange Fruit" was written by Lewis Allan, the pseudonym for Abel Meeropol, a high school teacher at De Witt Clinton High School in the Bronx.[8] The dance was initially performed to the accompaniment of the poem, and readers at various times included noted actors Gordon Heath and Vinette Carroll. But when Pearl performed "Strange Fruit" in silence the dance developed its greatest impact. The audience could hear the gasping intake of breath, her fists beating on the floor, and her footfalls as she runs and then throws herself to the ground. Arching her back, she reaches toward the space defined as the lynching tree, expressing over and over both fascination and horror. Her serpentine movements embody and reflect the twisted tree, as her thrashing on the floor is punctuated by thrusts of arms and legs. The words "Pastoral scene of the gallant south" are juxtaposed with frantic traveling turns that draw her closer and closer to the forbidden tree. Crawling, arching, falling back to the earth, suddenly she sits up as the narrator says, "Scent of Magnolias sweet and fresh," when in reality the air is filled with "the smell of burning flesh." The dance ends with a run that Pearl described "as gathering the consciousness of mankind to this act of cruelty and injustice." Finally, under "the unbearable weight of the act," the dancer succumbs and falls to the ground. With a final thrust of her fist, it is as if she is stating that such despicable acts must never occur again.[9]

The dance titled "Blues" was the precursor to "Hard Time Blues," which grew out of Pearl's protest against sharecropping. Pearl adopts the perspective of a black man resisting his degraded condition. In conveying this protest, it was as though she was also defying the very laws of gravity. "Protest against lynching takes us to the ground in our anger. Protest to the system that creates sharecropping . . . takes us to the air in our anger," Pearl said. In "Hard Time Blues" the dancer enters beating fists in the air as Josh White sings, "Went down to the commissary store . . . ," then spins and leaps in frustration. The pace accelerates as he introduces the chorus, "Great God a-mighty folks are feelin' bad, lost everything that he ever had."

She leaps in place, walks determinedly upstage right and then takes off on a run, not a dancerly run, but a fist-pumping, angry run, slicing the stage on the diagonal. Halfway across the stage, "Pearl takes a running jump, lands in an upper corner and sits there, unconcernedly paddling the air with her legs. She does it repeatedly, from one side of the stage, then the other, apparently unaware of the involuntary gasps from the audience . . . ," Margaret Lloyd wrote.[10]

The choreography creates intense dynamic contrasts, full body swings low to the ground followed by a series of jumps in place, knees high, drawn close up to the body, fists punching the air overhead. She finishes in a wide second position plie, similar to the stance at the end of "Negro Speaks of Rivers." The arms slowly cross in front of her body, hands flash and whip across each other quickly as if to wipe out pain, and then slowly extend outward, palms inverted, pushing away invisible walls. For Joe Nash the gesture where she is moving slowly downstage, directly facing the audience, in a deep contraction beating her hand on her thigh, meant, "Give me food, give me shelter, give me something." Pearl's angry demandingness, which could be disruptive in other life situations, found forceful meaning in this aesthetic context.

A handwritten program note calls "Rock Daniel" "a lesson in jazz." Dancing to the music of Lucky Millinder's Orchestra ("Come out tonight, Rock Daniel, won't you come out tonight . . ." sung by Sister Rosetta Tharpe), Pearl forms exuberant and joyful swirls, big smile flashing. With her head tilted way back, arms and fingers stretched at her sides, expressive palms facing the audience, she conveys a contagious energy. A moment captured by dance photographer Barbara Morgan shows her with knees bent, perched on her right big toe, her left foot just off the floor, as her joy and delight seem to lift her to the heavens. In another Morgan photo, her knees bend to one side as her skirt twists around her and flies up in back. Her arms lift at the elbows and, as her hands cross her chest, again there is the flash of a palm tilted toward the audience as her fingers spread and reach. Her head tilts downward as a big smile breaks across her face. With her eyes closed, we feel her sensing the inward pulse of the exuberant rhythms of the orchestra. She was costumed simply in a flowing skirt extending just below the knee, a striped top baring her mid-torso, and gold hoop earrings, and her hair was pulled back, secured by a large flower. Adelaide Kerr wrote that in this dance Pearl "blends the hallelujah gestures she saw in Harlem churches and the jitterbug she learned in Harlem ballrooms."[11]

"African Ceremonial," one of Pearl's "primitive" dances, was based on a fertility rite of the Belgian Congo. Pearl spent six months researching this dance, and her study gave her great pride in the beauty and dignity of ancient African cultures, their rituals, village life, and social and artistic constructs. She developed steps based on her study of African sculpture and artifacts and then went up to the International House at Columbia University to show the African students her creations. This dance was informed by a legend that told of a priest who would appear every year before his people on a high and distant rock, perform his ritual, and then vanish. In her powerful solo, Pearl became a living sculpture. When the dance opened, Pearl was standing still, "a carving in ebony," wrote Donald McKayle. Then, "powerful, yet sparse" movements coursed through her body. "Every curving of her spine, every thrust of her hips, every flapping of her loins, every wave of her heavily bangled wrists was a gesture from an ancestral ritual of unknown origin."[12] For the 92nd Street Y performance she used recorded drum music, but after that she often worked with Norman Coker and Alphonse Cimber, both extraordinary percussionists who profoundly influenced the development of African dance and music in New York.

After her debut at the 92nd Street Y, John Martin wrote in the *New York Times* that she "walked away with the lion's share of the honors," that she "is a remarkably gifted artist. It would be hard to think of a Negro dancer in the field who can match her for technical capacity, compositional skill and something to say in terms that are altogether true to herself both racially and as an individual artist." He ends with the endorsement "If ever a young dancer was entitled to a company of her own and the freedom to do what she chooses with it, she is it. Last week's audience literally yelled for more of her."[13]

Like other artists, including Harry Belafonte, Ossie Davis, Ruby Dee, Langston Hughes, Odetta, and Pete Seeger, Pearl performed for labor organizations and at rallies throughout the 1940s. She was also inspiring careers in dance. Donald McKayle, then a high school student, would go with his friends to meetings and to sing at Pete Seeger's hootenannies. He first saw Pearl dance at the age of sixteen and was instantly hooked. From that moment on, he knew he wanted to become a choreographer. When he heard that a scholarship was being offered at the New Dance Group, he went to audition, but those in charge of the audition demurred, as he didn't have any training. McKayle said, "If you don't like me, tell me to leave and I'll go, but you can't kick me out without seeing me." After he wore her down, executive secretary

Judith Delman said, "Go upstairs and change." Thus this celebrated dancer, choreographer, director, and educator got his start. McKayle went on to a career of great distinction, formed his own company, won many Tony and Emmy Awards, and is considered one of the "Irreplaceable Dance Treasures" by the Dance Heritage Coalition and the Library of Congress.[14]

McKayle retained vivid memories of Pearl's performances at American Youth for Democracy (AYD) rallies. Originally called the American Youth Congress, the AYD was an outgrowth of a movement made up of young people who were "Jewish and Christian, Negro and white, Democrats and Farmer-Laborites, and communists and young people without any political affiliation."[15] In October 1943, five hundred delegates from the Congress gathered in New York to found the American Youth for Democracy, and then returned as activists to cities and towns all over the United States, where they ran cultural events and picnics. In this era of Jim Crow laws, their rallies were part of the political environment in which the New Dance Group functioned and in which Pearl created the legendary solos that catapulted her to the forefront of the growing modern dance movement.

A 1945 brochure for the American Youth for Democracy, called *Dust Off Your Dreams,* puts forth "The Program" for this radical organization. Its ambitions included educating in the spirit of democracy and freedom; promoting cultural, recreational, sports, and social activities; cooperating with and helping to build the labor movement; fighting for youth's right to jobs, security, job training, education, and recreation; advocating the right to vote at eighteen; and standing for United Nations cooperation. They opposed "fascist-minded monopolists" and a host of prejudices ranging from anti-Negro practices and anti-Semitism to anti-Catholicism and Red-baiting.[16] In settings like the AYD rallies, Pearl performed "Hard Time Blues," many times.

Pearl's protest dances were electrifying, and there were many other occasions for performances. She danced at the First Negro Freedom Rally, which was held in Madison Square Garden on June 7, 1943, and which was organized and directed by M. Moran Weston, a Columbia University alumnus who later worked alongside Martin Luther King, Jr., and other prominent civil rights figures. Also performing at this rally were Duke Ellington, Paul Robeson, and Langston Hughes. Hughes wrote the lyrics for a song titled "For This We Fight," with music by Herbert Haufrecht, the composer of many folk songs of the era, and Pearl danced two dances at this important event. Langston Hughes eloquently described her in a piece called "Here to Yonder," written for the *Chicago Defender*.

On Leaping and Shouting

The young lady who leapt so high in the middle of Madison Square Garden a couple of weeks ago at the Negro Freedom Rally is named Miss Pearl Primus. She was in the very middle of the Garden on a star-shaped stage, and twenty thousand people were sitting around her. Every time she leapt, folks felt like shouting. Some did. Some hollered out loud.

Pearl Primus is a dancer. She was dancing a dance called JIM CROW TRAIN, and another dance called HARD TIME BLUES to records by Josh White and Waring Cuney. She is a dark brown young lady. She got low down on the ground, walked, turned, twisted, then jumped WAY UP into the air. The way she jumped was the same as a shout in church. She did not like the Jim Crow train, so she leaped way up into the air. And it was like a work-weary sister suddenly shouting out loud on a Sunday morning when the minister starts singing, JESUS KNOWS JUST HOW MUCH I CAN BEAR.

Dancing and shouting have a lot in common. Both are kind of relief, an outlet for pent-up emotions, a savior from the psychiatrist. Rhythm is healing. Music is healing. Dancing and shouting are healing. Father Divine knows this, so does Rev. Cobb. Exhorters and gospel singers know it instinctively. Shouters know it in their souls. Folks who work hard all week, all year, all their lives and get nowhere, go to church on Sunday and shout—and they feel better. Colored, and poor, and maybe born in Mississippi, JESUS KNOWS JUST HOW MUCH I CAN BEAR, so you holler out loud sometimes and leap high in the air in your soul like Pearl Primus does when she dances Jim Crow Train which is a pretty hard thing to bear, especially when you got relatives fighting in North Africa or New Guinea, and you at home riding in a Jim Crow car.

"Lord, I wish this train wasn't Jim Crow!" the song cried on the record. The guitar cried behind the words and suddenly the strings hit a hard and stubborn chord and Pearl Primus jumped straight up in the air! And folks cried out in the Garden—where there were twenty thousand people sitting in the great arena, having met for the cause of freedom.

Paul Robeson had just got through singing WATER BOY, JOE HILL and a Russian song which he dedicated to the Negro fliers who took off recently from the soil of Africa to bomb Italy, having ridden on the Jim Crow trains of Alabama themselves not so many weeks before. Robeson also sang OLD MAN RIVER that keeps rolling through the heart of the South. Then the lights went out. When they came on again—centering on a star-shaped stage—there stood a brown-skin girl going down to the station to catch a Jim Crow train.

Did you ever ride on a Jim Crow train? Did you ever go to see your mother on a Jim Crow train? Did you ever go to college on a Jim Crow train—Fisk, Tuskegee, Talledega? Did you ever start your furlough on a Jim Crow train? Soldier boy, training for fight for freedom, on a Jim Crow train. Did you ever take your vacation on a Jim Crow train? War-worker from Detroit going home for a visit on a Jim Crow train? Did you feel it in your soul, that Jim Crow train?

Did you ever see a dancer dance a Jim Crow train? Dance the rocking motion of a Jim Crow train, coach up by the engine on a Jim Crow train, half the coach for baggage on a Jim Crow train, other half for Negroes on a Jim Crow train, white conductors, candy butchers, baggage men and brakemen taking up the

seat room in the colored half-coach of a Jim Crow train, cuss-
ing, spitting, smoking, on a Jim Crow train, Uncle Sam's own
soldiers Jim Crowed on a Jim Crow train, sign says THIS COACH
FOR COLORED on a Jim Crow train, colored women Jim Crowed
on a Jim Crow train, Washington D.C., change to the Jim Crow
train, Pearl Primus dancing on a Jim Crow train, dancing she
don't like no Jim Crow train. Jumping in the air about a Jim Crow
train, shouting in her soul God help that Jim Crow train?
Where is freedom going on that Jim Crow train?[17]

When Pearl danced "Jim Crow Train" she was dancing for herself, for
her family, and for all those Jim-Crowed. The political was deeply personal.
One example was Pearl's brother Edward, who served as a corporal with the
American Air Force Weather Service, at the Tuskegee Army Air Field in Alabama, "the only Negro weather detachment in the entire AAF Weather Service." Acclaimed documentary filmmaker William Greaves remembered that
"dancing in Pearl's group before thousands of people under those powerful
spotlights was an awesome experience." Dance was a weapon.

In a very short time, Pearl went from political rallies to Broadway, and,
within eighteen months of her debut at the Y, not only was she performing
at Café Society, she also had a show at the Roxie Theater. This kind of rise
was almost unheard of in dance, especially for a young black woman. As
dance historians have noted, John Martin raised the issue of race even as he
pronounced Primus the premier dancer of the season. In spite of the sheer
brilliance of her dancing, the critics needed to define her as a Negro dancer,
associating the immense energy and precision of her movement language
with racial categories.

Although Pearl became widely known as a pioneer in the intensive
study, teaching, and performance of African work, throughout her life she
railed against reductive labels. She treasured her training by the early modern dancers, performed with many of them, and always considered herself
a modern dancer, not limited by racial or ethnic typing. She appeared in
concerts throughout the 1940s with a great range of artists, including the

composer John Cage and a pantheon of modern dancers: Martha Graham, Merce Cunningham, Hanya Holm, Doris Humphrey, and José Limón.

Pearl thoroughly embraced the modern dance ethos in which she was immersed. Julia Levien, one of the leading proponents of Isadora Duncan dance in America, shared the stage at the Y with Pearl in 1943, performing Duncan's "Prelude and Etude" (Scriabin) just before Pearl danced "Strange Fruit." Levien also performed "Two Dances from 'Hebraic Heritages'" to the music of Leo Smit. After Levien performed the "Prelude and Etude" in flowing chiffon, Pearl was overheard to say in the wings, "I want to do that." Pearl was promoted by the New Dance Group as an emerging personality, and was encouraged to include her knowledge of African dance in the spectrum of modern dance innovations.

The idea that African traditions could be encapsulated and set apart from the central thrust of modern dance aesthetics was alien to her training and her developing sensibility. Early modern dancers Ted Shawn and Ruth St. Denis had created a theater based upon ethnic dance forms, but their ethnicity was never a question because they were white. Joe Nash pointed out that "all white modern dancers are ethnic," going back to Ted Shawn's "Juba," an African American folk dance found on the southeast plantations and in Haiti. He indignantly challenged the stereotyping of black dancers:

> Was [Shawn] called an ethnic dancer when he choreographed that for Martha Graham to dance? When Helen Tamiris created her "Spirituals" in 1927, did you call her an ethnic dancer, because she used black materials? No. When Lester Horton on the west coast did his "Voudoun Ceremony" did you call him an ethnic dancer because he used Haitian material? No. So why does anyone say that American black modern dancers, when we use the same material, become ethnic dancers?

In other words, the artists working with folkloric materials were transplanting material in the tradition of American modern dance, to create something new. "This is what modern dance does," he insisted. Modern dancers were inspired by Native American, African American, Asian, Indian, and other cultures. They used elements from these cultures, integrating them into new forms. "This is the history of American modern dance, create something based upon your inspiration from a variety of sources, not just one source." Today, we call this "fusion."

The modern dance solos Pearl created in the 1940s formed the backbone of her early repertory. The best known of the early works include "Hard Time Blues," "Strange Fruit," and "Negro Speaks of Rivers," which were restaged as solos at various times during her career. "African Ceremonial," another early solo, was restaged later on as a group ritual for her company.

"Negro Speaks of Rivers" was set to the Langston Hughes poem of the same name. Pearl remembered meeting Hughes on a segregated train, where she told him about some of the works she had been thinking of creating and he talked about his poetry, in particular about "Negro Speaks of Rivers." While Hughes was talking about his dreams and travels in Africa, Pearl began to visualize the movement that became this seminal dance.

Margaret Lloyd described "The Negro Speaks of Rivers," with its "undulating rhythms," "deep-flowing currents of movement," and "whirlpool spins." "The pale soles flash, the brown toes clutch and grasp, the dark fingers spread wide, the whole body sings: 'I've known rivers ancient as the world and older than the flow of human blood in human veins. . . . My soul has grown deep like the rivers.'"[18] Throughout her life, when Pearl recited this poem, the gestures of her hands and eyes and the resonance of her voice would mirror the physical energy with which she first created and performed this work. Her performances and restagings demonstrated her complete command of technical theater, from light design down to the smallest movement details. The gold and bronze highlighting of her dark skin suggested the texture of the river itself. Even the tiniest gesture, from the cast of the eye to the subtle, pulsing rise and fall onto half-toe and back to the heels, enacted the river's flow, the current carrying its charge.

Choosing a poem that had personal meaning and suggested movement possibilities was right in the mainstream of the modern dance aesthetic of the times. On the shared program at the Y, Nona Schurman, a Graham dancer, performed to two poems of Walt Whitman. Martha Graham had premiered "Letter to the World" set to poetry of Emily Dickinson in 1940. Pearl's movement, too, echoed modern dance vocabulary of the moment. The closing posture in "Rivers" is similar to one of Doris Humphrey's, the wide second position stance, arms bent at the elbow, forearms parallel to each other at chest height, across the body. The music for "Rivers" was created by Sarah Malament, a pianist who played for classes at Hunter College for many years and created recordings of "Music for Modern Dance."

⌒

In 1938, Café Society, "the first mainstream nightclub in a white area to cater to a mixed-race audience," opened downtown under the direction of impresario Barney Josephson, who sought out new and emerging talents, singers, instrumentalists, and small musical ensembles. Josephson offered "a career boost to a host of performers, including Lena Horne, Hazel Scott, Josh White, Jimmy Savo, Pearl Primus, and Zero Mostel." Café Society "soon became a gathering spot for the left."[19]

Café Society was a small club; you entered by going downstairs, where there was a bar, the usual seating, and a small arena for the dancer. Joe Nash remembered that Pearl in 1943 appeared at the club's doorstep before a performance looking like a bobby-soxer. She said, "Wait, I'm the young girl who just made my debut at the Y." Josephson said, "Oh, I heard about you. Come in and let me see what you can do." He engaged her on the spot. On her first night, though, she was initially frightened and her music repeatedly failed. Describing her experience in 1979, she said, "I dissolved into tears and then this huge man emerged from the audience. It was Paul Robeson. . . . He made me get up and keep dancing that night."

Café Society was not a dance venue as such, but when Pearl danced there, the room became quiet, focused. Joe Nash recalled that "people stopped the clinking of their glasses. Those who were standing turned around to look." Pearl communicated with the same emotional intensity as she did on the concert stage, but "did not distort or overplay emotions for the sake of the audience." Joe remembers being stunned. "She awed the audience, reached people emotionally, spiritually and intellectually." Jacqueline

45

Hairston, a student at Brooklyn College, found Café Society the most exciting place she had ever been. "The atmosphere was open and alive . . . when she performed 'Strange Fruit' we were enthralled, ecstatic, unbelieving. It was all part of black people being welcomed." Originally scheduled to last three weeks in April 1943, Pearl's run was extended for months, through February 1944.

After seeing her at Café Society, John Martin wrote in the *Times,* "It is possible even now to say that no other Negro dancer has in any comparable degree touched on an art so aware of its racial strength and so true to it. She has studied with a number of teachers not of her race . . . but she has been marked by none of them in style." He praised "her superb elevation, her speed, her dramatic power, all of which are the result of talent, good teaching and—good studying."[20]

In July and August 1944, Pearl undertook her first fieldwork, a research trip to the South, to deepen her understanding of the culture and the communities whose work and rhythms she was intent on re-creating for the stage. Before she left, Paul Robeson had told her to make sure she had a return ticket with her in case she needed to escape quickly. She traveled through Alabama, Georgia, and South Carolina, passing as a sharecropper and studying church life, attitudes toward prayer, family, work, and recreation. Her two-month tour "left her bewildered and numb." "The Jim-Crowism I encountered affected me like the shock of a fist hitting me full force in the face," she wrote. "The discrimination is so vicious that it hangs like a blanket of darkness over all the colored people all the time." At times she wished "a helicopter would drop down from the sky and take [her] home fast." She was amazed at the extent of the poverty for both black and white ("equally bad"), the intensity of the hatred and fear that existed between the two groups, and the lack of cultural activities.[21]

Pearl experienced black Southerners as "begging for education" and "waiting for someone to awaken them to their own strength and potentialities," with a need to be reeducated "to learn of their noble culture." She stated boldly, "Our culture is equal to the culture of any other race, but we must take the time to study it and recognize it. It will help us in our battle for freedom." Pearl returned with the conviction that a group of artists should tour the South. She had found people wary of those from the North, but "say you're from the next town and they'll ask you to 'set' and tell them all about books like 'Strange Fruit.'" She thought a chorus would be an effective way to start and the local churches a good place to recruit. "There are some wonderful voices down there—talent going to waste." In thinking this through, she decided "there would be no objections to this as the singers would only be singing spirituals at first. Later on, they would be educated to learn the social meanings of songs, which would be very effective." Convinced that black artists performing in the South would give people "renewed courage, fortitude and pride in their race," she set about fund-raising for this idea and proposed Dean Dixon, a prominent black orchestra conductor, to head it up. "They need education, culture, and strength to fight for democracy; and we artists in the North have got to give it to them," she proclaimed.[22]

In 1946 Pearl formed a small company that toured extensively, including stops at historically black colleges and universities as well as other venues. The idea for this tour germinated during her 1944 study and travel in the South. Joe Nash and Jacqueline Hairston traveled with her along with percussionist Alphonse Cimber, singer Helen Tinsley, pianist Kenneth Drew, and lighting and stage manager Sturge Steinert. This tour took them to college theaters from North Carolina through West Virginia, Michigan, Indiana, Pennsylvania, and north to Maine, Rhode Island, and New York, where they were seen at the 92nd Street Y as well as the Metropolitan Opera House and the American Museum of Natural History. They were sponsored by groups as varied as the Winston-Salem Music Association, the Philadelphia Art Alliance, and college arts presenters in conjunction with dance programs and the American Youth for Democracy. The program at the Metropolitan Opera House, then in Brooklyn, was a benefit to aid the Welfare and Rehabilitation Fund of the Knights of Columbus under the patronage of his Eminence Francis Cardinal Spellman, archbishop of New York. This concert was unusual in that Pearl's work "Dark Rhythms" was set in the context of a classical and operatic program. Imagine moving in one concert from Bizet,

Rossini, Saint-Saëns, and Verdi to "Haitian Play Dance" and "Caribbean Conga." Pearl was billed as "the dancing star of 'Show Boat.'" The original 1927 *Show Boat,* based on Edna Ferber's novel of the same name, was a groundbreaking presentation of racial prejudice within the form of musical comedy. Reviews of the tour ran in all the major newspapers.

The repertory was similar from place to place. The first half of the program, "Dark Rhythms," reflected Pearl's quest to create work based on African traditions, images, stories, and rhythms. In "African Ceremonial," their opening number, the curtain came up slowly to reveal a figure that looked like a wood carving, bathed in a mysterious blue light. Ever so slowly the figure began to rise and then Pearl would start a sudden movement of the hands, then the pelvis. Joe said that Americans tend to express the sexuality of the movement, exaggerating the pelvis or the shoulders, but that Pearl always maintained subtlety of movement, "more like Africans doing their folk dances than African-Americans doing African dance." "Strange Fruit" was a program closer. "When she didn't have a narrator you heard her breathing," Joe Nash recalled. "You would be seated on the edge of your seat with this figure, pounding the earth. Her rhythm seemed to be established by our own heartbeats."

The tour included "Haitian Play Dance," in which Joe looked up at Pearl, who was about to jump over him, and he would appear fearful, as if she was trying to cast a spell on him. Another dance, called "Myth," was based on the Pygmalion story, with Jacqueline Hairston as the statue and Joe performing an ecstatic dance of joy over the fact that he brought the carved figure to life. The program note, however, refers to this dance as an interpretation of a Melanesian myth of creation: "To-Kabinana dances before the figure he has carved. His passionate intensity brings it to life."

Some of Joe's stories had less to do with choreography than with the ups and downs of touring and performance. At the Y in New York, when performing "Te Moana (The Deep), Study in African Rhythms," Joe was just about to exit upstage left when he felt his costume begin to give. He said to himself, "Joe, your backside gonna be to the audience, get this curtain dropped!" The curtain came down as the costume went "kaplui." Pearl made her own costumes, and apparently this one was hastily fastened.

On the last day of an engagement at the University of Chicago, Joe was narrating "Negro Speaks of Rivers." By this time they were tired of the tour and of each other, and anxious to get back to New York. He was supposed to say the concluding line that signaled the curtain and the blackout, "My soul has grown deep like the river," but he was daydreaming and missed his cue. When he looked up, Pearl was storming off the stage. "Mischievous Interlude" provided comic relief. Joe was upstage of Pearl, whose back was to him, and as he performed wide second position splits to cross the stage, he was supposed to approach her unawares. "The audience would be guffawing about what was happening upstage, and suddenly Pearl would look up and catch me making a movement. I would do a double-take and that would be the curtain."

Another favorite of his was the "Dance of Beauty," based on the Watusis of Rwanda. "She wore a headpiece which she would switch with a sharp movement of her head. The elegance and beauty of this movement were astounding." This was one of the solos from her early days that Pearl rechoreographed for Joe.

"Trio" was not a success. Pearl had problems with the overall concept of this piece and got bogged down choreographically. Joe thought that the audience was not concerned with the relationships that the dance depicted.

Pearl choreographed directly on Joe and Jacquelyn as they prepared for that first tour of 1946–47. Jacquelyn described Pearl in rehearsals as demanding but pleasant, setting a high standard with challenging material. In a pattern that Pearl maintained throughout her career, she worked out the dances first, then brought in one drummer. Closer to performance time she would bring in additional drummers and, if part of the program, the singers. In spite of Pearl's training with the New Dance Group and her own self-assessment as a modern dancer, Jacquelyn thought of Pearl's work as primarily African.

At first the small company on the road was all black, but it was soon integrated. They traveled in a station wagon that had a little trailer attached for luggage, drums, and sound and lighting equipment. Jacquelyn recalls that in Pennsylvania they went from one location to another and couldn't find a place to eat or sleep. Finally they found one that appeared clean and safe, but on "the low end of the totem pole." The management allowed them to come in after dark, but they had to leave before the other guests got up in the morning. Once the company was integrated, the white members of the group would bring food out from restaurants to the rest of them. In some places, they had reservations in advance, but this was not always possible. There were some towns where they couldn't find a place to stay together. Their experience recalls the war stories of black GI's who were ordered to escort German POW's to restaurants where they themselves were forbidden to eat.

They never got to see much of the towns in which they performed. After lodging, their next concern was the size of the stage and the condition of the floor. Pearl kept herself separate from the company, and would meet critics or tend to obligations while the company worried about food and sleep. When performing at colleges they stayed on campus, but there was always an undercurrent of anxiety as they drove into a new town and wondered how they would be received. It was easier to be accepted as an interracial company in the cities than in the small towns. At the black colleges and at colleges generally, they were looked upon as celebrities.

John Martin had said that this was one young artist who deserved to have her own company. After her 1944 research trip Pearl had imagined bringing art to this region, and she succeeded. She was on her way—creating, organizing, performing, traveling, meeting all the demands she placed upon herself. Her drive was always to bring an authentic form of dance to places where it had been lost.

⸻

Despite the way that Pearl's body challenged contemporary notions of beauty in dance, reviewers appreciated her creative energies. A Cleveland review by "E.F." described Pearl as "no fragile, fairy-like sprite, but a stocky girl with a beautifully disciplined body and great power of projection."[23] Similarly, Ralph Lewando, writing for the *Pittsburgh Press,* praised "the primal dance expressions of the dark-skinned natives of the far-flung regions of the earth . . . the simple folk who live by dancing as well as by food."[24]

Other reviews are filled with superlatives, yet they also reflect the effort to find a language befitting the experience of Pearl's dancing. J. Dorsey

Callaghan, for instance, in the *Detroit Free Press* describes "Pearl Primus, the dusky little dancer from Trinidad" who performs "primitive and modern dance," studies anthropology, and is "making a unique contribution to Negro culture in the United States." Dusky little dancer? "She has resisted the temptation to create a floor show from the materials at hand . . . her display of dance and rhythm is a forthright demonstration of the vast heritage of African culture." The review continues: "Joe Nash . . . created a picture that is unforgettable in his 'Dance of Beauty.' In it, he showed the almost decadent elegance of motion that is the mark of the seven-foot-tall tribesmen of the Belgian Congo."[25] Decadent elegance? By contrast, in a review of a performance at the North Carolina College for Negroes, this elegance is directly applauded. "In the 'Dance of Beauty' Joe Nash assumed the role of a member of a tribe of seven-foot people who live in the hills of the Belgian Congo, and whose dignity and beauty bespeak an elegant past."[26]

In a review from Charleston, West Virginia, Bayard F. Ennis praises Pearl's "bold brilliance" and "genius." Then he adds, "Miss Primus does not try to go beyond bounds . . . and that is to her credit. She has a definite contribution to make in the field for which she is best equipped."[27] In other words, although a brilliant, bold dancer, she knew her place. Another review from Detroit is succinct in its praise but then pigeonholes Pearl's artistry in terms of race. The writer says, "Miss Primus, short and strong, doesn't look like a dancer until she begins the dance. . . . She deserves to rank among the fine artists who are using her race's incomparable gifts of rhythm and music for its betterment."[28]

Reviewing the company's premier to a sold-out audience at Jordan Hall in Boston, Phyllis Watts calls Pearl "the dancing doctor from Trinidad," "lightning-limbed," a "25-year-old primitivist . . . of whom the Negro race can be justly proud. [I]n the space of a mere five years, [she] harnesses the dignity and the vitality of that race in the motions of two bare feet on a plain stage." She praises Pearl's "choreographic flair . . . in spite of the fact that as a serious-minded anthropologist she sets out to prove that the Negro 'soul has grown deep like the rivers,'" and concludes by saying, "Her dances can do what a gilt-edged campaign for her race never could."[29]

Pearl's concerts began to follow a customary sequence as she clustered pieces she called "Primitives," then segued to dances of social protest, abstract modern pieces, and suites of spirituals. "Primitives" included the dances based on research into the African traditions as she was studying them with Asadata DaFora, Belle Rosette, and other dancers in New York. They blended Pearl's understanding of African forms with her modern dance studies. In 1945 and 1946 she performed "African Ceremonial," "Afro-Haitian Play Dance," "Caribbean Conga," "Dance of Strength," "TeMoana (The Deep)," "Legend," and "Shouters of Sobo," among others. Her programs often had notes to orient the viewer to the dance. Of "Legend" she wrote, "In the tense blackness of the jungle Onishagun prepares her brew of fire and hate. Those who would pass must give warning that she may cover her pot. He who sees the smoke from her evil brew will have his guts ripped out and will wander forever a soulless man." In "Shouters of Sobo," set to a Trinidadian chant, "The priest having prepared the feast in the forest goes out into the street and by the ringing of a bell, calls the people to worship."[30] Pearl herself danced the priest, "with loquacious body and swinging bell summoning the people to the forest rites."[31] "TeMoana" was a study in African rhythms, and "Myth," as already noted, was a Melanesian Pygmalion story dance. With larger casts, "Caribbean Conga" and "Afro-Haitian Play Dance" explored "changing rhythms . . . syncopation that fathered jazz."[32]

A 1951 program shows the last part of the concert comprising a West African social dance, "Country Dance," followed by "Study in Nothing," "Mischievous Interlude," and then "American Suite," which included the folk songs and spirituals "Lonesome and Weary Traveller," "You Pray for Me," "Gonna Tell God All My Troubles," "Freedom Train," "Great Getting Up Mornin'," as well as "Strange Fruit (a man has just been lynched)." This suite, and others like it, directly prefigured Alvin Ailey's "Revelations," perhaps the most well-known American dance suite of the twentieth century. "Everybody Loves Saturday Night," billed as "a Country Dance from the West Coast of Africa," was featured in many of her "Dark Rhythms" concerts. Having learned the song and dance in West Africa, Pearl was never credited with introducing it into the lexicon of American folk music. Pete Seeger and the Weavers made the song famous in the popular hootenannies of the 1950s.

In contrast with the anguish of her own "Strange Fruit," and the African-based dances she called "Primitives," in 1946 Pearl performed in Sophie Maslow's "Folksay," set to music of Woody Guthrie and Tony Kraver. Like other New Dance Group members, Sophie Maslow was loyal to her cast of interracial dancers, which cost her performing opportunities in the South. Billie Kirpich, who also danced in "Folksay," remembered that Guthrie and Kraver sat downstage right, "Woody was the bum and Tony the gentleman." Their dialogues were interspersed with dance and music. "Is it far to the next town?" "Are you walking or riding?" As the dance opens, two lines of dancers come downstage doing a folk step, turn to the person opposite them and then break into a circle. The musicians continue playing and talking, two girls pass, flirting. A fight ensues. Muriel Manings recalled that Pearl was "fearful of the moment in the square dance part when two boys take you, throw you, lift you and you have to jump off." Ironically, Pearl had become known for the strength and height of her jumps.

Pearl made another foray onto Broadway with *Caribbean Carnival,* which had a New York run of eight days in December 1947, for a total of eleven performances. It was produced by Adolph Thenstead, with music by Samuel Manning and Adolph Thenstead, lyrics by Samuel Manning and Adolph Thenstead, directed by Samuel Manning and Col. John Hirschman, and choreographed by Pearl and Claude Marchant. The show was influenced by the success of Katherine Dunham, and all the dancers were recruited from a Dunham show, including the stars Josephine Premice and Claude Marchant. Dance historian Richard Long, who was living in Philadelphia at the time, described Thenstead and Manning as "two old vaudevillians." They hired Pearl to choreograph something that would look like a Katherine Dunham production, but conflicts ensued. Pearl was teaching in New York and going back and forth between New York and Philadelphia. At one point, it was arranged that she would stay with a friend of Richard Long's, since it was still problematic for blacks to stay in hotels. Richard's friend was looking forward to Pearl's visit with great expectation, but when she arrived, the friend called Richard and said, "I don't know what to do with this woman!" Pearl was in and out for two weeks and having great problems with "the vaudevillians," who thought the show didn't have enough erotic sizzle and had hired a snake dancer—i.e., a belly dancer—from vaudeville. By the time *Caribbean Carnival* opened on Broadway Pearl threw up her hands and had had it. Fortunately, her Broadway experience was very different by the time she choreographed and was the assistant director for "Mister Johnson" in 1956. In that show the director deferred to her African experience.

This tour of *Carnival* included several performances of a "Calypso" revue comprising work by Pearl, dancer Claude Marchant, and singer Josephine Premice. An extraordinary column in the *Evening Bulletin* in Philadelphia describes Pearl as "a buxom young woman of amazing flexibility and quivering muscles who gives exotic exhibitions of primitive African and native dances surrounded by a dozen active helpers."[33] A sampling of reviews suggests that this show was quite flawed, but apart from the structural difficulties of combining the work of the two artists, Pearl and Claude Marchant, the critics were still struggling with ways to speak about work that was outside their usual range of attitudes. Warren Storey Smith, writing for the *Boston Post,* reviewed a performance of "Calypso" at the Shubert Theater and said of the drumming, "If you can describe that one element as music, [it] is furnished by three drummers on the stage, who beat their tom-toms with their hands, inciting their companions on the stage to a frenzy that even affected certain members of the audience." He concludes condescendingly: "Frankly, the show is only for those who are willing to check along with their outer garments, everything but their most primitive instincts."[34] A paper in Boston describes "the savage dances of Pearl Primus," and "Miss Primus . . . a husky bundle of barbaric energy whose body shakes with the power of the whirlwind during the frenzy of the dance."[35] Pearl commented over the years that she perceived Boston as a particularly racist city, unwilling to support black artists.

Billie Allen, who became an acclaimed actor and director in New York, took Pearl's classes at the New Dance Group and then performed with Pearl in

Caribbean Carnival. She recalled the opening image, with Pearl elevated on a platform or a tree stump, and, as the lights came up, there she was "in all her glory and strength." Her costume was draped fabric in earth colors. Her legs were bare, "you could see her powerful thighs." The bodice was simple and loose so that "you could see the form of the body." One of Billie's friends once said, as Pearl came on stage, "My God, she's wearing rags. There were certainly no buttons or shiny things or bows." Pearl "electrified" the whole theater.

In the dance "Recumbe," composed of many leaps and contractions, powerful swirling and startlingly quick direction changes, Pearl was in complete control of her powerful body. "You could see her connection to the earth. She wasn't interested in being glamorous or pretty." Billie, who remembered Dunham as a good cabaret dancer, thought of Pearl as a concert artist. "Pearl used her sexuality in another way. You were always aware of this very powerful woman, very private, which made her more interesting, more provocative." Billie also recalled how Josephine Premice, wearing a red-orange silky sheath, sang a song called "Ice Cream Brick." "Come and get it and I'm sure you'll like it . . ." "It was quite provocative, not strictly Caribbean." There was no real "book" for the show, it was "slight." But the auditions for the dancers were stringent and exacting, and because there was not much happening for black dancers—especially on Broadway—they were able to hire top talent. The young dancers gave it their all but the directing was disorganized. Billie knew it wouldn't last, that it was a struggle on a shoestring.

Despite the show's shortcomings, Billie was captivated by Pearl's creative depth. "You always felt her subtext. She brought her self, the joy and the pain of her life, what she felt strongly about—it was expressed through her dance." Billie thought of Pearl as "the quintessential woman, as mother earth, not in the demeaning 'mammy' sense, but as perceiver, nurturer and doer. She had a very strong sense of who she was and she imbued the people in her orbit with that." "Pearl was very bright—in the sense that a light just shone through her. I always felt good in her presence."

Eloise Hill Anderson also danced in *Caribbean Carnival* and knew Pearl well in her early years as a dancer. Like Pearl she attended Hunter High, graduating in 1942. She first danced with a small group in high school and continued with Ethel Butler at Howard University. Returning to New York for the summer, Eloise found her way to the New Dance Group, where she met Pearl. She took to Pearl's style of movement and Pearl asked her to come to New York to study during the winter and ultimately to join *Carnival*. Pearl was transposing concert work to Broadway. Eloise auditioned and was cast as the understudy for Josephine Premice.

Carnival contained lyrical movements as well as Pearl's evolving strong and percussive technique, but the producers had a say in what types of dances they wanted to see. "We wore gorgeous dresses, but danced barefoot. Everyone wanted to know why we were barefoot!" Eloise recalled. "The show, with its mix of Primus' and Marchant's work, was really two different shows."

Pearl danced the lead in "Zinge," a piece about Shango, African God of Thunder. The story line focused on two warriors. As she did throughout her career, Pearl gave her dancers the background she was using for a particular dance. Another piece Eloise described was called "Night Scene," in which Pearl had a solo, "The Bat." She gave this solo to Eloise, who at first was thrilled but then realized that the dance was performed in the dark. The costume was giant wings treated so that their outline was visible on the darkened stage. This trick became a big joke among the cast, "not that we let Pearl know we laughed about it."

The show opened in Philadelphia and then went to Boston for two weeks, performing at the same time that *A Streetcar Named Desire* was opening. The two casts, including Marlon Brando, went to cast parties together. Performances in New York took place at the International Theatre, built in 1903, on Columbus Circle. But in New York there was a lot of criticism, and the closing notice was posted on opening night. Too many empty seats. Why are they dancing barefoot? It needs a book! Look at those costumes! After it closed, there were hopes that money would be sunk into it, but it came to nothing. Eloise felt that Pearl's choreography was more commercial than usual and that Pearl was clearly the star.

At this point Eloise was brought into the Dunham fold. For a time she

attended both schools, Dunham's and Primus's. She had Pearl's capacity for
elevation and enjoyed the training. But Pearl told Eloise that she thought she
needed a vacation from Pearl, and called Martha Graham to arrange a scholarship. Several years later, Eloise was performing with Dunham's "Shango" in
London when she received a note from Pearl that she, too, was in London
and was coming to see the show. They had a great reunion. Eloise had felt
a little guilty that she had left Pearl to go to Dunham. But Pearl greeted her
and said, "I know you were doing Dunham's choreography but I could see
my training in there."

When Eloise returned to New York, she became a teacher and later initiated a program that brought West African and Caribbean arts to the public
schools, including performances by Dinizulu, Syvilla Fort, Charles Moore,
Olatunji, and Lavinia Williams. After retiring she continued to teach at the
Harlem School for the Arts, which is diagonally across the street from the
Bentha Funeral Home on St. Nicholas Avenue, where funeral services are often held for the elite in black culture in New York. One day there was a fund-
raiser for WQXR Radio at the school. As a volunteer, Eloise was assigned
to greet celebrities. When she observed cars lining the avenue at Bentha
Funeral Home, she thought, "This must be a very important person." Then
she learned that this was Pearl Primus's funeral. "I could have dropped. Talk
about missing a moment in history. I went and donated money to WQXR
in Pearl's name. The others there didn't know how emotional it was for
me." "She did the work for all of us," Eloise reflected. Having danced with
both Pearl and Katherine Dunham, she resented the comparisons. "Physical
beauty was still on the table for most dancers. We knew Pearl in the raw."

After graduating from Brooklyn College in January 1948, Renee Cutler, now
Renee Cutler Meer, became the piano accompanist for the 1948 tour. Renee
thought of herself as "a nice Jewish girl who came from a secular background
where culture, music, and literature were always very important." She met
Pearl at Camp Wo-Chi-Ca in 1942, when Pearl was the dance counselor
and she was a Music and Art High School student. Pearl "took a shine" to
her, and when Pearl performed the newly choreographed "Strange Fruit,"

with Paul Robeson as an honored guest, she asked Renee to sing the verse. Responding to "a certain zing" she heard in Renee's folk dance and square dance music, Pearl invited her to accompany another dance, "Motherless Child," and ultimately to tour with the company.

Several years after their first meeting, Pearl asked Renee to be her accompanist on a tour that was being planned for the South, the North, and the Midwest. Renee lasted six months because she was a nervous performer and it put great strain on her. On the road, she and Pearl always shared a room. "We had a similar sensibility; she had more to talk to me about." Yael Woll, Pearl's husband, drove but, as an interracial couple touring the South, they did not share a room.

At Howard University in July 1948, Renee was struck by "the fact that the fraternities were so clearly colored delineated, the light skinned blacks and the darker blacks in different groups. I thought I was sophisticated but Pearl would say, 'Hey, stop being so naïve. There are color lines within our group, you know.'" Not only was Pearl very dark-skinned, but Renee felt that Pearl suffered from being short and muscular. "Yet as small as she was, she successfully depicted power and strength in her dance." Her work habits, however, proved problematic. When hired to teach, Pearl would often "come in late or not show up. There was a lot of negative talk about that."

Despite her periodically erratic behavior, Pearl kept up a full performance schedule. In New York on April 10 Pearl performed in a dance series at the Central High School of Needle Trades, where the cast was augmented by additional dancers, including Matt Turney and Charles Queenan, both of whom had distinguished careers, the former with the Martha Graham Company.

She also presented at the American Museum of Natural History for a program called "Around the World with Dance and Song" on April 22. This was billed as a concert and lecture, perhaps the first time she entered into a lecture-demonstration format, which was to become a staple in her later work. "It was the most regal and wonderful presentation, always with a lot of drama to it, capturing your imagination and interest to focus on what she was saying in a dance," Renee said. Performance stops for this program included the University of Illinois, Howard University, Hampton Institute,

Middlebury College, Smith College, Phillips Academy, and the University
of Wisconsin.

$\sim$

The 1940s were an immensely productive and vital time in Pearl's life. She
had graduated from Hunter College and was studying and teaching at the
New Dance Group and all over the city. She was a camp counselor at Wo-
Chi-Ca, mingling with many other brilliant young black and white artists
and activists, and she was performing at Café Society and attending and
performing at rallies. Twice she formed her own small company, in 1946–47
and again in the second half of 1948, and toured through the northeast states,
the South, and the Midwest, performing at many of the historically black colleges, among other venues. At the end of the 1940s she received a Rosenwald
fellowship and left for Africa, a trip that would transform her life.

In this period she met Yael Woll. Although Pearl is remembered as
having been married to Percival Borde, the Trinidadian dancer/percussion-
ist who became her partner in life and art, in fact she was first married to a
Jewish man, the son of Russian émigré parents whose father was a Hebrew
teacher and later principal of the Down Town Talmud Torah School on the
Lower East Side, and whose mother was the daughter of a rabbi. Although
Pearl had talked to several people about this marriage, and Yael was part of
the early dance days in New York, in a public interview at the University of
Michigan she denied it. To the question, "Was Percy your only husband?"
she replied, "Yes."[36] But early on Yael was her husband, her lighting designer,
and then her stage manager.

Yael's father, the eldest of eight children, was the first to emigrate, and
it was his responsibility to bring his brothers and sisters and, if he could, his
parents. His father had wanted to be a doctor but needed to make money
right away, so he became a Hebrew teacher. He moved first to Sioux City,
Iowa, where Yael was born, and then to Omaha, Nebraska, before returning
to New York. Born in 1923, Yael was younger than Pearl.

Yael described his mother as "very interested in the Pioneer Women for
Israel." She was "an activist for womankind." When he was about ten years
old, "my mother left for Palestine with me and my sister. My father stayed

home." They lived for two years with one of his aunts on the outskirts of Tel
Aviv. Yael went to school in Tel Aviv. "I used to hitch a ride on the back of
these Arab driven carts," he recalled. "I rode it until the driver turned around
and yelled at me. That became my customary way of traveling to school."
Yael enjoyed Israel enormously, especially being away from the authority
of his father, but after two years the father arrived to bring them back to
New York.

Yael enrolled in City College but was expelled for low grades and told
to come back after six months. He volunteered for the Army Air Corps, then
took a course with the Signal Corps and got a job inspecting radio crystals.
Although a good navigator, he had a depth perception problem and couldn't
become a fighter. Yael later went back to City College to finish his degree and
studied at the Film Institute under the supervision of Hans Richter, eventually replacing him as head of the Institute. There he met his future second
wife, Marian, with whom he had three children. Yael became a director and
eventually the national vice president of the Director's Guild.

Yael met Pearl in 1942 or 1943. In New York in the midst of the war
there was a strong sense of community and common purpose. Sympathetic
with those on the political left, Yael was always ready to attend events where
performers like Woody Guthrie or Huddie Ledbetter would appear. Many
decades later, Yael could not recollect their first meeting. Rather, he said, "It
was, probably, one of those things that went on in the city all the time. There
was always an affair or something on a Friday or Saturday night." Pearl appeared at one of those and they did a big story about her in *PM,* the leftist
newspaper whose name stood for "Picture Magazine."

Remembering those "heady days" in New York, Yael confessed that
everyone from his background was violently opposed to his marriage with
Pearl. By the time they were married in City Hall, Yael was an outsider to
some people from his past. "I had removed myself from those circles and I am
sure I was considered a lost cause," he said. Although Yael's family was not
particularly religious, they had a very strong connection to Jewish tradition
and custom. When he told his parents about his relationship with Pearl, they
were very upset, particularly his father, who came out to the army camp in

Indiana and spent a weekend trying to talk him out of it. "That didn't work. They broke relationships with me. My mother wasn't happy with that and my father was adamant and so was my father's family. They sort of controlled the whole family. They lived in a community in the country which was socialist or left leaning, called Ra'anana."

Yael's relationship with Pearl's family was "fairly friendly," he recalled. "They did the best they could with a white face in the house and in time they got more and more used to it." He attended Pearl's father's funeral. When circumstances permitted, Pearl and Yael would drive out to Brooklyn about once a week.

What did Pearl's family think of this match? Virginia Primus, Pearl's childhood friend and sister-in-law, knew Pearl and Yael as a couple. The Primus family liked Yael and had no problem with her dating a white person. "Yael was a nice person. I don't know if it was her station wagon or his station wagon or what station wagon it was 'cause I never asked. Honey, I don't ask nobody no questions. He used to come and take us out to New Jersey to some friends of his mother's. We used to go out there and have lunch. I never knew she was married to him."

Pearl's friend and former student Merle Afida Derby shared her impression of Yael as a very sweet person, often catering to Pearl. He was always kind to her and the students and people who came to the studio. In fact, when they were on tour, he used to send postcards to Merle and her sister Joan. "Not many people knew she was married to him." Merle said Yael was "soothing balm" around the students, teasing Pearl as he took care of business around the studio. In the beginning students would talk more with Yael than with Pearl, as if they were "like one person, one entity." "She was more than our teacher. We put her on a pedestal, she was like a goddess to us."

Yael and Pearl agreed about most things, but Pearl was the leader. She had a career, he did not, and she was the source of most of their income. Yael took to stage-managing and lighting concerts as they toured the Midwest and the South, giving performances at many colleges and universities. He drove the new DeSoto Suburban station wagon that Pearl had bought in the early 1950s, no small feat for a woman in those days. It was just large enough to

carry them, the troupe, and the luggage, though occasionally Pearl's manager, Austin Wilder, would arrange for a bus with a professional driver. Yael
introduced Pearl to his friends Ted and Lee Kazanoff and Gloria Beckerman.
In the late 1940s, Ted was enrolled in the Smith College theater graduate
program, and Pearl and Yael would visit them in Northampton on weekends.
Lee remembered them all walking out of a restaurant when Pearl was asked
to enter by the back door, in a northern example of Jim Crow.

By the late 1940s, Pearl needed a place of her own for rehearsals and
classes, and they rented a large loft at 17 West Twenty-fourth Street with a
studio in the front and an apartment in the back. Yael thought Merle and her
sister Joan Akwasiba were charming when they came for lessons. Joe Nash
was part of the troupe as was Albert Popwell, who later went to Hollywood
for a successful acting career in movies and television, including playing a
bad guy in the first three of Clint Eastwood's Dirty Harry movies.

On the southern tour, Yael recalled the separate black and white gas
stations, and having to buy food for everybody because they wouldn't be
served together. "We were okay when we came to a black university. Everything was all right again, but out in the real world it was very ugly," he said.
In Ohio, either Cleveland or Cuyahoga Falls, "suddenly there were pickets in
front of the concert. The feeling was that a friend of a friend probably turned
her in somewhere, somehow, for being red." Yael didn't know the extent of
her involvements with Communist-sponsored groups or whether she was
blacklisted. "She was probably active in all kinds of areas. I don't think that
there was any notoriety connected to it." As far as he knew, she never was
asked to testify before the House Un-American Activities Committee. About
that past, he mused, "McCarthyism had a horrific impact. When I was young
I was sure the world would become aware of itself and the badness toward humanity would disappear. Now I look around and marvel at how naïve I was."

Yael never traveled to Africa with Pearl, but he did travel to Israel in
1952 as the company stage manager. They went from Paris to Marseilles,
meeting with distinguished people, and then on to Tel Aviv. There were
many concerts in Israel, and Pearl was "an absolute smash. People loved
and admired her. I did not see any of my family there," Yael recalled. The

question of an interracial couple, as best he could remember, never came up. Students may have seen the couple as united, but Yael and Pearl didn't socialize with too many of the same people. "In a way we led two separate lives," Yael remembered. "I knew very little about her involvements. We just had that kind of relationship."

Yael thought their breakup was inevitable. "Our relationship was not too personal . . . Pearl was off in her cloud and I was down to earth," he recalled. Regarding the marriage, the Kazanoffs felt that by the time Pearl and Yael split, there was "nothing left." They saw Yael becoming increasingly dissatisfied in his role as manager and front man whenever they went to a southern town. "He was the one who booked them into the hotels and did the shopping. That role began to wear on him, over a long period of time, and he didn't want to get stuck in it." Ted remembers Yael saying, "Well, I just got tired of driving them around." Lee felt that Pearl was so involved in rehearsals, performances, and teaching, she let Yael slip away. In fact, Pearl turned her back against her white, Jewish friends at this time. Another friend from this era, Gloria Beckerman, recalled being "bruised by the ending of the friendship. I thought if she hurt so much, there was no reason to try to continue our friendship." Many years later Pearl called Ted, who was then head of the Theater Department at Boston University, for some guidance regarding her son Onwin's college studies, but they never saw one another again.

Yael Woll and Pearl Primus were married in August 1950 and separated in January 1953. The divorce was finalized in November 1961. Yael stated unequivocally that he was the one who ended the marriage. Their time together had been intense and defining but, finally, not mutually sustaining. Pearl was driven by her own needs and her desire for self-definition through her dances, and later through her African identification. To continue to be in her presence, one needed to accept her definition of things. After Pearl and Yael separated, Yael was reconciled with his father. "He was very sorry I wasted life. We never discussed it."

Reflecting on Pearl's career, Yael said, "She was a blazing star. She never had the same ambitions as Katherine Dunham had. She wasn't into show business. She was into intellectual accomplishments and took pride in study with Margaret Mead." He felt that the dances she derived from Africa were connected to a higher purpose. "Pearl never seemed connected to a search for commercial rewards and all that goes with that," Yael thought. "She had this sense of authenticity about her."

⟋⟍

Pearl's search for authenticity had other, public consequences as well. Concerts were cancelled because of her political dances, especially "Strange Fruit," and pickets assembled outside concerts in the Midwest. Even before the McCarthy years, the United States government was watching her movements and performances, and employing informants to report on her activities. Reflecting on the force of Pearl's protests against racial injustice, Jean-Leon Destine remarked, "If you work in this way, you were marked, and could be in trouble at any time." Pearl's FBI file reveals the nature and extent of the surveillance. Hearing of the time, money, and manpower that went into Pearl's file, Maya Angelou threw back her hands and exclaimed, "Don't be naïve! This is the would-be United States of America."

The first entry in Pearl's file was made by William A. Costello on September 9, 1944.[37] The "Synopsis of Facts" states: "Subject a negress born July 1, 1917 at Trinidad, British West Indies. No naturalization record found. She has an AB degree and is a professional dancer. She has been in contact with CPA National Headquarters." The "details" follow:

> This investigation is predicated upon information furnished by Confidential Informant T-1, who advised that PEARL PRIMUS contacted [name redacted] at Communist Political Association National Headquarters on June 1, 1944, and asked if they knew anyone with whom she could stay for a weekend while in Bluefield or Princeton, West Virginia. The informant later advised that [name redacted] of the CPA National Headquarters told PEARL PRIMUS that Mr. Browder [Secretary General of the U.S. Communist Party] had received Pearl's ticket for her performance that night but was unable to attend. [name redacted] also told the subject that he had been unable to be of any assistance

concerning the West Virginia addresses but he would attempt to find out something further and let her know. The subject told [name redacted] that she would appreciate it as she had never been further south than Washington, D.C., and it would be her first experience on JIM CROW trains.

A second informant, "Confidential Informant A," reported that Pearl attended the Citizen's Emergency Committee for Inter-racial Unity at Hunter College on September 25, 1943, and said she was "prominently mentioned along with many known Communists and Communist sympathizers." The meeting was ostensibly in the interest of interracial harmony but was described by the informant as Communist in its inception and management. "Yet a third informant, "Confidential Informant N," reported that on November 15, 1943, "Pearl Primus appears on a list of sponsors of the Citizen Nonpartisan Committee to Elect Benjamin Davis, Communist Party candidate for City Council for Manhattan," and reports on newspaper stories in the *People's Voice* and the *Daily Worker* that describe Pearl's performances. The informant recounts her participation in the Negro Freedom Rally at Madison Square Garden on June 7, 1943, when she said, "I know we must all do our part in this war to beat Fascism and I consider the battle against Jim Crow in America part of that fight which is taking part on the battlefronts of the world. Each one of us can field a weapon against Jim Crow and Fascism and my special one is dancing. I shall continue to protest Jim Crow through my dancing until Victory is won."

Several paragraphs follow to verify her address, including information from the United States Post Office, which did not seem hesitant to report on Pearl's mail and inquiries directed to a rental company. "Confidential informant T-1 advised that Pearl Primus resides at 536 Madison Street, Brooklyn, New York, and her telephone number is Glenwood 5-3629." Additional biographical material indicates that the FBI had access to the records of the registrar at Hunter College. "It is noted on the [Hunter College] record that on November 22, 1938, she was a non citizen and denied some day privileges as a result." "Nothing derogatory appears in her file."

On August 29, 1944, a special investigator searched the files of the Immigration and Naturalization Service in New York "in an effort to ascertain whether the subject has ever been naturalized," with negative results.

It was noted that a September 2, 1944, issue of the *People's Voice* states that "the subject is presently traveling through the south on a tour entertaining the Army camps and that she is due back in New York to undertake an engagement at the Roxy Theater in September." There follows a description that includes her name, address, citizenship ("Alien"), weight ("110"), complexion ("dark brown"), occupation ("dancer"), among other "facts." It concludes: "This matter is being closed on the authority of the Special Agent in Charge, subject to being reopened upon receipt of further information indicating activity on the part of the subject that might be inimical to the best interests of the United States." Special Agent William Costello filed the report in New York on September 9, 1944. Confidential informant T-1 was known to Costello.

It is clear from this first lengthy entry that the FBI was trying to find out whatever they could about Pearl, possibly in the hope of locating damning evidence. That her immigration status was in question must have been particularly distressing to her, although we learn further on in the file that Pearl considered herself a naturalized citizen by virtue of her parents' attaining citizenship.

Even though the case appears "closed," the file continues two months later, on November 11, 1944, with another report by William Costello. Again he starts by identifying "Subject, a Negress, reported to be an organizer for the CPA." Additional information here includes that she participated in the twenty-fifth anniversary celebration of the Communist Party, is reported to be a member of the Party, and "attended the Leadership School of the Southern Negro Youth Congress in Atlanta in August, 1944." This second entry recounts Pearl's activities during the summer of 1944, with quotes from Pearl herself and from various newspapers that describe her activities and place her in social, political, and artistic contexts.

A confidential informant stationed in the Women's Army Corps in Georgia was in contact with "Pearl Primus, colored, of New York City" while Pearl attended a Leadership School in Atlanta. Pearl appeared "well-acquainted" with the person, who is described as being from New York and an active member of the Communist Party. The writer asserts that Pearl was in contact with "the National Headquarters of the Communist Political Association and the purpose of her contact was to invite Earl Browder to come to the theater" as her guest.

This entry includes a statement of Pearl's that appeared in the *Daily Worker*, September 28, 1944, after she returned from the South. In an article by Honore Sharrer she is quoted as saying: "I am not trying to create something new in the dance . . . I am only attempting to present the Negro in his own true light, as he was in the past in Africa and as he is now, a member of a fighting democracy. . . . In America's bosom we have the roots of Democracy, but the roots do not mean there are leaves. The tree could easily grow bare. We will never relax our war effort abroad but we must fight at home with equal fierceness. This is an all out war; we will not stop fighting until everyone is free from inequality."

The Sharrer article reports that Pearl "contributed her services to USO Camp Shows, dancing at Army camps, hospitals, and ports of embarkation," that she thrilled audiences in "concert halls, service men's clubs, Café Society, Tuskegee University and union halls." It quotes another dance radical, Edith Segal, as praising Pearl's work and relates "her credo as expressed in the words of Owen Dodson and read by Gordon Heath: 'Dignity in my past; hope in my future; I fight among fighters for a new world that will blossom in a bright new spring.'" Both Dodson, a poet, novelist, and playwright, and Heath, an actor, continued to figure in Pearl's life.

The informant suspects that Pearl "is a member of the Artists Group of the Communist Political Association or at least a fellow traveler. He had no definite knowledge of her membership." It was reported that all the Communists "love her" and many attend her recitals, that she performs at "Front affairs," but again, there was no definite knowledge of her membership, though the report concludes that when she performed at Madison Square Garden on September 28, 1944, an informant stated that Pearl "was a member of the Young Communists League when she attended Hunter College."

On November 9, 1944, Special Agent E. E. Conroy wrote to the director of the FBI to recommend that a "Security Index Card" on Pearl Primus be started. This was followed on December 11, 1944, by a letter from none other than J. Edgar Hoover to the special agent in charge in New York, notifying him that a Security Index Card had been prepared in the name of "Pearl Eileene Primus, Alien, Communist, Professional Dancer at Café Society." It gave her home address and her work address. The card was to be filed, "kept current at all times and the Bureau immediately advised of any changes made therein."

On December 18, 1944, follow-up research "failed to reveal any record of Pearl Eileene Primus" at the Central Office of Immigration and Naturalization Service in Philadelphia. "No record could be located" of her "having received naturalization papers through her own application or through derivative citizenship of her father or mother. There is no record of subject or her parents having entered this country or having registered as aliens in the report of reference. This matter is being referred upon completion to the office of origin." In January 1945 William Costello reported to the FBI that there was no record in the Philadelphia office of Pearl's having received naturalization papers. The issue was stamped CLOSED, "subject to being reopened on receipt of further information justifying such action."

The last entry during this period was on May 16, 1945, to J. Edgar Hoover from William A. Costello. He writes that "there is no information in the files to indicate that she is either a prominent or influential Communist," and recommends that the Security Index Card be cancelled.

A final note from this period, dated May 30, 1945, was a response from Hoover, accepting the May 16 recommendation and directing that "if additional information is received indicating that the subject is, in fact, dangerous or potentially dangerous, a new recommendation should be made for the preparation of a Security Index card." The file, however, is far from complete at this point and picks up again in 1951, after Pearl and her company toured the South and after her first, life-transforming trip to Africa.

THREE

African Transformations

JULIUS ROSENWALD, a philanthropist and president of the Sears Company, was drawn toward leftist causes. In 1917, he founded the Julius Rosenwald Foundation, which funded universities, museums, hospitals, public schools, the fine arts, social settlements, and many other causes. Rosenwald was particularly interested in Jewish and African American organizations and individuals, and he assisted Marian Anderson, Katherine Dunham, Zora Neale Hurston, Langston Hughes, W. E. B. DuBois, and Ralph Ellison, among others. "Not every Rosenwald fellow became famous, but the number of people who used the award to embark on their careers is remarkable," biographer Peter Ascoli observed.[1] Rosenwald did not believe in philanthropy in perpetuity, however, and wanted all the foundation's funds dispersed within twenty-five years of his death (1932). The Julius Rosenwald Foundation was in the process of closing down when its president, Edwin Embree, saw Pearl perform at Fisk University in Nashville, Tennessee, on April 28, 1948. The president of the university, Charles Johnson, his wife, and Marjorie Rawlings, author of *The Yearling*, were among those in attendance when Pearl's performance provoked the delighted Embree to award her his last fellowship.

Sometime between April 28 and her departure for Africa in December, Pearl described her feelings upon learning that she would receive a Rosenwald Foundation fellowship.

> Sleep sat back and laughed that night. . . . The concert was over. My muscles were still charged with electricity. I could have danced for three more hours. My performing company and various people from the audience were off somewere [*sic*] feasting . . .

It slowly seeped into my brain that a strange thing was being discussed. A trip to Africa! Was I the person chosen to go?

My soul hopped out of my body, swung on the lights, kissed everyone present, flew out of the window and screamed with the wind and vanished into the night like a thing insane. I tried to piece history together. The concert must have been a tremendous success. Dr. Embree had been in the audience. Mrs. Johnson planted the seed—this girl—Africa! The others watered it and now a little tree was growing. . . .

I managed to walk calmly and to talk a bit logically till I reached my company. Then like my soul, I burst into ecstasy, explaining with an incoherent tongue what had happened. Amazement stood in their eyes and sleep sat back and laughed all night.

I was drunk with excitement. Back in New York I shocked my family. I am going to Africa! My friends smiled strangely, my manager dismissed it as a joke I had concocted for myself. But I leaped over chairs, turned and turned till the whole world spun with me, sang to my cats, Faust and Chopin, and my dog Aggripina. Chopin turned his head and yawned, but Faust and Grippy raced up and down the studio with me.

After this burst of exuberance she more soberly detailed the enormity of planning the yearlong trip. "Plans—maps—conferences! Clothing—medical supplies—camera—film—recording machine! Visas—questions, questions, QUESTIONS! Inoculations and their drastic reactions." Yet even in the cascade of practicalities a sense of momentous responsibility emerges.

I have been chosen to go on a serious mission . . . to learn from [the peoples of Africa] the basic truths of dance and life, to salvage for America the beauty, dignity and strength of a threatened culture—to bring back music, folklore, dances, and to interpret them honestly for the audience . . . I have put aside my books—. I shall fold my costumes away at home and with great humility I shall go into the land of my forefathers. My heart will be filled with the music and drums and my soul will dance with the people.[2]

Pearl saw an almost divine mission in this journey, and she expressed its implications for her sense of identity when Mrs. Johnson asked her to speak with a group of children in a small chapel at Fisk. Pearl wrote, "This was a special group. These Negro children were blind."

THE PROMISE

Have you ever opened your mouth to shout but found Silence sitting on your tongue? In the stillness which follows has your mind ever raced through the centuries? This has happened to me . . .

I heard my name announced and I heard the applause. My feet raced down the aisle of the Chapel, and there I was standing before my audience. Then it was I opened my mouth to shout, but silence closed it.

Over the years my thoughts ran—back to a dancing people—a people so strong and beautiful that the trade in "black ivory" became the life stream of great nations. Poured like so much cattle into strange lands, these people were stunned. Warriors, kings, artists, doctors, hunters, women of extraordinary physical beauty—all passed through the melting pot of the slave market.

Some escaped into the jungles of South America. Some were slain. (It is said that on each tree of the row of palms extending from the onetime slave market in Charleston a head of a slave was suspended as a warning to any who entertained thoughts of freedom.)

Suddenly my mind came back, back to the tiny Chapel, back to my anxious audience. I looked into their sightless eyes and in a voice which crept slowly from my throat I said:

Once I gazed upon the faces of children and in their eyes

71

I found a question. I find it in yours also. "Who are we?" I promise you when I return from Africa, I shall come back here. For
your ears I shall bring the music of Africa, and for your thoughts
the answer to your question . . .

Handwritten beneath this: "Someday she will become proud of you."

Pearl left New York in December 1948 and was away eighteen months.
She traveled first to Nigeria and then from May to August 1949 to the Belgian Congo (then Zaire, now Congo). Her travels also included Gold Coast
(Ghana), Angola, the Cameroons, Liberia, and Senegal. Tribes cross the
borders of these states, and the study of a particular group, for instance
the Yoruba, would have taken her to several countries as she went from village to village. Ultimately, she studied at least thirty culture groups on this
journey.

Pearl's diaries from this period are small books in which, in tiny script,
she recorded notes and impressions, poetry, questions, beginnings of choreographies, descriptions of costumes, language usage, and many drawings—of
dress, homes, trees, people. And lists, always lists: gifts to buy, medicines
to organize, letters to write. She wrote and wrote—letters, essays, magazine pieces, poetry and lectures, and later a doctoral thesis—and in them
she refined the raw impressions of her experiences. The beginnings of her
"Statement" are in note form in several places; drafts of letters with correc-
tions are saved along with copies of final versions, as are draft after draft of
essays, grant applications, project descriptions. She was as much a woman
of words as she was of movement, and a saver of virtually everything. Unfortunately, the letters she wrote to those back home from Africa are not among
her collected papers.

We glimpse the tenor of her experience through letters from family and
friends. Pearl's mother, described by all who knew her as kind, sweet, warm,
and caring, comes through in all these ways. She is anxious but proud, and
associates Africa with their Caribbean origins: "Dear where you are must
be like some parts of Trinidad, red, yellow, white, black dirt of all colours.
We are very glad you are happy among *our* people." "Fannie is dying to hear

from you is very worried too, as not being near to see about her darling's hair. She . . . knew all along that the people of Africa would love you, because you are wonderful and yet so unspoild [*sic*]. Don't ever change." On March 28, her mother sends news of Pearl's spreading recognition, noting her fellow dancer Hadassah's report of "the lovely things that is [*sic*] written about you & her & many others by Margaret Lloyd in her book named [*The Borzoi Book of Modern Dance*]," and conveys the drummer Cimber's "very best compliment." "We also have 4 pages of you in pictures in the center of the magazine called 'Colour.' Very nice," she adds.

It would be tidy if the period from her marriage to Yael to her meeting with Percival Borde coincided with the changes in her heart and soul when she lived and traveled in Africa. But life is not that neat. Pearl married Yael upon her return from Africa, not before the trip. In their divorce document, the marriage day is dated August 31, 1950. Even so, the letters Pearl saved from Yael to her in Africa contain telling details about their relationship and the sustaining role he played for her. Their communication was tense, but the relationship survived their separation. Yael alternates between the ongoing concerns of everyday life (e.g., getting a car out of storage) and discussions of their relationship. Most poignantly, he expresses the desire to know of her experiences, and not simply to hear about the practicalities of what needed to be done either in the States or in Africa.

Yael's writing shows a quiet wit and, at times, an almost self-effacing irony. He accommodates Pearl's needs, tolerates her flare-ups of anger, and voices a steady concern for her well-being: ". . . and I don't doubt that by now you've had fried cockroaches for supper. Don't let any of those foreigners step out of line. Just give them that old 'Battler' treatment." He expresses concern about her attractiveness to others: "It's nice to hear that you look lovely but don't look too lovely because you know what happens to too lovely looking people . . . be well, and don't get so angry so easy. . . . Don't worry about those kisses. I'll have you crying for mercy, and of course will show you none. You'll sleep for three weeks after I get through with you."

Yael also expresses the growing tension and anxiety about loss of emotional contact. He writes, "I want you should be home in September. Can you make it?" He doesn't want her to curtail vital research, "but seeing that I miss you so, and find there are many others who do also, it would be greatly appreciated, especially here, if you did manage it by sometime in September. Not only animate things miss you, the big fat heavy car of yours misses you more than all the others—it seems." As Yael's loneliness finally turns into exasperation, he is unhappy to learn that she is "disconsolate" over their separation and urges her to cut her stay short. "Enough is enough. . . . There is no need to become a martyr. . . . Let there be some wholesale choppings and eliminations in the agenda . . . if you are not back by Xmas you have stayed too long, no matter what."

Sometime later, Yael responds to what must have been an angry attack on Pearl's part. Though he does not state the cause, we can sense an intense rift and Yael's attempt both to express and to contain his hurt and anger. In very strong language, he describes the "awful shock" of her letter and how miserable and alone he felt after receiving it. "It was as if someone had come up to me as I lay sleeping and hit me with all his might right in the middle of my stomach." He writes that "bitter arguments arose in my mind." But basically he "worried half to death in those three weeks I hadn't heard from you."

He worried that she was "sick or in trouble" and felt "unprepared for the letter." Acknowledging that "bitterness remains," he also says that although "everything you said was true in the most stark and unpleasant sense . . . your point of view is in doubt. Also your right . . . to say it the way you said it remains in doubt. . . . I'm only trying to explain as best I can how I couldn't write to you sooner. If you wish, we can discuss this thing and thrash it out good and clear when you get back. If you've tried to get even in some way for all the hurt I've done you, you've succeeded." He acknowledges that "my life has changed very little from the one you knew when you left. . . . Of you and myself, I can say nothing, for your letter is, to me an insurmountable barrier. Only this—that I think of you incessantly in many different ways. My days are full of your image. Even now as I write these first few days reaction comes back. Pearl dear, I can't love you because you won't let me."

Yael responded as best he could through the vast separation he and Pearl were enduring, coaxing her to return, threatening her with kisses, trying to humor her even as he expresses deep hurt, anger, and dismay in response to a letter whose contents we can only surmise. His shocked response echoes a moment of deep personal crisis in Pearl's life. Although they married after her Africa trip, many years later Yael recalled that it was "all over by the time she returned and I, unequivocally, was the one who ended it." Though this may have been Yael's self-protective memory, their official marriage was probably intended as much to rescue as to confirm their bond.

Pearl's papers from Africa include an invitation from President William Tubman and his wife to "witness and participate in the striking of the Library National Ensign and the United Nations Flag by battalion of the Liberian Frontier Force," as well as invitations from other officials of townships throughout West Africa, but such ceremonies were only the surface of her experience. Not yet thirty, a rising star in New York, the darling of the critics and the downtown, left-wing artists and intelligentsia, she was forging a new sense of herself when she withdrew to immerse herself in African cultures. It is hard for us in the twenty-first century to imagine the distance that Pearl Primus traveled when she went to Africa for eighteen months. That continent was further away then than it can ever be again. On January 25, Hadassah and her husband, Milton Epstein, voiced the sense of vast, exotic difference that all of Pearl's friends and family must have felt at the time. "You have been on our minds a great deal lately. We are therefore sending this note into space, to seek you in the vastness of this universe, to find you, and inquire of your welfare. Perhaps this note will find you on the back of a camel surveying the Sahara Desert. Who knows? It may even be that you will read this note with one hand while you hold a lion's tail with the other."

Camels and lion's tail aside, Pearl expressed her perceptions of life in Africa in a statement dated September 28, 1949, and published in the *Observer* in December. It ran under the banner headline "AFRICA DANCES A letter from Pearl Primus."

> I am indeed fortunate. Tonight I write by the light of a tiny lantern and a sputtering twig dipped in palm oil. The village is

Kahnplay—hamlet of Paramount Chief Mongrue. He has adopted me as his daughter and to use his own words, "Whatever I have is yours for you are my child—you call me father." It is here I met the devil dancers. They came down the trail like fantastic giants hovering over the pointed huts—they came with drums and singing to meet me. Now everywhere there is dancing—the air is filled with music—this will continue for days till I leave here. So it is everywhere in Liberia. The people run down to the rivers to sing you across—and when you join in their dance you are lifted in their arms. You are welcome—chicken, eggs, native-made cloth and cola nuts are presented to you.

This is a new life to me. The dancer is still very important in the lives of the people. The dancing is basic—not primitive. (I shall never again use that term when speaking of African dance forms.) It seems to hug the earth, leaving it fleetingly only to plunge into its guts again—, the feet move faster than any other form I've seen. Often I must peer through narrowed eyes to see if the feet touch the ground at all. For the most part I would say the dance here shows mastery of subtle movement—Oh—the tiny movement of the back, the use of the hands, and the minute ripple of the neck. I have been amazed and overjoyed, for when the spirit entered me the reason for the dance became my reason to move. I danced as I have never danced on the stages of America. *Myself was transformed; yet underneath all this a deep process of analysis was taking place.*

I have been taken into many tribes and shown many wonders in certain societies. Now I am being prepared for initiation into the Sande, one of the most powerful of the female cults in Africa. The members are marked down the back and over the shoulder down the front to the pubic region. I shall plead for fewer cuts—though the design is beautiful I don't think I could endure all. Unfortunately I am sworn to secrecy and therefore cannot tell you too much.

For those of us who are performers this is really one of the greatest classrooms, for *the true dance aims at effect*—the rapid movement is suddenly halted—the spinning dancers suddenly stop still before the chief, and the woman in trance suddenly screams through the stillness. The costumes are splendid. No theatre has produced anything like those of Mushenge or Benin—designed again for effectiveness! The make-up is most interesting. Certain places in eyes are emphasized—in others it is the hollow of the cheeks—and where make-up fails, the mask is worn.

This is a course in choreography. The basic patterns of life—the circle which is the embryo—the force of the straight forward line which is birth—the spiral, the Xing, the jagged line which denotes growth and struggle—the return to the circle again—the shrinking of the circle to a tiny speck and the dropping of that speck into the vastness of eternity which is death.[3] [Italics added]

"Myself was transformed, yet underneath all this a deep process of analysis was taking place." Earlier Pearl's artistic focus had included African-derived work, but her most powerful dances reflected the black experience in America. Now African life itself became a source of strength, self-knowledge, and a profound source of inspiration. In the heart of Africa, Pearl found rebirth and enlightenment rather than the darkness that Western eyes associated with the continent. In the cultures of the villages she consolidated her identity. The Rosenwald grant allowed her to study the style of dancing, the rhythms, the masks, and the life of the people. The Oni, the king of Ife in Nigeria, named her "Omowale," "Child Returned Home." Wherever Pearl went in West Africa, she was announced by the drums with another new name, "'Little Fast Feet' is on the way."

She told Joe Nash that Africans were incredulous that an American could capture the feel of authentic African movement so accurately and that if she failed to do it right, they would poke her so that she could find the center of the movement. She mastered a polycentric approach to movement in which the dancer develops the ability to concentrate and isolate several parts of the body simultaneously—the shoulders, the head, the torso, the pelvis, and the feet, all with complex counterrhythms.

Through her travels, Pearl became a griot, and learned to tell African stories in her own inimitable way. "You become the persona of the story. Your whole personality is taken over by the content to be communicated. Pearl—through her eyes, her head, her shoulders, her feet, her body—she told a story completely, in the true tradition of the griot of Africa. The African spirit became part of Pearl," Joe said. When she returned, her work expanded in its narrative range. Instead of concentrating on the small recital stage, she brought together a company to develop the ideas she had studied in West Africa.

—⁓—

"Many Africans believed Miss Primus to be the returned spirit of one of their own people," wrote dance critic and journalist Walter Terry, who became her great friend and supporter. Pearl's "immediate sense of kinship with the dance rhythms, the philosophies, the art-beauties of her African hosts" derived from a "mystical, ancestral, [and] artistic" rapport. In Africa she was able to discover "the motivating forces behind such dances" as well as the "amazing technical, stylistic and thematic scope of African dance." Pearl had been instructed by individual experts, and in her journals she had drawn pictures and indicated rhythms. She also used photography and film to record movement and the great varieties of costumes and instruments. Terry wrote:

> Miss Primus's explorations uncovered court dances (some as stately as the West's pavane), nature imitations, abstract ceremonials, fertility dances, dances of the aristocracy, children's dances and dances of birth, puberty, death and motherhood. Acrobatic, social, hunting dances were to be found as well as ballets narrating story and legend, ecstatic dances, humorous dances and many others. The American dancer, then, witnessed not only complex rituals but also such diversified dance expressions as a pre-marital dance in the African equivalent of a beauty parlor where the bride-to-be was subjected to mudpacks by other help-

ful aids; jitterbugging, brought to Kano, Nigeria by GIs, and there Africanized by the local inhabitants, and a humorous dance at planting time in which the dancer, dressed as a miserable beggar, indicated to the gods that such would be his lot if the gods did not look with favor upon the crops.

Terry then detailed the body positions Pearl mastered "with the goal of academizing these techniques for use in the America educational system," and recounts the range and diversity of her researches. "Geography and climate as well as tribal customs governed certain dance forms. There were lightning dances in Liberia, fire dances in Senegal and dances evocative of the motions of the seas among the peoples of coastal regions. Among the Benis of Nigeria, Miss Primus found a dance almost Javanese in style, and the Efik of the same land recalled Hawaii, while the Ibo in his dance resembled most closely the general conception of African dance as a vital, vibrant and highly energetic activity."[4]

Terry's advocacy enabled the public to share her shift in self-perception, to witness her transformation. By highlighting her embodiment of African cultures, he opened the way for Pearl to re-present herself for the remainder of her days. In keeping with the African sense of spiritual kinship, many people would come to call her "Mna"—"mother who did not born you," a name she chose for herself.

—∞—

In Africa, Pearl absorbed an enormous amount of material. Uncannily, she seemed to have known the cultures already, and she deepened her belief in her own spiritual powers. She didn't announce these powers, but many people came to recognize them as part of her being. The sense of her as spiritually connected to worlds unseen was especially palpable to the African kings who adopted her, to the African dancers who felt she knew their dances before they were taught to her, and also, over the years, to some artists, colleagues, students, and close friends.

In her journal, Pearl experimented with how she wanted to present this new self publicly. She wrote:

PEARL PRIMUS, internationally famous dancer, has many names:
"Omowale"—Yoruba for "child has returned home"
"Adaora"—Ibo for "daughter of all"
"NKuyo"—Efik for "one born in to darkness faces the light"
"PEARL PRIMUS, internationally famous dancer was renamed
"Omowale" by his honor the Oni of Ife, the Spiritual Head of
the Yoruba people of Nigeria and also "Adaora" by the late Mr.
Mbonu Ojike."

In an undated journal entry we find the beginnings of her "Statement," which
was first published in *Dance Magazine* in 1968:

Dance is a language—:
    words   /   music
    painting   /   carving etc—
    I believe 1) language is for the purpose of communicating
ideas—moods—
2—No universal language of words—
3—Art is universal—
    No race, creed, level of society
Dance as part of art is universal and must not only communicate
but *must* communicate *to all*
Dance is in my opinion in America is a lang [*sic*] but speaks only
to sects—Graham—Weidman—Limon cults. . . .

In her journal Pearl also first sketched a plan for a school or an institute, with a curriculum based on ideas that may have originated at the New
Dance Group but that were strongly influenced by her African experience.
The closest realization of this school was the African-Caribbean-American
Institute of Dance Arts [Earth Theater] developed with Percival Borde
much later in her life, but at the time of her death she was still attempting
to create a complete institute, with a board of directors, a curriculum, and a
faculty.

However, all was not speculation about the distant future. Pearl corresponded with a man named Arthur about shipping film up and back, and—on stationery with the lettering *Esquire, The Magazine for Men*—Arthur responded to requests for magazines and perfume. He alluded to other anxieties as well: "Pearl, from your letter I can just imagine what you have been going through. I am terribly upset about it and only wish there was something I could do. I do think you are right to stay and face it out. I know you will feel better about it that way and I know that what you learn will be invaluable for you in your career and your life." He wrote reassuringly about her supporters, the possibility of a Guggenheim Fellowship, the availability of agents and concert venues, including television. He also saw fashion opportunities. "Keep an eye out for any native print material or styles that *Vogue* might be interested in . . . anything that might be adapted for resort or evening wear in headgear, blouses, skirts or sandals. . . . Have you come across anything in hats, shirts, trousers, trunks or shoes . . . any native-dyed, hand-blocked fabric that would be good for sportswear or the beach?"

Pearl did bring back fabric and clothing and "native styles," but not with an eye to exploiting African culture. Upon her return, she wore African garb as a manifestation of her discovered identity and never again appeared in public in Western attire. She saved a letter from Akanni Olatunji in Lagos, who tells her, "The most impressive part of your achievement is how you paid homage to the King of the Ife who gave you a new name, Omo Wale which mean[s] child returns."

The Africa diaries show Pearl's way of condensing her research in calendar books, each page with a day and date on it. Diary entries were outlined on note cards that became the basis for many future lectures and performances. One series of cards outlines a presentation about "Bushasche," the war dance of the Bushongo people:

The Function of Dance in Two African Culture   (BUSHONGO 1)
The two peoples whose culture I have chosen for this study are the Bushongo and the Watusi.
I shall first give a brief background on both groups then move on to a discussion of their dances.

I have visual material up here but in order to avoid confusion will keep it up here for you to observe at the end of the hour.

Not much actual performing today as I must learn how to make a point with words not movement.

The Bushongo People Bakuba   (BUSHONGO 2)

   Geography

      Some say flat—I say gently rolling

   Describe road—rising, plunging, brand new scenery suddenly then long

      Stretches of sameness . . .

      Giant trees and vines clinging to them—lush

      Then gnarled skinny trees struggling for existence in sand—

      Then fragrant cool forests

   Earth—Sandy—sand snatches at everything except the blue of the sky

   Location—between Saskuru and Kasai Rivers

   Climate—hot—scorching during dry season

      But cooler during rainy—

   . . .

People   (BUSHONGO 3)

Bushongo—Bakuba—People of the Lightning because of knife-throwing knife used with deadly accuracy

Language—Bantu

   Physical characteristics—medium height tho' many nearing 6′ are found among men. Stocky—exceedingly well built

3 sub groups or sub tribes

   Bambala—People of the Cloth

   Pranga—People of the Leaf

   Gwembe—People of the Mole

Capital Mushenge

   Built on series of concentric circles

Walls of city woven from plant fibers
    Servants and subordinate members of community
      (growing in import)
(drawing)   king

The lecture notes distill many pages of journal entries addressing geography, food, social organization and customs, political organization, work, physical characteristics, and so on. Although Pearl didn't formally begin studying anthropology until she returned to the States, she was systematic in her study of African cultures, the Bushongo being one example of many. She was anticipating and helping to shape a new field of study, dance anthropology.

The journals are also filled with personal entries ranging from mundane jottings to telling observations. For example, on Thursday, March 10, 1949, Pearl wrote: "Rose early this AM—packed—waited for his royal highness to arrive with the chariot and—By now I am so sick of him I could scream." On July 14, she is more focused on the dance: "Murami tells me I may work with dancers this afternoon—for he has seen my work and is moved—but it must be a secret—for tradition is broken—Dancers astonished—But he explains 'She is as the 1st in my company.'—He leaves—we work—dance together—they challenge—I accept—head rolling—hats at my feet—I am excited beyond expression—Eyes danced—mouth curved—Soul sat under tree very pleased indeed—Return home—exhausted—eat and bathe—then off to sleep—Dancers still dancing—hats waving—sounds—costume and the ecstasy on their faces—the grinding of teeth—the polished ebony—the music—and picture of soul sitting smiling under that tree." In lectures and classes over the years following this journey, Pearl loved to tell this story of being proclaimed part of this company. In order to be taught these dances, she had to be considered a man, for these were dances taught only to and danced only by the men of the village.

While Pearl's engagement with the dance and music embodied her experience of Africa in one way, her poetry articulates it in another. One poem is written on stationery from an ocean liner, perhaps on the return voyage, and expresses her response to the pain of separation.

Again—
>Again the knife stabs
>>And again I laugh——
>Pain spreads thru me
like slow poison——
>I am numbed
>>Laughter is a Mighty Camouflage
>>People will pass——Some
>>Will stop to laugh with me
>>But none will guess
>>That there—beneath the smile
>>Pain spread
>>Like slow poison——
>>>I am numbed.

The following poem, perhaps the most beautiful Pearl ever wrote, would later be incorporated into award-winning choreography, "Walking with Pearl," by Jawole Willa Jo Zollar, founder and artistic director of Urban Bush Women. It, too, is a poem of separation, but also of (re)birth, as Pearl readies herself for her return journey to New York. Moving from the natural beauty of the nurturing land, to the voices and rhythms of village life, the poem sings poignantly of her anguish and fulfillment. It would be hard to imagine a richer statement of the depth of Pearl's attachment to Africa.

Now that I prepare to leave you,
>Mother——
Now that I fold the curtains
>And pack away the many little things
—which would make a home——
>I feel my heart will burst
>>Inside me and—
My tears will crash the walls of
>Reason——
(It is not good to pack away wet things.)

Now that I prepare to leave you,
Mother,
The crimson Bougainvillea blooms redder still
—each brilliant flower smiles
upon the branch—
The birds sing longer, clearer, sweeter—
And
A plant I threw away for dead—
Put out new leaves.
Oh Mother—now that I prepare to leave
—It's mango time—
Remember that first Mango time I spent with you?—
A child among a hundred toys—
Memories are hanging from each branch,
This mango time—
Pineapples will soon be full—
And—
A little guava tree beside the house
(it was so small when we moved in)
Now it prepares its first soft fruit
—as I prepare to leave—
As I wipe and pack away my books,
The voices of my brothers
Take on new meanings—
The patient laughter of my sisters
Form into words—
The market places shout their living songs—
And thatched houses stand in stubborn silence
Among new concrete and hard stone—
I could pack faster——but
The earth clings firmly to my feet—
The red earth—brush it as I may
—holds to my feet—

The palm trees have wrapped
   Their arms around me—
The drums and winds have caught the rhythms
Of my heart——
   Caught them in a magic web of dreams——
                  Invisible.
And from the work left rotting in the
   Sun and rain——
The leopard of sorrow has jumped upon
   My back—
Sinking its teeth and claws into my
   Flesh

      ——

Oh Mother——
   Speak!!——
   Tell me you love me.
   Call me with your soft voice——
   Call me once——"Omowale"
      It will be hard to go in Mango time
    Leaving the guava ripening on the tree
    Shutting the brilliant flowers from my eyes——
    Hearing the voices of my kin
      Fade in the night.
   It will be hard to go leaving my heart
    Caught in the magic web of winds
      And drums——!!
I know that I can never scrape
   The red clay from my feet
   Or tear the leopard of sorrow
    From my back——
   Or dry the tears which fall
    Upon my face

As I prepare to leave you
—Mother

⌁

There is a sense of inevitability about Pearl's journey to Africa, which wove together the narrative threads of her life story. But the unity of the next phase of her life is harder to discern, and she too struggled to find it. She was changed by her immersion in African life and she was returning to a society that was also changing. She wanted to perform, lecture, open a studio, establish a school, pursue a doctorate, lecture, write, and travel, but the Cold War was intensifying, McCarthyism was creating a climate of fear, and the Korean War was on the horizon. All this affected her sense of possibilities and added to the stress of more immediate concerns. How to organize what she had learned for teaching, for performance, for education? How to advance her career? Who to turn to for help?

It was at this time, in August 1950, that she married Yael Woll. Although their relationship had been tense, he accommodated her changed self, continued to serve as stage manager, accompanying her troupe on their first European tour in 1952. Walter Sorrell captured her new state of mind:

> As with many exiles, the American dancer felt acutely the dichotomy between here and there: "I now feel as if I had two mothers. I am unable to give up either and must try to explain one to the other." The American-born black with his cultural roots in Africa cannot help feeling the heritage of exile. An Afrostyled hairdo alone will not do, it is like trying to carry one's soul in the buttonhole, an empty gesture of protest that in reality turns against one's very being. A black ethnicity can only be a cultural amalgam between here and there. . . . Pearl Primus seemed to have been able to reconcile the realities of her existence on this continent with a heritage lying beyond time and distance. Her success in life was that she was not only a "child returned home," but that she remained an "adult never having left herself."[5]

In order to put "the realities of her existence" to use, Pearl would develop a technique for teaching forms of African movement in a lecture-demonstration format and would continue to offer concerts called "Dark Rhythms," a suite of dances performed as early as 1948, but expanded in number and range after her return. Always appearing in her African dress, she became her own work of art, learning to interweave seamlessly the telling of stories with the dances themselves, and she deepened the meaning of each movement. Her internal relationship to the material had changed in a newly embodied sense of self, a felt identification with ancestral spirits. Pearl was finding gestures that became her rituals, her mantras—the chants, the poetry, the dance itself. "Fanga," in particular, was her signature dance. Each time it was performed, it held the possibility of a richer resonance, like a prayer.

"Fanga" was central to Pearl's school, her performances, and her lectures. A dance of welcome that she brought back from her first trip to Liberia, it was probably a variation on a traditional dance that she continued to change over the decades. Pearl's student Lynn Frederiksen emphasized that "'Fanga' comes from a place of giving, of confidence, of strength. . . . It is at once a statement and an invitation, a passageway opened to the possibilities of human connection and growth."

Virtually every community black dance company in America now has its own version of "Fanga," and most use the chant "Fanga alafiyah, ashe, ashe, Fanga alafiyah, ashe ashe" as its accompaniment. This chant, however, was added by LaRoque Bey, a percussionist in New York in the late 1950s, and was not part of the original work. Pearl used two other chants, "gehbeddy jung jung jung, gehbeddy jung jung" with a strong, active, insistent rhythm, or "dum dake dake dum dake, dum dake dake dum dum dake," gentler, and with a swing and a sway to it.

There is controversy over whether Pearl truly was the first to perform "Fanga." In her PhD dissertation, dance historian Marcia Heard claims that Pearl first learned "Fanga" from Asadata Dafora, who taught and performed a version of a welcome dance he called "Fugule."[6] Asadata Dafora was from Sierra Leone, and we do not know whether his was the same version Pearl danced. In "The Story of Fanga," Sule Greg C. Wilson, a percussionist who played with the Nigerian drummer Babatunde Olatunji, also says that Asadata Dafora first staged "Fanga."[7] Pearl insisted—not without some bitterness—that her "Fanga" became part of Olatunji's repertory and was popularized by the sisters Merle Afida and Joan Akwasiba Derby, who had studied and performed it with her and then left for Olatunji's company.

Ultimately, what matters is that "Fanga" came to represent for Pearl her very essence, her soul. Conventional wisdom in dance history, especially the history of black dance, has credited Pearl with introducing this dance into Western culture, although it entered the mainstream through Olatunji's explosive popularity in the 1960s.

The genealogy of "Fanga" in the United States may go back to Pearl's students Merle Afida and Joan Akwasiba Derby. With Pearl's encouragement, they began to study with other dancers at the New Dance Group and at other studios. They were also friends with some of the Nigerian students who lived at the Africa House, near City College. Merle remembered:

> Asadata Dafora had been headquartered there and Nigerian students practiced there. So we learned a lot of traditional dances and the African posture, which was always the body toward the earth and in plie, something that we had acquired from dancing with Pearl. Through the Nigerian students we met Olatunji, who is also Nigerian. It was only natural that he should be drawn into that circle. Sometimes we would have conflicts and wish we were dancing with Tunji and Pearl didn't like it too much, yes.
>
> It wasn't like ["Fanga"] was in the common domain, because it was hers. "Fanga" was definitely Pearl's, but Tunji borrowed it and it was different. It didn't have the same essence. I wouldn't say it was more commercial but the drumming was definitely different. . . . The drummers Pearl used were primarily Moses Mianns and then Cimber.
>
> Moses Mianns changed it considerably. It was a little faster. Pearl always did it so you could see the articulation in the hands and each gesture was symbolic of something. Mostly she did it

herself. Once in a while, she let the company do it, but you were very aware of each movement. The placing of the hands, whether it be from my heart to you, from my head to the heavens, from head to my heart to the earth. They were very articulate and very exact.

But the dance was rushed as it passed from Olatunji to other companies. Pearl used to say, "Oh they bastardized my work," which was true. It's hardly recognizable the way they do it.

From Olatunji it went to the Dinizulu and his company, African Dancers, Drummers and Singers. He did it completely differently. Oh my goodness! Then it started going to variations. The Dinizulu Company tried to emulate Pearl's presentation, but they did it pretty scholastically. It was correct, but there was only one Pearl.

Both Joan and Merle continued in the field of dance and developed as performers and college teachers, dancing in the original cast of "Revelations" with the Alvin Ailey American Dance Theater.

Mary Waithe, Pearl's longtime student and friend who was very much on the scene in the early days of this work, said she never heard of Asadata performing "Fanga" before Pearl did. "Asadata may have performed something similar but not in the context that Pearl did. NO!" Mary Waithe also recalled that Merle Afida and Joan Akwasiba had taken the work to Olatunji. "When Kwasiba went to dance with Olatunji, doing 'Fanga,' Pearl got upset," she declared. "I think that daunted Pearl because these people had worked with her, Kwasiba and Afida, from the time they were eleven years old."

In fairness to Merle and Joan, there was also considerable crossover in the drumming scene in New York in the early 1950s, when Olatunji came to New York. Dances and rhythms were cross-fertilized as the drummers worked with Dafora, Dunham, Primus, and Olatunji and studied with each other. We know that Cimber and Mianns functioned less as accompanists in the African dances than as coequal partners in the creation of performance. Indeed, poet and playwright Rashidah Ismaili AbuBakr and others described

Alphonse Cimber's role as pivotal. Cimber, who was a central figure for a growing community of drummers, became Pearl's close friend and associate and often accompanied her work. When Cimber would play his drum solos in Pearl's concerts, he would bring down the house, and when he would sit in on classes with Moses Mianns "the roof would lift off the studio," Mary Waithe remembered.

The relationships among the drummers were complex. Moses Mianns, who had emigrated to New York from Nigeria in the 1930s, performed with both Dafora and Pearl. Mianns's student was Olatunji's accompanist, Taiwo DuVall. According to ethnomusicologist Eric Charry, DuVall "met Olatunji shortly after the latter's arrival in New York and they began playing together informally. DuVall, whose grandparents were from Jamaica, had learned from Moses Mianns as well as Alphonse Cimber, a Haitian drummer who performed with Primus in the 1940s . . . DuVall played with Dafora and Primus and taught at Olatunji's center before moving to Washington D.C. in the early 1970s."[8]

This interweaving of performance careers also involved another important member of the African American drumming community in New York, James Hawthorne, called "Chief" Bey, who learned drumming from Isamae Andrews, who had danced with Dafora. "Montego Joe" (Roger Sanders) came to New York from Jamaica in his youth, studied with Mianns and Cimber, and performed with the Dunham and Primus dance troupes.[9]

Pearl continued to teach "Fanga" throughout her career. In 1984, Lynn Frederiksen, Pearl's graduate student, performed in a staging of "Fanga" in which Pearl danced the solo lead. Lynn remembered the complexity of the rhythmic phrasing and was surprised to discover that most people viewed "Fanga" as a much lighter, social piece than what she learned from Pearl. She described a sense of ritual form with a clear, downward, earthy feeling throughout.

Having mastered the form, Pearl could play with it. But Pearl's play, though seemingly spontaneous, was choreographed for maximum effect, from the raising of her eyebrows, to the slash of the scarf, to the stamp of her foot. She often would divide the performance into three parts. As the drumming began, Pearl took center stage to speak to the audience.

Now comes my part, my time to greet you in the language I know
best, the dance.
You'll notice the open hands; I bear no weapons in my heart
for you.
From my heart to you—all that is good in me. And from my head
all that I can think of for your comfort.
You are welcome.

She would tell the audience that for her performance of "Fanga" she was
awarded the Order of the Star of Africa medal by William V. S. Tubman,
President of Liberia.

When set on a company, the dance itself begins with a women's chorus,
entering and performing the welcoming gestures, hands to heart, gestures to
the earth and heavens, formal movements in all four directions to indicate the
corners of the world. With small jumps and arms extended upward and thrust
downward, the movements become wider and broader, combining ease and
power to link cosmos, dancers, and audience. The chant "gehbeddey jung
jung jung gehbeddey jung jung" is heard throughout.

Then comes Pearl's solo. The drum rhythm accelerates, and, with
scarves swirling, Pearl circles the stage. Her jumps and stamps becoming
increasingly emphatic, she adds complex shoulder and torso undulations,
full body vibrations, and pelvic thrusts, along with rhythmic nods of her head
in a movement conversation with the drummers. The force of the dance is
conveyed in subtle currents of bodily rhythms, counterrhythms, and a play of
facial expressions, especially her eyes. Simultaneously her feet express vary-
ing contacts with the earth, from a flat-footed stamp to a forced arch quick
rhythmic step as she crosses the stage. Then, drawing inward with her scarves
close to her face, she moves downstage with a smile of joy, as if to embrace the
audience. As her movements grow larger and faster, she forcefully circles the
stage and is joined in a circle by the dancers. Finally, with a downward slice
of her arm and a flash of the scarf in the direction of the drummers, there is
silence before the audience erupts in applause.

Today, the dance called "Fanga" that is taught in classes and workshops from Boston to Brazil is based on the first part of Pearl's staging, the opening choral sequence. DeAma Battle, cofounder with Bamidele Osumarea of the Art of Black Dance and Music in Boston, fears that it has been watered down, and although "Fanga" is written into the Massachusetts Standards for Arts Education, in which sixth-graders learn to perform dances from around the world, it is incorrectly identified as Nigerian rather than Liberian.

Then there was "Baba" Chuck Davis in 2005, teaching "Fanga" as he had learned it from Pearl many years before, this time at sunrise on a beach in the Gambia. Chuck said, "Pay attention, students. This is how Mama Pearl taught 'Fanga' before it was taken over by everyone." Chuck said it was in the early 1960s that "Fanga" began to be performed at "warp speed." He began, a soft, slow chant. "Dum dake dake dum dake, dum dake dake dum dum dake," and the group of ten dancers swayed with the rhythm of the ocean, feet hardly disturbing the sand. "To the earth, to the sky, we welcome you to the land." Chuck evoked imagery he remembered from Pearl. "When one arm is reaching up in front, the other reaching down in back, experience the body as a trumpet, connecting heaven and earth through the heart. Body as a long reed." The dancers' bodies tilted toward the earth, then reached skyward, one young dancer in particular, a member of Chuck's company, looking and moving like a young Pearl.[10]

Perhaps in the end it isn't crucial that her name is attached to the work. Perhaps what is important is that it is still performed by professional companies and taught in schools, workshops, and community dance groups around the world, and that all those who encounter it are, for the brief time they dance it, finding connection to those they dance for and with, and to others around the globe. That the piece is part of a world repertory bespeaks her genius for having tapped into such a great, universal longing and for finding a way to give it expression.

─✺─

Pearl did not need to keep creating new dances. In this, her artistic drive aligned with traditional cultures. John Martin had concluded a 1948 review saying, "Miss Primus offered no new numbers, but danced the old ones—a suite of spirituals, 'African Ceremonial,' 'Hard Times Blues,' 'Santo,' 'Shouters of Sobo,' two 'Songs of Protest'—in top form. Indeed, she stopped the show on both occasions, and rightly so. Both technically and dramatically, she has rarely, if ever, given a more brilliant account of herself."[11]

When she returned from Africa, however, she did respond to audiences' desire for fresh experiences. Promotional material for a benefit concert for the New Lincoln School, February 2, 1951, Hunter College Assembly Hall, announced, "All her dances, new this season, are based on her personal African experiences. She has promised to do one dance never performed before. Her deep understanding of the primitive people she lived with comes through in exotic dance patterns. Pearl Primus is recognized as one of the most exciting dancers in the world today." The emphasis in her repertory on the early works had to do with their profundity, their meaning to her, and her audience's desire to keep seeing them. Think of Alvin Ailey's "Revelations," one of the first dances he choreographed, when he was twenty-nine years old. Born of the desire to create a particular statement, this dance remained unparalleled in his later career. Likewise, Paul Taylor's "Esplanade," a mid-career work, became a signature piece. The more contemporary "Rush Hour," by Robert Battle, also has cultlike following. Such works become icons in time and space, and take on a life of their own as dancers move through them. Pearl danced her early solos over and over, but she held them close to her; no one else could easily have their power or could understand them, especially after they had been imbued with the deeper rhythmic embodiments she absorbed in Africa. She staged many of the African works first seen in "Dark Rhythms" for the next forty years, but only in her last years was she finally able to transmit the early solos to a few other dancers.

Yet, unlike other modern dances, Pearl's African work usually attracted the same kinds of racial qualifiers that had labeled the early protest dances: "Tribal Africa," "primitive people," "exotic dance patterns." She was brilliant, the critics wrote, and she was pursuing a PhD in anthropology from Columbia (that her degree was from NYU is another chapter), but the linguistic codes usually insisted that her dances were still black exotica. Unsurprisingly, an eloquent exception was in *Ebony* magazine: "Her powerful movements were thrilling to see as she achieves a freedom on the stage akin to flight. Her soaring, high leaps into the air have made audiences audibly gasp and her deep concentration while performing an African ceremonial dance holds people in hypnotic fascination. She combines in her work carefully thought-out choreography and a wonderful, free emotional drive."[12]

This statement appears in a publicity release soon after her return from Africa for the opening of the Pearl Primus School of Primal Dance, 17 West Twenty-fourth Street, which announced the introduction in America of "The Initiation," "Fanga (Liberian Dance of Welcome)," "War Dance," and "Dance of the Royal Court of Benin," and boasted that Pearl had been engaged in a host of other educational and artistic endeavors. The scope of her achievements is genuine, but the promotional excess also derived from financial anxieties. Of all her myriad activities, it was the dances gathered under the heading "Excerpts from an African Journey" that became her most financially successful in concerts and lecture demonstrations.

In 1951, Pearl presented "Dark Rhythms" at Hunter College as a benefit for the New Lincoln School. A version of the suite was often staged over the next few years. A typical program might contain her mission statement:

> Throughout the ages man has danced. He danced because he had something to say, and he danced for the joy which comes with rhythmic movement. As he pounded the grain, as he prepared for the hunt, even as he worshiped, he danced. He translated into this language of gesture his longings, his ecstasy, his tears, his laughter, his prayers. Man danced!
>
> Tonight we dance with a twofold purpose. We wish not only to entertain you but to bring to you a part of ourselves, that we may grow closer in the bond of brotherhood and so move one step closer to world peace.

A full program began with "African Ceremonial," "The priestess blesses the land and prays for numerous children and fertile crops." This was followed by "Chants" and a suite entitled, "Excerpts from an African Journey." Over many years, through her last concert in 1992, Pearl would adapt the program to the setting, time constraints, and skill of the dancers when she presented "Excerpts." This early presentation included:

> "Egbo-Esakpade." The dancers of the court of the Oba of Benin dance the elegance and pride of their people. This is one of the most ancient of the court dances of Nigeria, Africa.
>
> "Prayer of Thanksgiving." Let us walk into the fields and view the harvest, then let our voices rise with the drums to thank God.
>
> "War Dance." The warriors challenge the God of War and destroy him. By his destruction there will be peace.
>
> "Fanga." I welcome you. My hands bear no weapons. My heart brings love for you. I stretch my arms to the earth and to the sky, for I alone am not strong enough to greet you. This is a dance of welcome done in the hinterland of Liberia to welcome a chief.
>
> "Everybody Loves Saturday Night." A Country Dance (West Coast of Africa).

The first part of the program concluded with "Drum Talk," a solo for either Moses Mianns or Alphonse Cimber, the two drummers with whom she worked most frequently; "Conga Interlude"; and then "Santos," a solo for Pearl. The program description reads: "The dancer is compelled to obey the rhythms of the drums. These rhythms speak the language of the serpent. In Cuba the worship of the snake was forbidden by Christian masters, and this led to tremendous inner conflict among the slaves."

Pearl's modern dance and blues pieces, performed after the first intermission, included "Lamentation," "Creole Songs," "Study in Nothing," "Mischievous Interlude," and "American Suite," which included "Lonesome Traveler," "Hard Time Blues," "Folk Dance," and four "Spirituals." Some of the pre-Africa pieces then much in demand were performed again. Of "Hard Time Blues" she wrote: "In the south of the United States many people still live in extreme poverty. They are forever indebted to the landowners who live far away. This dance is a protest against the system which robs the people of the fruits of their labor." Of "Spirituals" she anticipates the connection between civil rights and the global civil humanitarian movement: "These are the songs which carried the Negro people in America through their period of slavery. Embracing every known emotion, these spirituals developed as powerful songs of hope, and were used as weapons for freedom. Today they are called America's great folk music and are used to express not only the prayers of the American Negro but also the emotions and hope of all peoples of the world."

This vigorous program continued after a second intermission with "The Initiation," described as a dance of self-mastery inspired by puberty rites in the African interior. In this dance, Pearl performed the role of the Initiate with the powerful men of the company, Charles Blackwell, George Shipman, and Charles Queenan, presiding over the ritual observance. With the driving rhythms of the drums supporting the choreography, the masked figure looms over the initiate, who falls before him, on her knees, in a backbend. Back arched, arms outstretched, she opens herself to the fearsome challenge presented by this rite of passage. The program states:

> Throughout the long centuries man has searched for methods of understanding and conquering not only his environment but also himself. He has not limited this search to the physical only. He has ventured into the psychological and spiritual realms of life. In spite of all this, each individual must at one time or another pass through his own jungle. He must meet Fear. He must conquer or be conquered, for Man cannot live with Fear. This meeting is called "The Initiation" . . . the period through which the individual must struggle if he is to really live.

"Folk Dance" followed, and the concert ended with "Impinyuza":

> Let us dance the elegance of our people. . . . Let our feet fly over the earth and our faces reflect our ecstasy. (Dance of the Ishyaka, Batwa, Corps-de-Ballet of the King of the giant Watusi, in the Belgian Congo.)

"Impinyuza," also called "The Incomparable," is a dance in praise of "the elegance, invincibility and beauty" of the Watusi monarch that Pearl was taught "as a man." In turn, she taught it to Percival Borde, who performed it as his signature piece until his death in 1979. Pearl staged it successfully for the Alvin Ailey American Dance Theater in 1990.

FOUR

Teaching, Traveling, and the FBI

IN DECEMBER 1950, *Theater Arts* published an article entitled "The Voice of the Earth," which reads like a description of Pearl's developing technique and new school, the Pearl Primus School of Primal Dance. Clearly Pearl's writing, it is both an etiological myth and a promotional statement:

> Man struck a hollow tree with his club and as the intruder boomed forth he leaped into the air! The first musician! He crouched low and slowly approached the tree again—for surely there was magic in it, and he must be cautious. He struck it again—and again the deep thunder plunged through the air.
>
> Man felt this sound inside him—He felt something in his bosom answering this—He heard his heart booming. Then his feet took up the pattern—and from his throat the thunder rose to blend with the thunder of the tree—
>
> So it was that the first drum, the dance and the song met. The hollow tree was the music—the rhythm came from Man's heart—and the dance emerged as response to the power within him. . . .
>
> Pearl Primus has taken this voice as the basis of her work.
>
> . . .

The statement goes on to extol the dance as a defiance of oppression, drawing on the forces of nature and the human drive for self-expression. "The music is everywhere." "The dance is everywhere." Her technique will enact a "studied and intellectualized spontaneity," bringing the experience of primal forces to the space of the studio and the theater.[1]

This aesthetic vision also informed studio rehearsals. When presenting new movement, Pearl did not teach from a distance but came to the students, letting them feel her body, her back, where the contraction was. Initially she demonstrated a movement, but then gave directions verbally and with gestures, and she didn't differentiate between teaching technique and teaching particular dances. The technique was embedded in the dance itself. When teaching the African dances she began with the song or chants, integrating the music, song, and dance, as she was taught to do in Africa. When she didn't have a drummer to accompany a class, she would develop the rhythms with vocal and body percussion. The rhythms were key to teaching and learning the dances.

After teaching a few counts of movement in this way, Pearl would disappear upstairs for about half an hour, leaving the dancers to work on their own. Not knowing when she would come back, they would often sit down to rest, and nervously jump back to work when she returned. When she felt the dancers had grasped what she wanted them to learn, she would sit down, put all the steps together, and have the dancers perform them.

She also worked meticulously with props—the slash of the scarf for "Fanga," the placement of the sticks for "Impinyuza," the thrust sword for "Bushasche," the rhythm of the maracas for the "Engagement Dance," and the skirts for "Everybody Loves Saturday Night." Once Pearl began teaching a particular dance, anthropological lessons preceded any movement instructions. Were these farmers from a particular village? Were they hunters? Were they warriors? How did they walk upon the earth? What was the meaning and function of the dance's symbolic objects? When teaching "Impinyuza," for example, Pearl would tell the women about the Watusi social structure and belief system, though only the men in the company were to perform this dance. Pearl's student Merle Afida Derby described the men as "the most elegant things in the world, they just made you sigh when they did it. She nearly worked them to the ground, but it was worth it, because they were just fantastic." Charles Blackwell was the tallest at six feet, five inches, but it was generally agreed that Charles Queenan fulfilled this dance in a singular way, embodying the essence of the movement and the Watusi culture.

"Impinyuza," which praises the king's powers and the deity he represents, announced its premier in 1952, though it had been performed earlier.

Pearl developed what she called "the earth studies," a series of progressions where the dancers learned to glide across the floor, envisioning the floor as the earth, to be danced upon with rapport and respect. She often ended class with another, demanding progression, "Agu, the Dance of Strength," which involved a difficult chugging, gliding motion in which the dancer had to articulate her feet, using her toes to propel herself forward. This was performed in a deep contraction and then the dancers would take to the air. Pearl would spend hours on this because she wanted the dancers to achieve a precise position above the earth. Merle said that Joe Commodore was the only person she ever saw achieve this in the way Pearl performed it.

Rehearsals on the weekends started at eight in the morning and might go until midnight. The dancers would provide their own sandwiches and Pearl would make peppermint tea and bring it down to the studio from her apartment. In a practice that continued throughout her career, Pearl began using a close friend and dancer as a rehearsal mistress, and Mary Waithe had the role during this period.

Decades after Pearl's return from Africa, her students at the 17 West Twenty-fourth Street studio remembered her teaching vividly. As a young girl, Merle Derby, who had an illustrious career as a dancer and teacher, along with her younger sister, Joan Akwasiba Derby, studied and performed with Pearl. Mary Waithe was Pearl's student while she was in high school. When her parents couldn't afford to send her to Michigan State University, Pearl suggested that she go to college in New York and continue studying dance.

Merle and Joan began taking ballet classes but their mother thought they needed something more African-oriented, and she found her way to Pearl's school. "That was a revelation; it opened a whole new world for us. Pearl's teaching was so complete, so thorough," Merle recalled. Pearl's earthy style contradicted ballet training and required a reorientation for dancers who came to her from more classical forms, as the Derby sisters did. Pearl's "meticulous and mesmerizing" teaching took place in a studio without mirrors or barres, a clear break with tradition.

Pearl's warm-ups were grueling, and she kept students working on a movement until it was perfect. Merle, who wasn't more than fifteen at the time, would occasionally break out in hives or have temper tantrums, saying, "I can't do this!" Pearl would speak softly, but she could also raise her voice. "If she got mad, her eyes would become like saucers, and then you knew she was disturbed." Mary said Merle would sometimes cry because Pearl would look at her angrily. "Pearl would holler at you and when she got through you felt like two cents. She tried to use that as a motivator or to bring you out of yourself," Mary said. "If she wanted a student to work on a step," added Merle, "she would put her in a corner or in another room. Then she would come back down and say, "Oh, it's coming, it's coming."

Demanding as Pearl was, Mary and Merle remained devoted to her and her work. "Your thighs burned so much, you couldn't walk down the stairs and you couldn't walk up the stairs," Mary recalled. "We would leave there at 1 a.m. We used to dance down the street and sing on the subway. We actually got to the point where we lived and breathed dance. She was more than our teacher, we put her on a pedestal, she was like a goddess to us, very, very special." Their friendship survived the rift that occurred when Merle and her sister joined Olatunji.

Rina Sharett, an Israeli student, also remembered the excitement of being in the studio and everyone's desire to acquire Pearl's special technique, which was not the prestigious mainstream style of dance of those days. "Pearl excelled in her analytic powers of dismembering and reassembling of movements and movement sentences, and of rhythms," Rina said. "The moment she sat down, the drum between her knees, raising her hand to hit the drum as a sign for the opening of the class, the atmosphere was immediately electrified."

These students remembered the group they called the Men's Company, which included Charles Queenan and Charles Blackwell as well as other dancers—George Shipman, George Mills, Joe Commodore, and Albert Popwell (a bit earlier). (The great dancer Charles Moore and charismatic performer Percival Borde came later.) The men who studied closely with Pearl became the embodiment of the power and elegance she had perceived in the African dancers as well as that of her own strong physicality. The photo of the men dancing "Bushasche" shows muscles rippling, the left arm braced, ready to thrust the spear, and the strong torsos and knees lifted high, as they advance on the forces of evil. Their stance epitomized Pearl's translation of African form to the concert stage.

"Bushasche" was originally titled "War Dance." Originating in Congo, it is a dance in which the warriors stir up the forces of evil in the compound with the aim of defeating them. A generational dance performed once every twenty years, the warriors cleanse the village for the next generation so that women will be fertile, crops will grow, and the gods will protect the compound. Fierce men enter upstage right, leaping over the imagined village walls of Mushenge, in Congo, with a kuba—or spear—in one hand and an intricately carved shield in the other. As staged by Pearl many times, first one hears the call "Kuplio," which is answered by the cry "Chi!" This is repeated as each dancer flies out from the wings, knees held high, spear thrusting outward. After several rounds of the chant, in unison they proclaim a loud, low, drawn-out "Aha!" at which point the drums announce their intricate rhythms and the dance begins. Leaping across the stage, thrusting the sword forward and back, swirling in fast-moving intricate patterns, they stir up the ground, engage in battle, and finally, victorious, raise the kuba to the heavens in triumph as they exit the stage. As they raise one arm high and thrust the other downward toward the earth, they become the human connection between heaven and earth, a concept Pearl taught in this and other dances.

Pearl was still with Yael when she returned from Africa and opened the Twenty-fourth Street studio. The dancers remembered talking more with Yael than with Pearl, as he continued to take care of business around the studio. Pearl was occupied with consolidating her understanding of all the material gathered during her Africa sojourn, and her manager, Austin Wilder, was arranging tours, mostly to colleges.

In addition to teaching and touring, Pearl continued studying. In the fall of 1950 and spring of 1951 she was enrolled in graduate classes at Columbia and she was also honing her lecture-demonstration format. Despite all her other work, she continued to write, and in October 1950 *Vogue* published her article "In Africa," and in December of that year *Theatre Arts* published her "Earth Theatre." She was written up in *Ebony* in January 1951, and in February she published "Earth Theatre of Africa" in *Monthly Magazine* of the Brooklyn Institute of Arts and Sciences.

There were other projects as well. In 1950 and 1951, Pearl began working with her friend Marjorie Rawlings, author of *The Yearling*, on the story line for a play entitled "The Woman of Zor," a project that would preoccupy her until her death. She thought of this work as the culmination of her studies and creative life, and in her last years she would travel to Barbados specifically to work on it. There was mention at one point of it being produced on Broadway by the radio and television personality Joe Franklin. But this work seems to have disappeared and is not archived with her papers.

Rawlings had hoped Pearl would be eligible for a grant from the Institute of Arts and Letters, but these were awards for work already published. "Never mind, you are strong and tough, vital and creative, and you will manage to create and to do the things you were born to do," she wrote. Rawlings, in her characteristically supportive way, identified with Pearl's passionate nature. "I think that one of the bonds between you and me is our mutual recognition of that inner flame that can never be put out, short of death itself." Responding to news of Pearl's emotional distress and financial anxiety, she encouraged her to keep writing, as "the book may well say better what you have to say, and as artistically, certainly in more permanent form, than the dance, however dear that medium is to you." Rawlings also saw a reflection of her own creative process in Pearl's struggle with an uncertain moment in her life:

> In my long life . . . I have found again and again that when things
> hit bedrock, there came an inevitable turn, sometimes with a
> great sweep of good luck. As you say, when one gets about so
> low, the only place left to go is up. So let me urge you with all I
> can command of my admiration for your varied artistry and my
> affection for you as a person, to do the book—now. Let nothing

interfere. And all cheers for your husband, who obviously sees things in proportion.

I wish I were a Rosenwald or a Guggenheim to finance you while you work, but at least I can insist that you call on me for a hundred or two if you are ever up against it. I think of you so often. My re-writing goes slowly, I can't tell yet, how well.

Pearl always seemed to need help financially, for she spent money as fast as she earned it, and her projects outran her budgets. The whereabouts of "The Woman of Zor" remains a mystery, but it seems to have been a story Pearl was intent on completing for its own sake, and also as a source of income in the early 1950s.

◦◦◦

In January 1951, Pearl embarked on a nineteen-week concert tour of England and Israel. In London, she gave a Royal Command Variety Performance for His Majesty, King George VI, at Victoria Palace, as part of a concert to aid the Variety Artistes' Benevolent Fund and Institution for Indigent Variety and Circus Artists. The tour also included sixteen concerts of "Dark Rhythms" at the Prince's Theater in November, followed by eight concerts at the Shakespeare Memorial Theater in Stratford-upon-Avon in December.

The reviews in England reveal ingrained racist attitudes toward "primitive" African dances. Photos accompanying one article bear stereotypical captions. In "War Dance," for example, "The frenzy is disciplined. The unison perfect. But this surge of emotion—in a programme otherwise quieter—has all the violence of the African original." A review from the Birmingham *Evening Dispatch* of a performance at Stratford-upon-Avon speaks of "the truly savage rhythms" of "War Dance," and an atmosphere that "sizzles." The "exotically named Moses Miann, with a drum, two hands and a wide grin he talks jungle talk." Pearl is "the buxom Miss Primus, herself the granddaughter of a voodoo doctor—and an M.A.," like a new version of a Noble Savage.[2]

A sympathetic writer, Garry Saunders, described Pearl with tears in her eyes as she said, "They don't understand what we're trying to do. We're trying to show the heritage and dignity of the Negro through his dancing and music—not pander to the lower kind of public taste. . . . This isn't, and never was intended to be, the Hollywood version of a jungle jam session. This is how the African dances to the rhythm of the drum—provided he has never been under the Hollywood influence." Pearl wanted her audiences to appreciate the muscular control and subtle movement of these dances, and was impatient with the desire for more "sexy" and less repetitive performances.[3]

From England, Pearl traveled briefly to Liberia. On January 4–6, 1952, she danced "Fanga" at a command performance for the Inaugural Ceremonies of President Tubman. On January 8 she opened her Israeli tour, which included everything from a command performance for the mayor of Tel Aviv to performances in Haifa, and at various settlements and immigration camps. Pearl's was the first modern dance company to appear in Israel. It wasn't until 1956 that the Martha Graham Company appeared on the way to their first trip to the Far East, which ultimately led to the foundation of the Israeli company Batsheva.

Pearl's appearance in Israel was sponsored by two producers who had a deep influence on the development of modern dance in Israel, Abrahim (Gingi) Bogatir and Ori Benadyr. Shortly after they introduced Pearl to Israel, they brought former Dunham dancer Talley Beatty, who performed his repertory as well as Katherine Dunham's. Bogatir and Benadyr gathered wealthy and important Israelis at premiers and postconcert parties. In 1956, they tried to bring Pearl and the company back for a return visit.

"She has taken the country by storm," announced Nadia Lourie, an Israeli journalist.[4] The admiration was mutual, as Pearl proclaimed her Old Testament roots and observed that in Israel she found "neither racial antagonism not color prejudice."[5] The original plan for eight concerts was expanded to thirty appearances in Haifa and Tel Aviv.

A young dancer, Ahuva Anbary, was caught up in the excitement created by Pearl's visit. She recalled sneaking with friends into the theater to see Pearl's performances at the Ohel and Habima Theaters in Tel Aviv. The theaters were always packed, but the students would arrive in the morning, bring sandwiches with them, hide in the bathroom, and stay for the performance. Their enthusiasm reflected the hunger of Israelis for artistic experience. Ahuva and her friends were "groupies, nudging [Pearl], running after her," and they would visit her hotel to talk with her. Ahuva responded to the seeming contradictions of Pearl's physical presence. "She was chubby, had short legs, and moved like an angel, so very light. All the young students loved it!"

Well over fifty years later, Ahuva could still vividly describe the falls in "Strange Fruit":

> I remember a solo, a wonderful solo. She did circle falls. She would fall and rise in circle five or six times. It was like Graham but different. Graham would slide down. Graham falls don't lead with the hips. . . . Instead of sliding into a split and then to a fall, she did it from standing up. She did a hitch forward, falling into the arm, going sideways a little bit with the body, going into one arm only. Then when she reached the floor, she would shift to her left leg and turn the right leg backwards, turning herself around. She would rise from the knees, into the body and then into the arms, using the arms to rise without putting weight on the knees. She pushed into the hips, into the knees, into the arms and always got applause on that.
>
> We then all took that move into our dances afterward. She was a great influence on us. We weren't choreographing yet at the time. We loved modern dance. The only modern dance then in Israel was Gertrud Kraus. Before that we saw only ballet companies from Europe.

After Pearl left, Ahuva and her friends began choreographing dances based on Pearl's work. In 1958, Ahuva went to the United States to study at Julliard and the Graham School, and later became the rehearsal director for the American dancer Pearl Lang. She went back to Israel to the Batsheva Company, danced with Bat Dor, and returned to the United States where she taught at the Interlochen Arts Academy and then at York University. She returned to Israel to teach at the Rubin Academy of Music and Dance in Jerusalem. When one thinks of Israeli modern dance, one doesn't think of Pearl Primus, but of Martha Graham and the development of Batsheva. But there was Pearl, first to arrive, first to inspire, first to ignite passion for a particular kind of movement expression at a powerful moment in the life of an idealistic young nation.

Rina Sharett was also a young dancer at the time of Pearl's visit. She was then a second-year gymnastics student at the Seminar Ha'Kibbutzim, a teacher-training institute in Tel Aviv where, among other subjects, dancers studied how to teach in the schools and on the kibbutzim of Israel. She first saw Pearl perform at the Rama Theater on January 10 in Ramat Gan, a suburb of Tel Aviv. Rina's father-in-law was Moshe Sharett, Israel's first foreign minister (1948–50) and its second prime minister (1954–55). Because she was married to Moshe Sharett's eldest son, she was invited to a farewell party in Pearl's honor on the evening of the last performance in Israel, February 11. "I introduced myself to her and related my deep impressions of her performance. I had no idea then that in the next year I would be living in New York and would be able to become her student. She was the most important teacher I ever had," Rina recalled.

When Rina returned to Israel, for three years she was in charge of the activity of all ethnic dance groups and for two years was the artistic director of Inbal Dance Theater, where her work was closest to the dance she studied with Pearl. Rina felt that although Pearl's group was well received, this was in part because Israelis did not see many artists from abroad. Some Israelis did not appreciate the Africanism of the work. Despite Pearl's disclaimer of racism, she and her company were not permitted to stay in the famous King David Hotel in Jerusalem for fear that some guests might be disturbed by their presence.

From Israel Pearl continued on to France and then returned to the States on March 5. The political atmosphere had been darkening. As early as October 19, 1951, a reporter named William Fulton had printed a story in the *Chicago Daily Tribune* under the heading "Reds Get Cash in Fund Set Up by Guggenheim," with the subheading "Party Followers Given Scholar Awards." The article named the Guggenheim Foundation and the Rosenwald Fund. A United States representative from Georgia, identified only as "Rep. Cox," demanded an inquiry into all the big foundations, as he believed they

were infiltrated by Communists and diverting money into un-American channels.[6] Cox accused the Guggenheim Foundation of "spreading radicalism
throughout the country," listing forty-five artists, scholars, poets, composers,
playwrights, and other luminaries of American culture who had received
Guggenheim support. He then claimed that Rosenwald funds "were diverted
to known Communists and leftists," including Langston Hughes, Dr. William
E. B. DuBois, and Pearl Primus.

A similar article, by John D. Morris, entitled, "House Unit to Hear
Dulles on Hiss Tie," appeared in the *New York Times*. It included the subheading "Seeks His Version of Carnegie Fund Post—Budenz Says Grants
Aided 23 Reds."[7] John Foster Dulles was about to be named secretary of state
and was on a committee that selected Alger Hiss as president of the Carnegie
Endowment for International Peace. Though Dulles refused to condemn
Hiss in the absence of proof, the article incriminated many individuals who
received grants from various foundations claimed to have Communist lean-
ings, including Dr. DuBois and Pearl Primus.

Pearl's FBI file, begun in the 1940s, has no entry between 1945 and
early 1951, but on April 12, 1951, it resumes with a letter from a Cincinnati
agent saying that a leading Communist Party member in Columbus, Ohio,
had contacted Pearl. "The purpose of this contact was unknown to the informant." No fewer than eight names are whited out in a brief memo. Someone
"reports," someone else "ascertained," someone else "advised" that "Pearl
Primus is a member of the Communist Party."

A memo of November 22, 1951, refers to a dinner in 1946 sponsored by
the American Youth for Democracy (AYD) as a "Tribute to Negro Youth"
in Philadelphia, where Pearl received an award. The memo claims that AYD
comes "within the purview of Executive Order 9835," and reports that Pearl
had had a conversation with a "leading Communist Party member in Columbus, Ohio, that it was his understanding that Pearl Primus was a member of
the Communist Party." This information, however, should not be considered
"clearance or nonclearance of the individual involved."

From October to December of 1951, Pearl and her company toured
England, Italy, and Finland. In January 1952, while they performed in Israel,

the legal attaché in London sent a memo to the FBI that Pearl was traveling on a passport issued in 1949 in Monrovia and renewed in 1951. She was "allegedly in Europe but, unfortunately her exact whereabouts were unknown. It was also reported by the Department of State that she is an organizer of the Communist Party." Then a large section is blanked out.

In Los Angeles, on April 12, 1952, Pearl's passport was confiscated, and she was told that "further travel would not be for the best interests of the United States." Her ability to tour would be impaired if she didn't clear her name. Although she was a citizen of the United States through the naturalization of her father, she was increasingly concerned about her freedom. Indeed, a subsequent entry in her file marked "Urgent," with three agents' names whited out, describes an appearance by Pearl "relative to reason why her passport was picked up by Security Division, Department of State Agent about April Twelve, Nineteen Fifty-two in Los Angeles." Pearl once again asserted, "she had never knowingly joined CP," and implied that she would contact the FBI in New York in the near future. An agent noted Pearl's comment that Communist groups seemed to be ignoring her since her return from overseas, but the *Daily Worker* did run a story noting that her passport was "lifted." There seemed to be a lack of clarity about how to handle a planned trip to Europe, Israel, and Africa, and about a request to the FBI to discern Pearl's willingness "to cooperate with the US Govt."

A letter from Pearl on June 13, 1952, to Monnett Davis, U.S. ambassador to Israel, sheds direct light on the "lifting" of her passport:

> You recall that I performed with my company in Israel early this year. You saw my performances. Someone in Israel wrote the United States State Department that I made the following statement. "The condition of the Negro in America is worse than in times of slavery."
>
> Acting upon this, the State Department withdrew my passport. Since I never made that statement I am most [word unclear]. Nothing could be worse than slavery. True, the condition of the black people here in America is not one hundred per cent

what we would like it to be—but *we are a free people* and in time
all the rights granted us by the constitution of our country will
be ours in reality. My work contributes to better understanding
of us by showing our beauty, our strength and our dignity.

She asked the ambassador to write to the State Department about
her program. He replied that he recalled the performances and with great
pleasure the walk he and his wife had taken with Pearl, and he would "make
inquiries with possible regard to possible sources of the story."

Herbert Levy, who was general counsel to the American Civil Liberties
Union as well as Pearl's lawyer and friend for many years, went to see FBI
agent Tolson. On September 23, 1952, Agent Tolson sent a memo to L. B.
Nichols "about a prominent New York entertainer who desired to make a
full confession of Communist Party activities, with the exception of one fact
which would place another close friend who was a big name in the entertainment world in the Party and lay the groundwork for a perjury action." Agent
Tolson continued:

> At that time I told Levy, we, of course, would be glad to receive
> any information that his client desired to pass on; that if the cli-
> ent was inclined to withhold information, that was the client's
> responsibility. . . . He called me today and identified his client
> as Pearl Primus, a very prominent dancer and one who particu-
> larly is highly regarded in the Colored entertainment world. He
> described her as one who has attracted considerable attention
> by doing the "authentic African stomp."

Also on September 23, another agent, someone named L. B. Nichols,
had written, "Levy had also told me that the passport of the Primus woman
was denied by the State Department in April, but prior to her notification
a story to this effect had appeared in the *Daily Worker*. Further, she had
told friends she was going to the FBI and talk and her friends were trying to
dissuade her from doing this. I told Boardman he should have a very competent Agent who has a background of the matter handle this interview and

he should carefully brief himself." An appointment was set up for Saturday, September 27, 1952.

Then, on November 3, 1952, a memo reports that the "subject" voluntarily appeared on October 2, that no signed statement was taken, and that Pearl had "come to the FBI in order to advise the FBI of her past connection with the Communist Party as suggested to her by XXXX of the Passport Division, U.S. State Department and Mr. Levy of the Civil Liberties Union." She brought with her a seven-page letter dated October 16, 1952, that documents the early part of her career and explains her relationship to the Communist Party and other left-leaning organizations.

In this letter she identifies herself as Pearl E. Primus (Mrs. Yael Woll), born in Trinidad, and claims her birthday is July 1, 1917. She states that she came to the United States in 1923 or 1924 on a British steamship to the port of Hoboken, New Jersey, with her mother, Emily, and brother Edward. Her father had come at least a year earlier and was a superintendent of an apartment building on the West Side of Manhattan. She recounts her high school and college education and her work as a riveter and burner in the Todd Shipyards at Hoboken. She dates her scholarship and studies at the New Dance Group from late 1941 or early 1942.

While at Hunter, she says, members of the radical group the American Student Union approached her, but she had no interest in this movement and "resented the aggressive approach used by these people." She declares that she had "no contact with Communism or Communist front groups during that period." She then describes auditioning and performing at the 92nd Street Y and at Café Society Downtown and Café Society Uptown for approximately a year (1943) and receiving a lot of publicity. At this time members of the Communist Party first approached her. "I had no interest whatever in their proposals," she wrote. Shortly after she began performing at the nightclubs she accepted an invitation to perform at the Negro Freedom Rally at Madison Square Garden. Right after this, she says, "I received wide acclaim as 'a dancer for Negro freedom,'" and she was asked to lend her support to organizations working on "improving the conditions for the Negroes in the United States."

Then she wavers. "I did, in fact, join the Communist Party; however, I have no recollection of ever having a membership card or of ever paying dues." She believed that "the lot of the Negro in the United States would be best served by the Communist Party." She states that while she appeared and performed at events they sponsored, she was "seldom, if ever, paid for them."

After her 1944 research trip through the South she turned to the *Daily Worker* as a place to publicize the appalling conditions she found and asked that petitions be circulated to end "Jim Crowism" and sent to the president and Congress. The woman at the paper refused, saying that "such an action might constitute sabotage," because the country was at war. Pearl wrote that at this time her attitude toward the Party began to change and she began to doubt its effectiveness in "improving the lot of the Negro."

In 1946, while she was performing in *Show Boat* at the Ziegfeld Theater, an unknown woman approached her and asked her to join the Party. "I found this confusing since it was my impression that I was already a member." But she told this woman that she was "no longer interested . . . for personal reasons," and she declares that this was the last time she was approached by the Party.

Now we come to a key passage: "Not long after my visit to *The Daily Worker* I suffered a nervous breakdown." Pearl does not describe this further except to say that she was incapacitated for several months and she did not hear from any of the people with and for whom she had worked. "This struck [her] as indicating a lack of interest in the individual by these parties or groups. My feelings against the Party increased." Pearl's "breakdown" seems to have been a depression brought on by the feeling of helplessness derived from the government's uncertain and potentially malevolent intentions. She had been spat on and stoned in the South and picketed in the Midwest, and now she lost bookings. She feared that her African notes would be taken from her, and she withdrew for a while from work and relationships.

"I am not presently a member of the Communist Party," Pearl wrote. She reiterates that between 1943 and 1947 her sympathies were with the party as she thought they would help the Negroes in the United States. "If the Communist Party . . . stands for the overthrow of the United States Government, I would not be sympathetic." "I will not list individuals with whom I became acquainted during these years for the reason that I was never sure as to who was actually a Communist party member." The interview report, from Nichols to Tolson, makes reference to "a rather clever denial of Communist membership, (although membership and sympathy during certain period were admitted) . . . and, of a denial of any Communist activities and furnishes no information about any associates . . . with the argument that she could not possibly furnish information about Communist membership on the part of an individual unless she was absolutely sure that individual was a Communist, and she was not even sure she was a Communist herself. . . . New York is closing the case on her and is taking no steps to develop Primus as an informant since the signed statement reflects no Communist activities for a long period of time. Action: None."

Pearl was never called before the House Un-American Activities Committee, nor did she name names of other artists and accuse them of being Communists. Her file supports a definitive "No" to suspicions about her compliance that circulated periodically in the entertainment world.

Though no longer actively investigating her, the FBI continued to track her travel and passport requests. An urgent memo dated July 11, 1953, states that the passport Pearl had been issued in Monrovia, Liberia, in 1949 would be validated for a trip she planned to Haiti only and would expire on July 15, 1953. However, Pearl planned on studying for ten to twelve weeks in Haiti and Trinidad, departing from New York on June 20, 1953, and returning on September 7, 1953. Retracing old ground, the FBI decided that she needed to be deposed yet again. She gave a lengthy affidavit on May 29, 1953, declaring that she did not recall signing a "CP" membership card or paying dues. The FBI was asked to furnish the results of the interview to the New York passport office.

Pearl's dealings with the FBI ceded little ground. At her deposition, Pearl acknowledged working as an entertainer or lending her name to organizations on the attorney general's current list, but pointed out that no list existed when she was involved with them. Although she would occasionally help someone, she "soon began to realize that this was inconsistent; that past favors should not be a reason for contributing to causes which, however worthy their apparent aims seemed, were basically out of harmony with [her] own convictions." By 1948 she ceased all such activities and, since then, she had not "to [her] knowledge in any way whatsoever been affiliated with any organization on the Attorney General's list." "From what I now understand as the true aims of the communist movement, I am thoroughly opposed to communist totalitarianism," she added. Once again, she denied a report that she had made derogatory remarks about treatment of American Negroes, attaching a letter from the American ambassador, Monnett Davis. She also wrote to the Emma Lazarus Jewish Women's Club confirming that she withdrew her group from participating in a Carnegie Hall concert scheduled by the club because there were "aliens" in her junior company and she did not want to risk their deportation. Finally, a copy of Pearl's long letter of October 16, 1952, was sent to the Passport Office at the State Department.

Fortunately, Pearl's life was not completely derailed by the government's harassment. She was still managing a creative public life, and it was during these years that Maya Angelou saw Pearl perform for the first time. Angelou had begun studying dance in 1945. After classes with Ann Halprin in San Francisco, among other teachers, she auditioned for Katherine Dunham and was accepted but could not afford to join the company, as she had a son to support. Then Pearl came to California to perform. "I had never seen anything like it," Ms. Angelou recalled. "I'd never seen such strength and the grace at the same time. I'd seen beauty but never almost a raw strength with the grace of a fish. I couldn't contain my tears at the beauty, and ecstasy is what I remember of Ms. Primus' dancing. She seemed to stand without a plie and lift herself and had those very thick thighs, and she was like a gazelle. And so she saw me and saw me weeping and she came over to me and I told her I was a dancer. . . . She gave me a time the next day and I came without music and in a leotard and I just danced. And she said, 'You are a dancer. You are a dancer.' I told her the little I had of training and she said if I would come to New York she would give me a scholarship to study with her. And that's all I could think of for months."

FIVE

Trinidad Communities

HAVING SUCCESSFULLY PERFORMED the delicate dance required by FBI surveillance, Pearl finally received permission to travel to Trinidad in the summer of 1953, her first trip back since leaving as a young child. Returning to the scenes of her origins, she was seeking to navigate her own route through the cultural crosscurrents that flowed between Trinidad and New York. Africanist culture returned to Trinidad via West Indians who moved to New York, traveled to Africa, and then went back to Trinidad, though the route could also start in Africa and move to Port of Spain, to New York, and back to Africa. Returning to Trinidad as both dancer and anthropologist, Pearl wanted to link her African experience with the ritual practices of the island and to bring her own performances to culturally diverse Trinidadian scenes. This journey became yet another transformative and exhilarating moment in her life, but her allusions to periodic breakdowns, her "going in," attest to her continuing struggle for inner harmony.

To fully grasp the personal and professional significance of Trinidad for Pearl, we need to appreciate the rich creative diversity of the island's artistic life, especially the contributions of the Holder family, Beryl McBurnie, Holly Betaudier, and, later on, others like Michael Manswell, a Trinidadian living and dancing in New York and partner of the late Cheryl Byron, Pearl's last "adopted daughter." The current of Pearl's life flowed through this creative culture, but by focusing on the "primitive" dance of the rural rituals, she expanded its range of movement and meaning.

$\backsim$

In Trinidad, Holder is a household name. Members of this family have received the highest awards the government offers, a street is named for them, and art galleries show their work proudly. The Holder parents, creative forces in their own right, encouraged the creativity of each of their five children, Jean, Marjorie, Boscoe, Kenneth, and Geoffrey. Born within a few years of Pearl, Boscoe was the oldest. Gifted as a musician, artist, and dancer, by the late 1930s he was producing shows depicting the music, songs, and dances of Trinidad as well as exhibiting artwork. Boscoe used traditional African Caribbean rituals—shango, bongo, and bélé—in his dances and as subjects for his paintings. In 1947 he visited New York, where he taught Caribbean dance at the Katherine Dunham School and had an art exhibition at a gallery in Greenwich Village. In 1950 he moved to London with his wife, the dancer Sheila Clarke, and their son Christian, where they lived for twenty years. Boscoe Holder was credited with introducing limbo dancing and the first steel band to Britain, where his company performed at the Queen's coronation in 1953. He returned to Trinidad in 1970, focusing on painting until his death on April 21, 2007; he was a man who was much revered for his graciousness, warmth, and generosity.

When Boscoe departed for London, he left his group in Geoffrey's hands. In the United States, Geoffrey Holder is an iconic figure in the arts—a choreographer, dancer, actor, visual artist, painter, sculptor, and costume designer. In 1951 Geoffrey took the group to the first Caribbean Arts Festival in San Juan, Puerto Rico, where they represented Trinidad to great acclaim. He then performed at a Hilton hotel in San Juan and at other Hiltons in the Caribbean, and he had his dancers learn the steel drums. From San Juan they returned to the Little Caribe Theatre, their performance home in Trinidad.

Agnes de Mille saw the company perform in Saint Thomas and initiated Geoffrey's coming to New York to audition for Sol Hurok. On the strength of that invitation he got visas to America. Marjorie and Geoffrey believe that he brought the first pan (i.e., steel drummers) to Broadway and got them unionized in 1952. Other dancers claimed that Pearl introduced the steel drum to the New York stage when she brought dancer and drummer Arthur Bart to New York in the mid-1950s.

In Trinidad, the Holders lived in the Woodbrook neighborhood, which reflected the European colonial influence, and the Bordes on nearby

St. Vincent Street, close to the Savannah, a huge park and gathering place in the center of Port of Spain. The Primus family initially hailed from Laventille, a poor neighborhood set in the hills above the port, but they and the Holders were acquainted from Pearl's earliest days. The Savannah is ringed by hills on three sides, and on the fourth the land slopes toward the downtown and the sea. Trees bloom in all shades of gorgeous flowers, deep vibrant orange, purples, and yellows. In the park's large center children play and the fields host cricket matches, festivals, and concerts. Just off one side of the Savannah was the Princess Building, where there were ballroom dances and where young girls made their debuts. Cornmeal would be spread over the floor to make it possible to glide for dancing. Underneath was a stable for horses.

The Holder's house was on Abercrombie Street, where everyone was like family. Marjorie Boothman, sister to Boscoe and Geoffrey, remembered the community as having no color barriers. "If one mother made ice cream, everyone ate ice cream." Before World War II British influence prevailed. "We imported everything—the curtsey, black stockings, dresses with bows, frills, knee highs. Young girls were ladies-in-training. We wore pantaloons, Panama hats with long streamers," Marjorie remembered. They lived in bungalows with big yards and fruit trees, but when apartment houses were built, a family might live in one room. Pearl's parents, Marjorie said, would have been of the "import the British" school. Meanwhile there were drummers playing the Shango in the African tradition and still observing the culture of the Orishas. When Pearl returned in 1953, she met up with renowned drummer Andrew Beddeau and other artists who were practicing Africanist cultural expression.

In the 1950s, there was a great infusion of Trinidadian art forms into the theaters in Europe and the United States. In Trinidad and on other Caribbean islands, the Pan-African movements were growing in art and religious practice. In the United States, the dance, the drumming, and the theatrical expression of African-based forms were continuing to influence theater and dance. Through her studies in Africa in the late 1940s and in Trinidad in the 1950s, Pearl was at the forefront of the flow of these cultural dialogues. Part of her life's work was to establish herself as a bridge among three points—Trinidad, Africa, and the United States—for those seeking cultural roots of creative expression.

Geoffrey remembered Pearl as "an energy, a force," having heard of her stunning performance in *Show Boat* in 1946. "What she was interested in was not chic," he said. "All her undertakings were big undertakings. Traveling to Africa by boat. This was not easy travel! She was independent, doing what she needed to do. We artists were too busy for much socializing," he continued, "but I helped her plan her trip in 1953." In Trinidad, Boscoe encouraged Pearl to travel to rural areas and study the Orishas and the ritual of Shango. People who came to study the Orishas and the rituals associated with them took religion very seriously, but the police persecuted those engaged in the practices. Caribbean dance did not become fashionable until after independence in 1960, and into the 1930s there had been a prohibition against using the drum. "However, it seemed very exciting to the artists," Marjorie said, and when Pearl brought her group, there was a party every night.

Another revered Trinidadian, Beryl McBurnie, founded the Little Caribe Theatre in 1947. She was born in 1915 in Woodbrooke and died in March 2000. In 1938 she went to New York to study education and eurhythmics at Columbia University, and performed under the name Belle Rosette. She and Pearl became friends in this period, and Beryl was one of the first to provide Pearl with background in West Indian dance. "I was influenced by Beryl McBurnie, who is the cultural dance teacher and driving force from Trinidad; so Trinidad is strongly in me," Pearl said.[1] Pearl performed in *Antilliana,* in which they re-created a West Indian market, and other McBurnie concerts. McBurnie told Pearl's student Eva Koonan Zirker that Pearl "stole the show," "dancing by herself."

Marjorie thought of McBurnie as an ambitious woman who found New York too big a place to master and returned to Trinidad in 1940, where she overshadowed her sister, Frieda McBurnie-Artman, a "real artist, a wonder woman." Beryl took over Boscoe's troupe, and Boscoe and Marjorie's mother did the costumes, Boscoe the choreography and music, and Beryl the business side. This was the beginning of what grew to become the Little Caribe Theatre.

When Pearl arrived, Beryl McBurnie was recognized as the Mother of Dance in Trinidad. Even though they had had a prior association and Pearl embraced her former home, particularly the raw folk culture of Laventille, the friendship between the two women broke apart after Pearl arrived, because Pearl was given government funding and, as Marjorie recalled, Beryl envied her. Although Beryl had come to be cherished in Trinidad, it took Pearl, a New York star, shaping the raw cultural basics of Trinidadian folk dance and giving a recital at the Princess Building, to legitimize the work.

Pearl's Trinidad study group consisted of ten dancers: Esther, Jeannie, and Olive, three African American women; Ora Bronstein, a sabra from Israel; Lydia, from Switzerland; a woman from Washington, D.C.; Lorna Burdsall; Eva Koonan Zirker; and two others. They paid what they could toward their airfares, and Connie Williams, a Trinidadian who had organized Carnivals first in New York and later in San Francisco, raised the remainder. The group established their headquarters in a place called the Cricket Wicket on Tragarete Road, in a diverse, bustling neighborhood opposite the Oval, the central cricket stadium. Marjorie remembered that a Chinese couple donated their apartment to Pearl for the duration of her stay, and she used it as both home and studio.

The ideal of racial cooperation was not always realized, however. The group Pearl traveled with was mixed, led by Pearl, who was very dark-skinned. A rich Jewish Trinidadian family that owned a department store took Ora in and catered to her because she was Israeli. "What are you doing with the *schvartzes?*" they asked. The prejudice against very dark skin in Trinidad was built into the social structure. The question Eva heard as the group studied African-derived dance was, "Who wants to bring savages here? This is not Africa." But Pearl was devoted to the restoration of original forms, and the integration of performance and authentic re-presentation of the dances. As a Trinidadian who grew up in the States and who had traveled to Africa, she was pioneering the Pan-African movement's acceptance of African culture in Trinidad, a trend that would spread throughout the Caribbean.

Pearl's guide was Holly Betaudier—Holly "B," as he is affectionately called—the famous host of Trinidadian radio and television programs who is fondly remembered as the down-to-earth, vivacious host of "Scouting for Talent." Pearl was interested in Holly's stories about the folk aspect of Trinidad, the superstitions and what he called "the macabre side," as well as folk medicine, herbal cures, and the work of the midwives, the one or two elders in each village who delivered the babies.

When Holly saw that Pearl was attracted to the limbo he put her in touch with Julia Edwards, the undisputed queen of limbo in the Caribbean. The dances Pearl brought back from Trinidad included "Limbo," originally a men's dance performed at wakes to draw out evil, "Belle Aire," also called "Bele," a formal, elegant folk dance with an orchestra of drummers and folk-singers, and "Picque," a saucy dance the women did to attract suitors. In "Cacao," a dramatic dance of slaves as they crush the beans from the cocoa plants, the women wear ruffled skirts that swirl around their ankles, and the men are bare-chested in work pants. Feet shimmy on the floor and hips and arms swing in opposition as they scoop up the beans and toss them overhead.

At the time, Trinidadians were discouraged from performing these dances, which had African roots, but when black Trinidadian dancers saw the white women in Pearl's group learning them, it was as if they had been given permission to learn the works themselves. Pearl found that the Shango dances and the Yoruba rituals she had learned in Africa had become deeply rooted in Trinidad, though not part of mainstream culture.

Lorna Burdsall, one of Pearl's American students in Trinidad, had been teaching at the College of William and Mary in Virginia when she met a music teacher at an all-black high school who suggested that her students perform at his school. "It was in 1953 and when the President of William and Mary heard about this, he called in my superior and said, 'What are our girls doing, going to perform half nude in front of an all black audience!'"[2] Furious, Lorna decided to leave William and Mary. An announcement in *Dance Magazine* caught her attention. Pearl Primus was seeking ten people to accompany her on an upcoming trip to Trinidad and Tobago to help with research for her doctoral thesis in anthropology. Lorna applied, was accepted, and at twenty-five embarked on her first trip outside the United States.

On July 4, 1953, Lorna wrote of the royal greeting they received and described going to "a bongo," a worship ritual that combined elements of

African and Christian traditions with songs and dances of Spanish origin. Bongo was originally performed by men to ward off evil spirits and continued to be performed as part of the Nation Dances of African origin during the Big Drum Festivals on the island of Carriacou, off the coast of Trinidad. Lorna then described their first Shango, which reminded her of what she knew about the Holy Rollers. Shango, an Orisha in the Yoruba tradition of Africa, became recognized as the god of thunder and lightning, whose power is symbolized by his staff, a source of unpredictability and violence. Shango rituals took place "secretly in the hills, [went on] for as many as three days, with animal sacrifices and possession . . . closely allied to hypnosis and other forms of psychotherapy."[3] Lorna was fascinated by every detail. In her eyes,

[it was] not a worship but a sort of outdoor party. People came from quite a distance to join in, singing hymns, playing crap games and dancing. Everybody surrounded a small space and the men began to hit bamboo sticks called gua-guas (never knew you could get such sounds from sticks!). One or two people, men or women, would become encircled by the crowd and show off their wonderful dancing. One guy even showed off more than his dancing when he gyrated so much his fly flew open, revealing an impressive surprise for the ladies.

Milling around were vendors selling delicious roast corn, boiled red nuts (sort of like chestnuts) and peeled oranges, producing a combination of smells that perfumed the air. The dancing seemed to be a mixture of Spanish folk and individual jazz styles. One or two men would start the songs, all sung in patois, the local French-based dialect. The rhythm simply gets you after a while and you find yourself dancing. I did it too, although I felt and am sure I looked like a prima ballerina. These songs and dances have been handed down through the years by word of mouth and are not easily recorded. I wish Pearl had brought the tape recorder, but undoubtedly we will be going to other bongos.[4]

On July 20 Lorna attended another three-and-a-half-day Shango fete. They slipped and slid through muddy, steep hills to reach the compound above the town of Arima, where the Yoruba practiced their religion, and from where they would watch the ritual with its Shango tent and altars. "Since Trinidad is a predominantly Catholic country, there was much Catholic ritual, but along with it the dancing and beating of drums. The High Priestess, called the Papa, presided and became possessed. She took on the characteristics of different orishas [African Saints]." Again, Lorna recorded the scene:

> The grass-thatched roof of the tent, the heat, the incessant beating of the drums and the sweating black bodies created quite an atmosphere. The four corners of the tent are very sacred and are cause for much ritual. It is believed that evil lurks in these corners and must be routed out by sprinkling water, myrrh, essences, oil, etc. Several women and one man became possessed.
>
> After dancing all night there was a lull between 4:00 and 5:30 AM and then preparations were made to sacrifice four chickens. We all had to take part in everything, so after sleeping soundly on a fifteen inch-wide bench for about two hours, I awoke to participate in the mass, which had to do with the offering of the chickens to St. John and St. Catherine. The Papa anointed my head with oil and stuffed a piece of bread in my mouth as I held a lit candle. In this mad frenzy of dancing the chickens were killed and drawn and thrown into a big pot to boil. These fat old women are such wonderful dancers . . . the rhythm of the drums simply takes possession of them and they perform the most miraculous steps. We all ended up eating the chickens with rice and green tea and the saints were also given their share.[5]

Pearl and her group departed in the early morning, leaving Lorna to make sketches of the Shango compound and to record the ritual secretly, since the believers discouraged writing about them. Sweaty and filthy, she made a quiet exit in a sudden downpour, but repeated the experience two more nights and wrote it up for Pearl's research notes.

Lorna also sent her family a vivid, physical description of Pearl:

> I am trying to collect my thoughts while numerous members of this happy dance family wander about laughing, talking on the telephone and Pearl traipsing around dressed only in her gorgeous brown skin but adorned with African silver draped on her buttocks, waist and bosom. She is trying to figure out what to wear for the lecture she will give tonight. She prefers to go as she is now. That woman is just not made to wear clothes, and yet she has boxes and boxes of African materials and jewelry and most of the time is trying them on. By the time I get back home I will have forgotten how to live in a western fashion.[6]

She also reflected on Pearl's personal style:

> She has to be handled with onion skin. . . . She is as feminine as they come—jealous, emotional, likes to be the center of attention, etc., and on top of that she is trying to lose some of the weight she gained in Africa while gathering materials for her Doctorate in Anthropology. She is magic! When she demonstrates in class the beauty of her movements dumbfounds us. She is an incredible jumper![7]

Pearl's costumes played essential roles as their experiences brought them from the poorest of places to opulent occasions. "Now I know why Pearl said not to bring sixty-six pounds of luggage . . . she needed the extra weight for her many African lapas, gold and silver jewelry, Chinese embroidered blouses and other paraphernalia," Lorna observed. "It takes her hours to get dressed and we feel like orphans in comparison. We go from dancing in the dirtiest of places to a millionaire Mohammedan's wedding. We have only one bathroom and cold water to clean up ten sweaty women."[8]

After her month of studies Lorna decided to head home. "I did get nostalgic when you talked about Martha Graham and Jose Limon and seeing their classes, but I shall never regret coming down here," she wrote.[9]

Eva Koonan Zirker became one of Pearl's assistants. The daughter of Polish immigrants, Eva was born in 1933 and always loved to dance. As her family left Poland to escape the horrific pogroms, people threw pennies for her when she danced on the train. At age eleven, Eva attended Camp Kinderland, one of the summer camps for "red diaper" babies outside of New York City. She met Edith Segal, who taught modern dance and had founded a group called the Red Dancers in 1928. Eva first studied with Pearl in 1952, having seen Pearl perform in support of dancers who were trying to form a union in the late 1940s. She was awed by Pearl's strength in "Great Gettin Up Morning" and instantly felt at home. Eva likened Pearl to Picasso, who drew inspiration from African arts, and was attracted to Pearl's way of looking for the thread of continuity from Africa to the Caribbean to the United States. "She talked about the color of black before anyone had and, along with Nina Simone and Odetta, Pearl was already leaving her hair natural," Eva remembered.

In New York Pearl and Eva became close friends. "One night Pearl took out a mask that had been given to her in Africa and she did something from Shakespeare with it. It was three in the morning and she was so hilarious I was screaming with laughter when two policemen came in with their guns drawn. They thought someone was being raped!"

After Pearl had returned from Africa, Yael observed that Eva moved like Pearl. He said, "You can pick up on the African dance itself. How do you explain that?" She replied, "It's because I had done the Yiddish dancing." Pearl recognized similarities between Jewish and African dance, saying somewhat cryptically, "It's like going from one room into the next room." Even in her eighties, Eva could demonstrate the vigorous stamping, arm pulsing, and reaching upward associated with ecstatic Hasidic dance, and then transform the same rhythm and body effort to the African dance, legs and feet never changing, body leaning over the earth, arms extending diagonally out and down.

In Trinidad, Eva said, "Pearl related to people who were down to earth, coming from backgrounds not middle class, the earthy people. She had that humanity." But the group also met with professional anthropologists and folklorists as well as leaders of African-based religious practices, arts, and dance. The folklorist Andrew Carr befriended Eva and took her to the ritual group Rada, which practiced the Ibo-Yoruba religion. She found herself watching the dances of possession and described them for Pearl in great detail, insisting that there was no need to "commercialize anything. . . . It's theatrical enough!"

> I had seen the Shango, which was a lot more militant. Here it was lyrical and soft and the faces were marvelous. And the drums! Papa Antoine, born in Dahomey, was eighty years old and still drumming.
>
> The next day, at six in the morning I was up and talking to the women who were wearing white. There was a great deal of camaraderie. The priest put a chicken between his toes and— Wham! The neck and the body was ripped off and the blood spouted! In front of my eyes, all of a sudden, the women changed. The eyes, the bodies and the dance started. It was magnificent. They were still doing African dance according to Pearl. Shango already had been bastardized with the French and Spanish influences, but not Rada. They were still singing the African chants. Pearl was familiar with the African chants from her time in Africa.

When it came time for Eva to dance, she started talking in patois and became possessed. Andrew Carr understood what she was saying. "He translated what the spirit was saying about me. My guardian was a long faraway African spirit. The Rada community had kept records dating back from the last century. The records showed that the last time a man from their compound had gone in possession was 1901. Andrew said that I was a reincarnation of that man." He told Eva that the people of Dahomey were her people.

∾

Against the drama and excitement of the religious rituals, personal dramas were developing. Boscoe Holder had discovered Percival Borde, a footballer (soccer player), and taught him to dance. Then Beryl McBurnie enticed Percy to join her company at the Little Caribe Theatre. When Pearl was in the mountains, Percy came into a class Eva was teaching, and she thought "he was gorgeous." After they "danced together beautifully," he invited her out and they started "roaming around" together, but Pearl told Eva to stay away from Percy, presumably so as not to interfere in a conflict between Percy and Beryl, but perhaps because Pearl wanted Percy for herself. Eva was in her twenties, with kids of her own, and in a bad marriage at the time, but she was having the time of her life and was angry at Pearl for telling her what to do. Nevertheless, Eva encouraged Percy to join forces with Pearl, urging him to get to Carriacou, where Pearl had gone to see the Nation Dances, and telling him, "You need the strength that Primus can give you." She takes credit for their union and, even though both Percy and Pearl were married, she was not surprised when the two returned from their trip to Carriacou and Pearl told her that Percy would be coming to New York.

In Trinidad families were deeply intertwined. "Pearl was like a daughter to my mother," said Marjorie Boothman, one of the Holder children. "Percy and his first wife, Joyce, were childhood sweethearts. Percy was everybody's friend." His family lived on Stanmore Avenue. Marjorie was close to Percy and described the Bordes as "semi-prejudiced." The Bordes were distressed by Percy's alliance with Pearl, not only because of his existing marriage but also because Pearl's skin was dark. But, Marjorie said, Percy "accepted his African ancestry, delighted in it and researched it." Trinidadian men were "chauvinistic," leaving wives alone with the children, while they left for weekends and Carnival parties. "Wives knew they were having affairs," Marjorie said. After Pearl and her group left Trinidad, Percy spoke to Marjorie's mother, who told him he shouldn't leave the marriage, that he had responsibilities in Trinidad. "There's a Calypso song about the wanderings of 'the Trinidad man.' Sometimes things started out innocently but then that was that," Marjorie concluded.

When Pearl returned to New York, she and Percy began making arrangements for him to follow her as a scholarship student, but he was also arriving as her lover, leaving a wife and three-year-old daughter behind. Percy's letters reveal that the planned deception weighed on him and might have also troubled Pearl. While it was Yael's recollection that he and Pearl were separated before Pearl met Percy, Percy's letters imply otherwise. Despite their anxieties, he and Pearl envisioned a life filled with dramatic new possibilities, in which music and dance would be the basis of their union.

Percy's many letters express the passion that brought them together, but also portray Pearl as the director and teacher. Some of Pearl's letters to Percy have notes in the margins next to references to the choreographies she had taught him, presumably for her small company. It is clear that she felt she would determine when he was ready to perform individual African dances, especially "Impinyuza," from the Watusi.

Percy's first letter expressed his concern about being "found out," his distress at their "deceit," and his response to her distress about what people might say and think. Then he turned to business, his work on the various dances she had taught him, the rehearsals, travel preparations, and forms he received and had to fill out before traveling north.

> It is now 4:46 pm.
> Alone in an empty office
> T.G.R-Trinidad
> 28-9-53

My love, my love,

The clock ticks loudly from the wall at my back. A fan hums unconcerned a little way to my right. The sounds of voices are heard now and then down the passageway as the messengers hurry on with their afternoon chores. Heavy irons clang against each other as the familiar sounds of an engine, shuddered just outside my window to the left. I am alone now with you amidst these noises, these empty yawning chairs, these ugly silent desks which I have now come to loathe. But now I forget them—I forget everything, let time tick away if it must for now I shall relive those hours I spent with you and dream of others to be spent again.

He worried that they would be discovered, and did not know whom to trust, but he was thrilled to receive a photo presenting "those eyes, those hips, that bosom. . . . Wait let me read your letter again."

Percy's letters are filled with defiant and hyperbolic language that conveys the sense that Pearl has rescued him, both psychologically and professionally. "I was incomplete until you came. Now I'll follow you to the ends of the earth and back again," he wrote. "Somehow I never cared what people said of me. But now—now it's what they must not say of 'us.' There is the difference. Here is the awakening I spoke of. . . . The fire you have left in me burns bright. I'll be worthy of you, by God." He then returned to practicalities, describing what he is up to with "Te Moana," "Bushasche," and "Limbo," and asking if he should try "Watusi." Pearl responds with a teacher's marginal notes: "Do not attempt Watusi as yet—please."

The next day, Percy revealed that Tante Silla, a relative, was in on their secret and enjoyed hearing from Pearl. Percy and Pearl looked at different visa possibilities, including his getting a student visa under which she would have collected all earnings for him until he could get a permanent one. He prepared to give notice at his job and worried about all the travel problems falling into place. "Oh Darling I am frantic as to know what else to do," he wrote. Percy's stream-of-consciousness letters continue in this vein as he narrated his moment by moment thoughts and feelings, and veered from the practical to the emotional and back again.

Pearl's lawyer, Herbert Levy, had been enlisted to help with Percy's visa, and on October 8 Percy informed Pearl that he booked passage for October 31, and he began counting down the days. "Thanks for the warm clothes you are bringing to the plane—but darling your arms will be enough," he wrote. Health issues and Pearl's mental state are a recurring theme in the period preceding and following Percy's arrival. Eva recalled that Pearl was "tortured emotionally" at the time, as she was "hounded and hounded" by the FBI agents who came to her loft with threats and accusations. There was also occasional tension between them, as when Percy wrote on October 10, "I shall ignore your remark about mongrels but do not let me hear you speak like that again—understand! Now you would look up with one of those wicked smiles and say 'All right' and I'll take you in my arms and kiss every part of you. Why are you so sweet. . . ."

On October 14 Percy wrote, "This heart alone must hold this love for you—my loveliness, my beloved," but he still worried about gossip and felt that they needed to make an announcement. "Something official should be said. If even for my Mom and Dad's sake. So I think it will be quite in order for you to do so." Finally, on October 20, on Yael's personal stationery, there is a brief, typewritten letter addressed, "To Whom It May Concern."

> This is to certify that Mr. Percy S. Borde is arriving in the United States as our guest and shall remain in our home with us for the entire length of his stay in our country. Thank you in advance for every consideration shown him.
>
> Sincerely,
>
> (Mrs.) Yael R. Woll [in Pearl's writing]

Percy arrived in late October, and Pearl was pregnant in March. Years later, he filed for divorce from Joyce, his first wife, in St. Augustine, Florida, and signed papers on October 13, 1961. Joyce Borde was granted custody of their daughter, Cheryl, with "reasonable visitation reserved" for Percy. Yael finalized his divorce from Pearl in Mexico on November 15, 1961, and on December 15 Pearl and Percy filed a certificate of marriage in Manhattan. On the certificate, Percy is named Percival Sebastian Borde of the Bronx and Pearl is Pearl Eileen Woll of Brooklyn. Joyce Borde never signed papers but did marry again.

⁓

Cheryl Borde was three years old when her father left Trinidad to join Pearl in New York. She saw him a few times in the ensuing years when he returned to Trinidad for performances and family visits, before her mother sent her north at the age of seventeen to finish her schooling, first to Baltimore and later to New York. Although she had loved Percy's few visits to Trinidad when she was a child, Cheryl's recollection of her "welcome" to New York was dismal. Pearl and Percy cleared a space in the basement amid costumes, boxes, props, artifacts, and instruments. "I had a bed, a dresser, a refrigerator.

My shower was a sink. I had an electric teakettle," Cheryl recalled. "I never set foot in the studio or apartment upstairs. If I needed something or needed to give them something, I would go upstairs. Pearl would open the door a crack and hand something out or take it in. I would glimpse down the long hallway, it was dark, dank, and gloomy. I was never asked in."

As can be expected, Cheryl's earliest feeling was that Pearl had ruined her life. "I put up a barrier and didn't let her in. She had told me that when she was pregnant with Onwin she always wanted a daughter. I didn't know if we ever would have become close." She did remember once going to the Village together and having fun, thinking, "I should let my barrier down," but "it never came down."

Tensions between Pearl and Cheryl were not the only source of anguish in the marriage. Soon after their son Onwin was born in 1955, Percy became involved with another Trinidadian woman—she was living in Brooklyn—and she had a daughter with him when Onwin was five years old. He supported this second family for the rest of his life.

On August 5, 1954, Pearl wrote to Tante in Trinidad, announcing her pregnancy, and explaining why she had not been able to attend her feast.

> . . . at that time I was so sick we had to call in specialists to discover what was wrong. First they discovered that I was very anemic and that I would have to build up my blood before I could dance again. Then guess what!! They announced that there will be an addition to the great family of the Orisha People. Now don't go running down the hill and announce this to everybody. It is still a secret. Furthermore the Powers have warned me to be careful. This is why you did not get your things. But as soon as I feel better I shall send them off to you.

She alludes to a visit to Trinidad by her mother, the only record we have that Pearl's mother returned to the island after leaving in the early 1920s. "I had thought of taking [the family] to Africa this year, but the doctors say I must rest." Pearl's emotional state was also precarious. She had written to a confidante called Norman (probably the publisher Norman Berg, who had had a close relationship with Pearl's friend and mentor Marjorie Rawlings, who had died in 1953) about her depression, having sunk "deeper into the chaos of nowhere." On Norman's advice, she called Scribners, Rawlings's publisher, and asked to speak to someone who knew and loved Marjorie Rawlings. She had previously been in touch with Macmillan Publishers about a book project that was in progress, but neither publisher was responsive. Shortly afterward she discovered she was pregnant, and now the trip to Africa that she had been trying to put together was out. She reassured him that she was becoming stronger. "Norman, let those who wish to laugh at the thought of a Divine Power, laugh—I cannot. Out of the shadow of hunger, the threat of losing a roof, the sickness, the inflexibility of a society—Out of the fear of losing my 4 legged friends and the frightening depthless pit into which my mind had fallen—I am emerging—stronger though still not strong—healthier and determined to face life no matter what it brings," she wrote.

She was pleased to be working as a specialist at New Jersey's Newark Museum, correcting its catalogue of African objects and assisting with an upcoming exhibit. "This is a wonderful achievement for at last my great knowledge in the field is being recognized among scholastic groups." She wrote that "Percy is teaching all classes at the studio," which she described as a blessing, "for I not only cannot teach now but have no desire to see a student. I have just about developed a block." She ended by asking what happened to Marjorie's animals.

Yet even as she was coping with her pregnancy, Pearl wrote about bringing "some members of that sad little group I started in Trinidad" to New York. She was distressed that "little Jeffrey," one of the younger drummers, would create a Shango dance "for some fly-by-night group. I have washed him off my books. I do not wish such weak people near me. Temptation is great in New York and if he can be swayed there, do you know what would happen here?" She then said she would try to get "Big Jeff" (Jeffrey Beddeau) and "Sam" (Sam Phils), two of the leading drummers from Trinidad. They must know that she is very strict, she wrote.

While in Trinidad Pearl had invited Holly Betaudier to join her group

top left: Pearl Primus, Port of Spain, Trinidad,
c. 1920. Source: American Dance Festival Archives,
photographer unknown.

top right: Primus family portrait, New York, 1920s.
Edward, Emily Albertha, Edward Onwin, and Pearl.
Source: Schwartz collection, photographer unknown.

left: Young Pearl on a park bench, New York,
c. 1939. Source: American Dance Festival Archives,
photographer unknown.

left: Pearl and her pets, late 1940s. "She had a cat that thought it was a dog!" said a friend. Source: Schwartz collection, photographer unknown.

bottom: Pearl and her first husband, Yael Woll, late 1940s. Source: American Dance Festival Archives, photographer unknown.

Formal portrait, mid-1940s, one of
many portraits taken during this period.
Source: American Dance Festival
Archives, photographer Gerda Peterich.

he Roxy Theater, November–December 1944, where Pearl first staged the solo "African Ceremonial"
r a full company. Source: American Dance Festival Archives, photographer unknown.

Studio images of Pearl and noted drummer Alphonse Cimber, mid-1940s. Of Cimber she said, "His hands played absolutely authentic rhythms." Source: American Dance Festival Archives, photographer Morris Gordon, *Picture Magazine*, April 4, 1944.

Pearl with Josh White in "Hard Time Blues," early 1940s. Source: Time and Life Pictures Collection. Getty Images, photographer Gjon Mili.

Pearl Primus performing to "Honeysuckle Rose," December 1942, with musicians Teddy Wilson, piano; Lou McGarity, trombone; Bobby Hackett, trumpet; Sidney Catlett, drums; and John Simons, bass. Source: Time and Life Pictures Collection. Getty Images, photographer Gjon Mili.

Pearl in a studio image entitled, "Hate and Fear," 1951. Martha Graham said that Pearl had the strength of a panther. Source: Hulton Archive Collection, Getty Images, photographer Baron/Stringer.

A joyous Pearl performing "Rock Daniel," 1944. Source: University of Massachusetts Amherst, copyright Barbara Morgan Archive, photographer Barbara Morgan.

"Calypso," Philadelphia, 194
Cast: *(left to right, standing)*
(dancers) Lillie Peace,
Pearl, Eloise Hill Anderson;
(left to right, kneeling)
(singers) Dorothy McDavid,
Helen Tinsley, Clara Hubba
(front, sitting) Alex Young.
Source: Courtesy of Eloise
Hill Anderson, photographe
unknown.

"Haitian Play Dance,"
performed by Pearl Primus
and Joe Nash, 1947. Source:
American Dance Festival
Archives, photographer
Gerda Peterich.

"The Southern Tour,"
1947–48. Company membe
included *(left to right)*:
Helen Tinsley, singer; Ren
Cutler Meer, pianist; Padje
Fredricks, dancer; Pearl
(center), Alphonse Cimber
drummer; Lillie Peace,
dancer. Source: Courtesy
of Renee Cutler Meer,
photographer unknown.

A dramatic moment in "Shango," performed by Percival Borde and Pearl, 1957. Source: American Dance Festival Archives, Moss Photo Service.

"Bushasche, War Dance, A Dance for Peace," 1940s, part of the repertory throughout Pearl's career. *Center:* Joe Commodore; *back left:* Charles Queenan. Source: American Dance Festival Archives, photographer unknown.

Pearl in Israel in 1952, where she was enthusiastically received. Source: Courtesy of Ahuva Anbary, photographer unknown.

Pearl performing one of her "Spirituals," 1940s. Source: American Dance Festival Archives, photographer unknown.

Pearl in a contemplative moment at Jacob's Pillow, 1950. Source: American Dance Festival Archives, photographer unknown.

Pearl performing "Caribbean Conga," 1940s. Source: American Dance Festival Archives, photographer Jay Florian Mitchell.

top: An exuberant Pearl performing "Dance of Lightening," Congo, 1949. Source: American Dance Festival Archives, photographer A. DaCruz.

left: "Bush Devil," Liberia, c. 1959–63. These dancing masks were the subject of Pearl's PhD thesis. Here her note reads, "'Bush Devil' dancer—symbolic of the materialization of a spirit form. Symbol of chief's authority for the Vai tribe in Liberia. One of various forms." Source: American Dance Festival Archives, photographer Pearl Primus.

right: Pearl as anthropologist in Liberia, 1952. Source: Leon M. Jordan Collection, University of Missouri-Kansas City Libraries, Dr. Kenneth J. LaBudde Department of Special Collections, photographer Leon M. Jordan.

Top: Pearl as teacher in Liberia, 1952. Source: Leon M. Jordan Collection, University of Missouri–Kansas City Libraries, Dr. Kenneth J. LaBudde Department of Special Collections, photographer Leon M. Jordan.

Bottom: "Impinyuza." Batwa dancer of the King of the Watusi, Rwanda, 1949. Source: American Dance Festival Archives, photographer Pearl Primus.

top: Percival Borde dancing "Impinyuza," his signature solo, 1979. Drummers: Earl Thorne (known now as Earl Robinson, or Ayan Layo), seated; Alphonse Cimber, standing. Source: American Dance Festival Archiv[e] photographer George M. West Photographic Studio.

bottom: Pearl dancing "Impinyuza," 1951. She was declared a man by the Watusi chief before being taught this dance. Source: American Dance Festival Archives, photographer unknown, Consolidated Concerts Corporation.

One of Pearl's demonstrations with anthropologist Ethel Alpenfels, her mentor at NYU, 1962. Source: American Dance Festival Archives, photographer William Simmons.

Pearl engaged in a lecture demonstration hosted by the Five College Dance Department at Amherst College, 1984–85. Onwin Borde is the percussionist. Source: Courtesy of Frank Ward, photographer.

left: Pearl with Percy and Onwin celebrating the opening of an exhibit, "Dancing Masks of Africa," September 1974. Source: Westchester Rockland Newspaper, copyright *The Journal News*, photographer Kirchoff.

right: Archbishop Granville Williams of the Sons of God Apostolic Spiritual Church in Barbados, 1986. The archbishop was Pearl's beloved friend and spiritual guide in her last years. Source: Courtesy of Stan Sherer, photographer.

in New York. He arrived in 1955 and found the group of West Indians she had sponsored living in Brooklyn in great disarray, while Pearl was trying to revive arrangements for a tour of West Africa, and seeking funding from the Rockefeller Foundation. "She had a very big vision and also wanted to send separate groups to the South, to the East and to the West," Holly said. She had invited ten people including Andrew Beddeau, Trinidad's best-known Yoruba, Shango, and African drummer, to join her. When one of her other invitees declined the invitation, she extended it to Holly. Building on the work of Beryl McBurnie in the early 1940s, Pearl had continued to work with the raw cultural basics of Trinidadian folk dance, which included Yoruba and Shango rituals, and to present them in New York.

Pearl wanted to know if a drummer named Montillo would be interested in working with her internationally.

> My work is guided by the Great African Powers. He will visit Africa with me some day. But I demand loyalty, honesty and sincerity. I know he drinks a great deal. Tell me, does this drinking get in the way of his work? Do you think he would cause me trouble with women? I know the man is a master. His hands are the hands of my brothers in Africa. He will play the African drums. But if he makes me unhappy, he hampers the work to be done. Write me soon for I am planning now for those I need to be here by December of this year.

Maya Angelou was Pearl's student when Pearl was pregnant. "We were friendly, but I think of the teacher as being in one caste and I never presumed that we would be friends in the sense that I wouldn't socialize with her." Ms. Angelou was aware that Pearl was having emotional difficulties during this period and commented, "All I know is that I wanted to be of help. Had she displayed her emotional upset in a really obvious way I would simply have assumed that that's the attitude and the personality of a master."

Far from displaying her upset publically, Pearl continued to perform. Eva related the following story:

When Pearl was pregnant with Onwin, in October of 1954, there were two women who arranged through Hunter College for Pearl to perform a one-woman concert in their theatre. One of the two women whose family supposedly owned King Solomon's mines sponsored Primus' one woman performance. At that time Pearl was enormous in her pregnancy. I was sitting in the orchestra of that small theater and heard a man sitting a couple of seats away say jokingly to the people who were with him, "I'm a doctor and that movement could bring on the birth."

After the concert, Pearl and Eva were invited to an exclusive dinner at the Fifth Avenue penthouse home of one of the sponsors. They took a private elevator up to the apartment, and were seated at one of several small tables, each of which had its own waiter. Among others, the wife of Ed Sullivan was there. "Pearl appealed to society women at that time." Eva then wrote, rather mysteriously, "There are some other things that Pearl told me that I have started to remember but which are best told in person." Eva, in her eighties, said she had come upon a memory that she found hard to talk about. She said that after this dinner Pearl told her about receiving a phone call from one of the women from the party who said she was pleasuring herself, i.e., masturbating, while talking on the phone with Pearl. Eva continued: "Her movement was so strong, women as well as men were sexually attracted to her and by her. Pearl was ridiculing these people because we both felt the same way about these snobby rich people, but these women adored her. Two women at the dinner were clearly in a relationship."

Pearl's dark skin and her tremendous strength as a performer are often duly noted, but not her power to stimulate her white audience sexually. Dunham's work may have been more overtly sexualized than Pearl's, but in her earthier, less-idealized body, Pearl's work was also deeply erotic.

Onwin was born on January 19, 1955, in Mount Sinai Hospital in Manhattan. Virginia Primus, Pearl's sister-in-law, remembered Yael arriving at the hospital after the birth, "taking one look at the baby, leaving, and not being seen again."[10] On the birth certificate the child's name was registered as Onwin Woll, as Pearl was not yet divorced. But Yael confirmed unequivocally that Onwin was Percy's son. Onwin never used the name Woll, except on Pearl's passport when she prepared for European travel in 1956. He officially changed his name to Borde in 1978, writing in an affidavit, "The reason why my last name is different from my birth certificate is that my original name of Onwin Sebastian Woll was legally changed by order of the Supreme Court, County of Westchester, July 1978." The petition states,

> The grounds for his application are as follows. "My true parents as I have long since been advised by them are Percival Sebastian Borde, father, and Pearl Eileen Primus, mother. However, at the time I was conceived and born the divorces of my mother from her then-husband, Yael Woll, and of my true father from his wife had not come through. As shown by the next affidavit from my mother, she put down as my father's name, her then-husband's name Yael Woll out of a sense of embarrassment.
>
> "However, I have virtually always known that Percival Borde was my father and he has treated me as a son. I, my mother and my true father all want to change my name."

Onwin was then twenty-three years old. Herb Levy, the petitioner for Onwin, noted that having a child out of wedlock in the climate of the 1950s could have been disastrous for Pearl's career.

Rina Sharett, one of Pearl's Israeli students, was pregnant around the same time. Pearl invited Rina to her apartment and very proudly showed off her beautiful baby, who was lying in bed. Rina was present at Pearl's first performance after Onwin was born:

> She came out to the audience dressed in a colored wide dress all radiant, and at once electrified everybody present as always, even before starting to talk and move. She addressed the audience, "Good evening, tonight you shall see much more of me," then she dramatically stopped for a while to suggest that she would give a longer program. She continued, "Because I am now in a post-birth

period and I have gained much weight." That is how she has totally captured everybody, beaming with her motherhood happiness.

The end of the marriage to Yael, the union with Percy, and the birth of their child together mark a decisive shift in Pearl's life. Although their loving relationship had an undercurrent of conflict and betrayal that was part of Pearl's life until Percy died, it also provided a professional partnership that enhanced the career of each. The greater talent was acknowledged to be Pearl's, but Percy's skill and charisma complemented her artistic life. They taught and traveled together, raised Onwin to follow his father's path as a drummer, lived for a long stretch in Africa, created a school and company, and shared many performances.

The work of identity formation that was propelled by her experiences in Africa was consolidated between the time she and Percy met and Onwin's birth. The subsequent years were ones in which the challenges of the early career continued but on new terms. With prodigious drive, she would dance, teach, study, lecture, write, travel, and raise her son simultaneously. While never on very stable ground financially, she was clear about her work and goals, and how she would function in her various pursuits. She transferred her graduate studies from Columbia to New York University in this period. Though the PhD was not completed until 1977, it would benefit from three decades of maturation since the first, seminal trip to Africa.

<hr />

Life settled in with Percy and baby Onwin and continued to be unreasonably busy. From October through December 1955 the company toured colleges throughout the northern and southeastern United States. Though Onwin was an infant, Pearl was planning a European tour and preparing for work on Broadway. In 1956 she choreographed *Mister Johnson,* a show set in Nigeria (then British West Africa) in which the distinguished black actor Earl Hyman played an African clerk who seeks to become an English gentleman. Historian Miles Jefferson thought Hyman's performance "absolutely authentic and persuasive," although "it was feared that the African dances and chants directed ably by Miss Pearl Primus, might convert the play into another one of those jungle orgies that the Caucasion [*sic*] thinks is the essential and ever-present element of African life. As it was, there was just a bit too much ceremonial frenzy, but hardly the excess shattering completely the play's capacity to move the spectator."[11] Pearl included Pearl Reynolds and Mary Waithe, along with several drummers from Trinidad, in the show, which ran in Broadway's Martin Beck Theater for twelve weeks. Although she was given much freer rein than she had in *Caribbean Carnival*, this was her last choreography in Broadway commercial theater.

Pearl's letters describe the staggering amount of work that went into planning the European trip, whose participants included Pearl and Percy, Trinidadian drummers Jeffrey Beddeau and Samuel Phils, Edith Bascombe, Arthur Bart, David Berahzer, Harold Nurse, Reginald Reid, Louise Gilkes, and Mary Waithe as dancers and Helen Tinsley, singer, many of whom had performed in *Mister Johnson*. Trinidadian dancer and drummer Arthur Bart, the designated babysitter, was also a steel pan player. Pearl's mother also traveled with the group to help with Onwin, and she was listed as wardrobe mistress. Norman Coker is listed as a drummer. Louis Naylor, a dancer-drummer, and Leslie Tamases, a stage manager, may also have participated. They sailed to Europe on the SS *United States* through stormy seas. "Everyone was seasick!" said Mary. They landed at Le Havre, France, in September 1956 and stayed in a small hotel in Paris, visiting the famed Moulin Rouge before making their way to Italy. In Rome they gathered at a pensione and then toured their way south to Messina. "The people in some of the small towns had not seen black persons before and would come out of the houses to admire the color of our skin," Mary remembered.

Mary said there were always police present at concerts, as this was standard in the Italian theaters, but the company would joke that the police came because they were attracted to Helen Tinsley's full anatomy. They presented a program similar to the one that had toured the United States, including Pearl's variety of African, Caribbean, spiritual, blues, and jazz dances. They were well received, but travel visas were curtailed due to the Hungarian revolution and instability in the Middle East. The company waited anxiously in Rome while Pearl tried unsuccessfully to get clearance for travel to Israel, but finally they disbanded and most of them returned disappointed to the States. Ultimately, Pearl and Percy were advised by the U.S. Embassy to return home. Mary described their relationship as "congenial, cooperative and harmonious" at this time.

Her depression having subsided, Pearl herself was relaxed and would participate in some of the social activities but remained very focused on the tour and caring for Onwin. The company would precede Pearl to the theater for preperformance preparations. Pearl and Mary would handle the costumes, even though each dancer had a responsibility for following a routine related to costumes under Mary's direction. In October and November, the company performed at the Quirino Theatre, one evening performance of which was in honor of President William V. S. Tubman of Liberia. Pearl also performed in an International Dance Festival Series in Rome.

Pearl and her entourage were supposed to travel from Italy to Israel in December. Pearl had fervent feelings for individual Israelis as well as for the State of Israel itself, and she had formed a warm and personal relationship with the presenters of her first trip in 1952, when Israel was not even five years old. Her commitment to this young country remained strong throughout her life. Abrahim Bogatir and J. Ori Benadyr, also known as Gingi and Ori, her Israeli producers, looked forward to seeing her and her entourage. In the spring, Gingi had assured her that "food is plentiful—and your son will find everything his heart desires." He acknowledged Pearl's request not to stay in a hotel, since her anthropological interest had surfaced and she preferred to live among the people. "In short," they wrote, "come to Israel and be our guest of honour." But, as she did so often, Pearl kept them waiting for a reply. Finally, on May 6 Pearl answered, first apologizing—"I am a miserable correspondent, that is all."—and then asking about the threat of war and safety for her group. They reassured her, as did Rina Sharett. They also reminded her that the standard of art in Israel was high, as world attractions like Martha Graham, Danny Kaye, The London Festival Ballet, and the Royal Dutch Opera had visited. But "[your] art is something special . . . [you are] still well remembered." Pearl proposed coming in September.

On June 18 Pearl asked for their cooperation in obtaining free passage with an Israel shipping company by offering to entertain on the trans-Atlantic trip. Ori and Gingi responded, but not with the news that Pearl wanted to hear. They hadn't made progress because they first needed a contract with her. They did put a request in to Shoham, the shipping company, but required a definite reply from her regarding dates. Pearl answered that the company would be ready to leave Italy at the end of November in order to be in Israel in December 1956 and January 1957. She hoped to fly from Rome to Tel Aviv or to travel by ship from Naples to Haifa. Apologizing for her lateness, she finally outlined the programs she would bring.

But after months of letters back and forth, on November 21, 1956, Pearl wrote to Ori and Gingi canceling this tour. Mary thought that the Hungarian revolution was at the heart of the cancellation. Indeed, Hungary had been in turmoil, with freedom fighters rebelling against Soviet rule. On November 4, Soviet tanks rolled into Budapest with overwhelming force to crush the uprising. But there was also major trouble in the Middle East. On October 29, in response to a possible Egyptian invasion, the Israeli Defense Forces had launched a preemptive strike into Sinai. By November 2 the fighting was over, and, after pressure from the United States and the United Nations, Israel withdrew to its 1949 boundary. While the decade after the 1956 war was a relatively peaceful one in Israel, in its immediate aftermath the United States declared Israel off-limits for travel. In the wake of this, Pearl's letter from Rome is deeply emotional.

> How can I write this letter? As I sit here I remember the young
> trees planted along the mountains and the faces of the little
> children from everywhere, building towards the future Israel.
> I remember the wrinkles on the hands of the new refugees, and
> the look of hope in their eyes as they spoke of the homeland. I
> remember the Mediterranean pounding against the shores and
> the piles of shells it left behind every morning. Israel is for me not
> just the tiny strip of land, but a promise fulfilled. I write all this
> because you asked for understanding, while it is I who ask for it

now. We are ready to come to your country. . . I have spoken to
my company about the warmth and the honest appreciation that
was mine on my former visit. . . .

The American Embassy in Rome refused permission for American
citizens to travel to Israel and, due to finances, Pearl could not keep the
company together. Nevertheless, she still hoped to travel there with a very
small group. She introduced Percy to Ori and Gingi as her "partner and
associate" and said he would take over communication as she "become[s]
emotionally upset by a situation such as this present crisis."

Ori and Gingi were moved by Pearl's depth of feeling, "her attitude
toward their struggles," and they shared her "noble words" with friends.
They continued to hope she would come as soon as the ban was lifted and
maintained confidence in her high artistic standards. In early January 1956,
they heard that the ban to enter Israel was to be lifted on the fifteenth. On
January 10, Percy wrote to Gingi and Ori from Barcelona, where Pearl had
gone to study Catalonian dance, asking that they continue to try to make arrangements on their behalf with Greece and Turkey and informing them that,
"heartsick and unhappy," Pearl had complied with the wishes of members
of the company and sent five of them home from Rome, leaving six—Pearl,
Percy, three drummers, and one wardrobe mistress (Pearl's mother). This
core group had traveled to Barcelona, and after performances there two others headed home, leaving four—Pearl, Percy, a drummer, and Pearl's mother.
Onwin was there as well. "Pearl feels quite dejected and unhappy about the
whole situation—especially since she had planned to come to Israel with a full
company." Percy informed them that Pearl had come to the painful decision
that they should postpone the trip until they could come with a full company
to present their full repertory. "Pearl's integrity as an artist would not allow
herself or her work to fall one inch below the high regard and expectations
of her Israel public—whom she loves dearly."

A year later, on January 18, 1957, Ori and Gingi sent a letter to Pearl and
Percy with suggestions for how they could perform without a full company
by incorporating local artists into their performance. This plan was based on

a format that had worked successfully for a recent tour by Eartha Kitt. They suggested that if there was still a ban, they should go to the local American Consulate for special permission to travel, "stressing the cultural and good-will importance of [their] appearance in Israel." They would then launch into planning for the full group to come the following year.

Pearl replied that she had been thrilled with their idea but "a trip to the consulate extinguished the fire." During the following months negotiations continued fruitlessly, and they finally collapsed in early May. The last letter, sent by Pearl to Gingi and Ori almost three years from the first one, is terse. "As much as I respect our past association, if I don't hear from you by May 24th, I shall have to take other steps to obtain bookings in your country."

But this was not to be, and here the correspondence ends. Despite the idealistic spirit, Pearl encountered complex difficulties in adapting her vision and style to the practical and political exigencies of the time. She was settling into a new mode of presentation, developing lectures and courses that would become staples in her presentations, but she needed intricate forms of cooperation as she sought to consolidate her educational aspirations, her work with Percy, and the demands of motherhood. Now in her mid-thirties, she had embarked on a life that would contain all three in various combinations and permutations. There would be other disappointments, and many successes.

SIX

Return to Africa

PEARL ASPIRED TO DEVELOP a heightened awareness among African cultures of the power and majesty of their native arts, and she wanted to bring African groups to a level of performance that would enable them to tour successfully for African, European, and American audiences. In the late 1950s and early 1960s she worked tirelessly to realize this vision, raising money, drafting proposals, and enlisting support of government and private agencies as well as businesses.

In 1958, Pearl proposed to form the First African Dance Theater. On Pearl Primus Dance Studio stationery, which, incidentally, identifies Percival Borde as the director, she celebrates the emergence of African cultures. "Now is the time when Africa must speak with many tongues. Her Dance is one of her strongest voices. With it she can tell of the dignity, the beauty, the strength that is part of the cultural heritage of the Negro People. With it she can capture the heartbeat of the observer and convince the world of her greatness." Pearl proposed that she and Percy become the artistic directors of the First African Dance Theater. They would work in Liberia, Ghana, and Nigeria and then present programs throughout the United States and other countries. She garnered the support of the ambassador and the consul general to the United States from Liberia, and sent her ideas to President Tubman of Liberia, as well as to American artists and agents. Kofi Mensah, the press attaché for Ghana's embassy in Washington, D.C., is quoted in the proposal as saying, "This is what the African people want, this is what the African people need." She wrote to the American Committee on Africa, the president of the Liberia Mining Company, the Ghana National Cultural Society, and the ambassador from Ghana, Daniel Chapman.

In March 1958 Ambassador Chapman wrote to a school director in Ghana: "Miss Primus' idea is this: first, that she and her partner should go over to Ghana some time this year to see what we have got and then give you some tips as to what you should do to get the appropriate way of staging the dances. This is a technical matter about which Miss Primus has a great deal of experience." Pearl's plan displays both the clarity of her thinking and the seeds of the controversy that came to full flower after extensive work in Africa. Pearl and Percy did not intend to impose their teaching on the African dancers, but their "appropriate staging" would cause questions about authenticity and appropriation to simmer and finally to explode.

The ambassador proposed that the director of the school "take a year's leave . . . and travel through Ghana with Miss Pearl Primus and her partner to let them see the variety of dances we have in the country. Then, after you have chosen the items which will go down very well with audiences in America, you select your troupe and give them the necessary training." In May 1958, as the details were being worked out, Pearl wrote to Ambassador Chapman, "This project will be the first of its kind in Africa and will bring the great culture of Ghana before the eyes of Americans and Europeans in a most spectacular and truthful manner." Letters went back and forth, in the same manner as they did in the Israeli correspondence, but now they were successful, and Ghana became a crucial part of Pearl and Percy's travels during the 1959–62 sojourn.

Liberia was another key locus of their work. In 1959 Pearl attended the First International Conference of Negro Artists and Writers in Rome and, at the request of President Tubman, she and Percy, with young Onwin, went to Liberia to found their new school, the Konama Kende Performing Arts Center. From 1959 to 1962 they based themselves in Liberia, though they traveled extensively within Africa and between America and Africa.

In April 1960 Pearl and Percy celebrated the grand opening of the Konama Kende Performing Arts Center, where Pearl was chairman of cultural activities and director of the African Center of Performing Arts, and they gave eighteen presentations in Monrovia. She also gave a command performance for Ethiopian emperor Haile Selassie. In 1961, visiting back in New York, she and Percy gave sixty-eight presentations for private organizations of a work called "African Carnival," sponsored by the African Research Foundation. From December of 1961 to the fall of 1962, she conducted a Pearl Primus Dance Tour of Africa, sponsored by the Rebekah Harkness Foundation, giving scores of concerts in over a dozen countries.

As the director of Konama Kende Center, Pearl suggested a program for the Inauguration Ceremony of His Excellency President William V. S. Tubman during the week of January 3, 1960. She wanted to present dance music and dance dramas of African countries and Caribbean islands, creative dances of the Americas (blues, jazz, spirituals, and shout songs), and historical dance, based on the founding of Liberia. Pearl invited the president to the first recital of the Performing Arts Center on March 17. "By your consent to be Chief Patron of Konama Kende, the First African Performing Arts Center, you are initiating a Golden Age for the Arts in the history of Liberia and all Africa." He agreed to attend, but after moving the date forward to March 23 and 24, the first concert was abruptly cancelled. Pearl issued the following announcement:

Konama Kende

I regret that, due to unforeseen circumstances the programs scheduled for tonight and tomorrow at the City Hall have been postponed. A new date will be announced shortly.

Pearl E. Primus, Director, The First African Performing Arts Center

The above was written in capital letters, as was the follow up announcement:

First African Performing Arts Center: A Community Development

A misconception seems to have crept into the public's mind about Konama Kende—the official name of the First African Performing Arts Center.

It is not a center of two persons, namely, Pearl Primus and her partner, Percival Borde. It was not their "recital" that was postponed but the performance of nearly one hundred Liberian artists from the interior and Monrovia. This in itself will prove in no uncertain manner the all-embracing nature of the project.

Its Aims and Purposes

Konama Kende will be a name to be reckoned with in the near future. Because what took generations to build up the acumen, knowledge and vast experience serves the present generation in good stead. Therefore, art, drama, poetry and dance can be assimilated quicker by the latest methods of teaching and imparting them. Only unstinted co-operation is necessary.

Konama Kende, meaning "a new thing—alive" is here to put Liberia on the map of world art. The Center desires to modernize the indigenous performers by assigning to them the job to raise the standard to a high degree of performance and to the wearing of appropriate costumes.

The Dance Is a Language

Konama Kende wishes to teach academic students the supreme importance of the beautiful rhythm of the body as expressed in the language of the dance. This language is well known, studied and developed to great perfection in Europe, India, Japan, China, Russia and America. The Liberian government has invited Miss Pearl Primus and her partner, Percival Borde to come and assist Liberia, and through her, Africa as a whole. This cultural expression is the physical entity.

Do not fail to see them. The date of the performance to be announced.

Describing the inaugural of Konama Kende, Pearl proclaimed that "if by her good will gesture and faith in her race Miss Primus can develop and carry to great heights this historic human expression of the spirit within man, Liberia will create an immortal niche of fame for herself in the new civilization that is in embryonic form in modern Africa."

Pearl believed so fully in herself as "Omowale"—"child returned home"—that she was blindsided by the idea that she and Percy had exploited an African cultural space for their own benefit. Despite this conflict, however, several important articles appeared in major New York newspapers celebrating the opening of the African Performing Arts Center. John Martin of the *New York Times* described the project as

> the first of its kind in Africa, rich in potentialities, and, apparently, almost as rich in problems. . . . The purpose of the center [is] to perpetuate the African arts . . . , to identify them as African and as art in the eyes of the Africans themselves as well as the rest of the world. This involves the collection and preservation of material, the presentation of it professionally before audiences, teaching, training teachers, training artists and constantly advancing, with virtually opportunistic zeal, as new fields open.
>
> . . . since there never have been professional performances of native art, there is no audience for them. The great mass of people, then, to benefit by the awareness of its own cultural creativeness must first be awakened to the fact that it has a cultural creativeness to be aware of.[1]

The tension for Africans grew out of the distinction between dance as a "form of life" and dance transposed to the stage as performance, a movement from ritual to theater. To describe this transposition as an awakening can carry the implication of "progress" toward Western aesthetic values. Martin's language hits on a central ambiguity in the "authentic" staging of ritual dances. Can the art native to village culture be staged for urban audiences without being transformed in the process? While the work was considered "revolutionary," it might also be seen as one of the first steps toward what Yvonne Daniel and other anthropologists analyze as the "commoditization" of traditional arts and its effect on indigenous culture.[2] The purity of Pearl's aspiration to legitimize the dances on the stage for both Africans and Westerners was not always accepted. For her, the language of the body retained its power through translation to the stage, like the transmission of a message from a transcendent sender to a human receiver.

Martin cites Pearl's intention in establishing a National Liberian Dance

Troupe "to represent the country at home and abroad; to create a theatre that will evolve a native art but also will borrow from the best theatres of Europe and America." At the first concerts of the center Pearl and Percy danced, and they presented Sawatowa ancestral spirit dancers, Sandi girl dancers and mimes, Fanti drummers and singers, the Naffi Tombo "Devil" Dance, and groups of students from the school. "If the newspaper reviews indicated a degree of incomprehension," Martin wrote, "they also reported high enthusiasm and deafening applauses throughout the show. . . . Miss Primus has been given a new official name; it is Jay-bondu, which means boss-lady of the dance. Mr. Borde also has been rechristened, affectionately if not officially, Jangbanolima, or the man who would rather dance than eat."[3]

One of Percy's innovations was preparation of an indigenous dance group for performance in the Pepper Bird, the one hotel and nightclub in Monrovia owned and operated by Liberians. The other clubs in the city were owned by Europeans and featured what Pearl called "cheap shows of sixteenth rate wiggle-dancers imported from Spain." Percy was also scheduled to perform in August in a nightclub in the "luxurious air-conditioned Ducor Palace Hotel, on the highest peak in Monrovia," and he attracted interest from Nigerian and Kenyan visitors.[4]

A Liberian newspaper said that Pearl "is a divinely appointed inspirer. She is aflame with her mission, shunning the annoyance of politics." "But in spite of everything," Martin concluded, "she evinces a profound sense of the values involved in going to a new country, which is also one of the oldest, to establish the oldest art, which is also the newest." Walter Terry reported that Pearl sought "to discover a unity for the tribal cultures and the culture of the Western-minded Negroes of American descent. To this end, Miss Primus is working toward a dance expression which will incorporate all the cultures of Liberia and she feels that a modern dance form is the device which can bring together basic African and basic American art manifestations."[5]

In her first trip to Africa, Pearl had been initiated into some of the very groups whose dances she would now want to present in theatrical settings. Now she had a further ambition, "that Liberian performing units can be sent

abroad as cultural ambassadors representing the art heritages and achievements of their homeland." She hoped to draw artists from other African
states to train at Konama Kende, and they would then return to their own
countries as "valued professionals."

Pearl was now a teacher, with fifty-five students in Monrovia, as well
as a researcher of tribal dances, legends, and songs from the interior and a
recruiter of dancers from the villages. She told Terry that "before I was permitted to teach or look for possible recruits for the center, I had to prove my
supremacy as a dancer by entering a dance contest with natives of the area.
I guess it worked out all right because at the end of it, I was given the title
'leader of the dance.' And I must say that I've had wonderful support from
all the tribal peoples, including the 'bush devils' who are superb artists."[6]
When Pearl encountered obstacles in Africa during this period, it was not
in the bush but in the cities, where politics were changing, and the legacy of
American and European influences aroused suspicion.

When Pearl returned briefly to the United States for fund-raising, both
the *Times* and the *Herald Tribune* carried stories in their Sunday editions. "I
have two homes . . . America gave me the technique and Africa gave me the
heart—and to each, I must explain the other," the *Times* reported her saying.[7] In the *New York Post,* Joseph Wershba voiced some skepticism: "After
almost two decades of the dance, Miss Primus still hasn't decided whether
she's a modern, a primitive, a primitive modern—or a modern primitive."
Yet he seems deeply admiring of her self-presentation: "Pearl Primus is a
vibrant, soft-voiced, cream-complexioned woman. Her hands dance constant
accompaniment to her words, her wide brown eyes reflect the continuous re-
newal of emotion. Her head is turbaned in a scarf, Mandingo style. She wears
shell-shaped ivory earrings, a string of large amber beads, silver bracelets—
serpentine fashioned—and a multi-striped cloth stole called a lappa."[8]

This was a pivotal moment in the larger dance world. The work of the
early moderns had been established, but the postmodern aesthetic had yet
to emerge fully in the work exemplified by Merce Cunningham. African and
Caribbean arts and culture had made inroads with the dances pioneered by
Asadata Dafora, Katherine Dunham, and others, and by Pearl and African

artists, particularly Olatunji from Nigeria, who were also making their presence felt in New York. Within this competitive flux, Pearl risked falling between worlds as she sought a unique synthesis that would transmit essential meanings of African dance as it was re-created for Western audiences. She was enacting an aesthetic vision in which the revival of art forms of various cultures would promote indigenous dance companies and would hold a key to communication across cultures. She needed to strike the right balance between transposition and translation.

Pearl was living and working in a shifting political environment as well. The activism of the 1940s and the conformities of the mid-1950s were giving way to the epochal cultural changes that would become "the '60s." The civil rights movement had erupted, and equal rights and educational opportunities for black Americans were emerging as major issues of the day. Meanwhile, there were conflicts in Africa as colonies or groups within colonized countries struggled for independence. The support of critics like John Martin, Walter Terry, and Joseph Wershba helped Pearl navigate her passage between continents and define a space for her work within this volatile environment.

—✺—

The African tour that began in 1960 took Pearl and Percy to at least ten African states including Liberia, Ghana, Cameroon, Dahomey, Togo, Senegal, Mali, Ivory Coast, Nigeria, and Southern Rhodesia. With them was the drummer James Bey, known in the States as Chief Bey, who later performed with Olatunji and jazz musicians Max Roach, Art Blakey, and Herbie Mann. The tour continued until the fall of 1962, with a return trip to the States in 1961, during which Pearl and Percy were married on December 15. The entire trip was backed by the U.S. State Department, as the project accorded with the policy of "international cooperation for cultural advancement." "Our main purpose," Pearl wrote, "is to work directly with the leaders of the performing groups and through suggestions and concentrated private instruction to give to these leaders advanced principles of choreography and staging techniques."

The performances throughout West Africa that were part of a project Pearl called "Venture into the Soul of a People" consisted of five "variety shows":

• Earth Magician—a show depicting an African ritual priest who comes to bless the earth so that it will bring fruits for the whole community.

• A dance of welcome from the hinterland of Liberia called "Fanga." It is generally arranged to welcome important Chiefs in African villages.

• South American Congo.

• American folk dance called "Lisa Jale" [*sic*]—based on a folk-tale about a lovely girl who is dressed up for a Sunday fair.

• Dance from Congo—Waluzi—Rwanda—Urundi—a dance of the Congo King telling of his grace and invincibility.

In the "Introduction" to the final report, Pearl's voice sings: "We named our project 'Venture into the Soul of a People' for man will dance of feelings he cannot speak and of things his consciousness has forgotten." The arts will serve to bring people together:

> Africa today is smiling, lifting her arms like one who has long been deep in thought and who now rises to put those thoughts into action. Against the fast changes which confront her Present, the voices of her great traditions shout from her Past to guide her. Half smothered, neglected, or seemingly destroyed during the colonial period they waited for the dawn of freedom.
>
> But they, too, must face today. They too must realize tomorrow. . . . They must adapt themselves to the stages of the world without losing their power or their authenticity . . . traditional dance in Africa now faces the challenge of becoming a spectator art.

This challenge led to many successful experiences but it also engendered hostilities, some of which were expressed in the press. A journalist named Peter Pan wrote an outraged story in the *Daily Times* in Lagos. His scathing article ran under a huge, bold headline: SHAM! SHAME! The writer is full of passionate intensity:

All week I have felt very conspicuous. Everyone I have met has seen the Pearl Primus show. The smart cocktail party set, the bright intellectuals; the Very Important Socialites. . . . Who is Primus? If you haven't heard of her I wouldn't blame you. Although if you take my advice, you shouldn't say it, because she is publicized as the "world famous exponent of African traditional dances." . . . Miss Primus is an American.

HER NATIONALITY IS A PRICELESS ASSET IN NIGERIA TODAY AS FAR AS CULTURAL ART GOES, ESPECIALLY AS THE COLOUR OF THE SKIN HAPPENS TO BE BLACK.

He then rails against Pearl's celebrity status. "Miss Primus and the whole lot of them who are coming to sell African culture to the Africans should get out of the continent," he proclaims. "We are fed up with being treated as children who must be humored. And then the condescension, the hypocrisy; and the amateurishness sickens me." Olatunji too is caught up in his invective and he also decries "a man called Geoffrey Holda [sic]. He was billed to do some voodoo dance or some other rubbish like that." Then he gets to the heart of the matter, without realizing that he speaks of himself: "To put it frankly, too many people are obsessed by an inferiority complex of a very sorry nature. A carry-over from yester-years when only the white man's art and culture were considered the best."[9]

For Sam Akua as well, African dignity was being denigrated. He wrote in the *Daily Times* under a bold headline, PRIMUS DANCES—TO A DEGREE:

Damn it. Why does everyone want lollies all the time like babies. They were there in full force—the smart society people who go to shows because the right people go; and they filled the J. K. Randle Hall to overflowing on Sunday night at a joint concert given by the Pearl Primus Troupe,—the American negro lady who is dancing her way to a doctorate degree and the Nigerian National Dancers' Association.

He criticizes what he sees as "absolute contempt and depreciation of Nigerian artistry," except when Nigerian dancers perform it, declaring, with unintended irony, that you "can't carry 'coals to Newcastle.'" But then he softens his critique with a thoughtful conclusion: "This sort of show is all right. At least it confronts you with an opportunity for a re-orientation of our values."[10]

However, in the *African Pilot,* F. I. Okonkwo writes that "true Nigerian lovers of art and cultures should be grateful to Pearl Primus."

> Pearl Primus came to Nigeria not to teach the African dances as ignorantly interpreted by our able journalists, not even to improve on them nor did she come to pose as the champion of the African dances, but rather to assist the Nigerian dancers to know the stage technique i.e. the best method of presenting these dances on the stage as distinct from the present open space dancing method. There is no doubt that Pearl Primus had gained from our dance just as we have also gained a lot from her stage experience, technique and demonstration.

"I ask," he concludes, "Is it fair and proper to treat Pearl Primus who came all the way to assist and to be assisted in the way our journalists have done?"[11]

Between rejection and acceptance, there was also satire, as in a notice in *The Service—Nigeria's First National Magazine,* which shows a picture of Percy in a traditional costume, raffia at the waist, legs parallel, one leg in front of the other, bent knees, arms reaching forward. The caption says: "Any idea what the man in the above picture is up to? He is not a Tarzan of the jungle going out to rescue his lover from wild beasts. In fact he is Percival Borde, husband of the Afro-American dancing priestess—Pearl (Omowale) Primus who recently stormed Nigeria with her weird dances."

But the controversies over the African performances were not confined to verbal sparring in the newspapers. Pearl left among her papers a vivid, unpublished story of an experience that confronted her with the real terror of being misinterpreted in her deepest intentions. On the night of August 3, 1962, perceptions of nations, cultures, and human freedom collided, with Pearl smack in the center, fearing for her life.

On a Friday night in Harare, Pearl and Percy went in different directions, he to a performance of the Ivory Coast Theater Group and Dances, and Pearl to rehearse one of the five groups of dancers they were preparing for a concert the following week. Pearl was using a new space, Stodart Hall, because the State Congress was in session at her usual rehearsal space in the National Gallery. Percy was to meet her for continued rehearsals later in the evening, and, after he departed, Pearl's work was going well. "Certain things began to click on that stage," Pearl wrote. "We were actually getting things done and I was feeling very happy." She sensed a process of refinement in her dancers, like the cutting and polishing of a diamond made of "the raw cultural material we find here in Southern Rhodesia."

Except for a nearby beer hall, the rehearsal space was isolated in a clearing. Without warning, waves of people accompanied by drummers began intruding, and an ominous, noisy scene emerged. Pearl begged for silence and tried to welcome the crowd, when a man claiming to represent the Zimbabwe African People's Union (ZAPU) began accusing her of doing the business of white people and declared that "he would immediately stop it." Antagonistic comments flew at her as mob energy coalesced in the room. Pearl was astonished:

> At this point my mouth fell open. This was something I just couldn't figure out. . . . In my wildest dreams I had never imagined anything like this. They were drunk, some of them with eyes almost closed. One man came up to my face and began just pushing and leaning against me, in a harsh voice threatening me, saying that I was actually working for these Europeans. . . . Don't I realize that African people are fighting for freedom and anybody who was going to work for the Europeans is not on the side of the people?

Pearl tried to explain her intentions, but to no avail. Dressed in her lappa, ceremonial beads, and bracelets, "the traditional fashion of our great ancestors," she stared at them in their European garb and wondered, "Who are these young men who dare to speak to me this way?" Then she confronted them:

> Some of you were not born and some of you must have been
> babies in your mother's arms when I rose almost 20 years ago as
> a lone voice speaking for the great dignity of the African heritage
> in dance. I am no small girl! Where is your respect?

Even in her anxiety and confusion about the currents of political turmoil surrounding her, Pearl recognized a misguided search for freedom in the crowd's
rage at anyone contaminated by contact with white people, but her desire to
transcend the racist division was met only by an escalating threat of violence:

> "Can't you see, can't you see," I tried to shout, "through the
> dance, through the proper projection of an art form, through
> your dances, your sculpture, through your music, you can . . .
> tell the world who you are and what you want. Don't destroy
> this work, it is not for white or black people, art belongs to all
> people," but no one was hearing me, no one was listening.

As the struggle continued, Pearl failed to moderate the assault, and "the
faces swarmed into mine. I had never seen such anger," she wrote. She felt
overwhelmed:

> I've seen the mob scenes in the movies, I've seen hate and an-
> ger in the scenes dealing with violence—German concentration
> [camps]—Little Rock—but this hungry anger I had never known.
> . . . Not from the people who are my people. Not from the people
> whose cause I have defended all my life.

Forced to flee the scene with some of the dancers, Pearl finally hailed
a taxi but was still followed by the murderous mob before the police finally
arrived and she was reunited with Percy.

Beyond the strong physical terror of this incident, Pearl suffered a
traumatic threat to her identity. She realized how the mob mentality she had
resisted elsewhere had come home to Africa, to "my own people." Her fear
for herself was also a fear for them. It was fear of the unknown that the rituals
of adult initiation she had studied were meant to master.

Pearl did conquer her fear, and she persisted in her work. Her "Reflections" on "Venture into the Soul of the People" tell us why:

> When people dance—people who have never bartered the fierce freedom of their souls for the superficial dust of paved city streets—people who have not doomed themselves to the robot-like existence of modern shadow beings by strangling their hunger for rhythmic movement and frustrating forever their own physical response to music and song—
>
> When these people dance, Time stops!! Even the air draws back and the Past, the Present and the Future merge and shine like a single indescribable jewel in Eternity . . .
>
> Even as their feet caress the earth—even as their arms defy the waiting air—they know they must someday pay for this ecstatic freedom. . . . [Yet] a hunger consumes them and a thirst to reach the center!!
>
> "The dance is a spirit. It turns the body to liquid steel. It makes it vibrate like a guitar. The body can fly without wings. It can sing without voice. The dance is strong magic. The dance is life!!"

SEVEN

The PhD

The single most important thing for me to say is that I both profoundly
admired and deeply loved Pearl Primus. As a young African American
student of anthropology, I was looking for "sheroes" anywhere I could
find them.

—Johnnetta Cole

"SHEROES" IS A FEMINIST TERM for women who inspire other women, and
this African American woman, an anthropologist and inspiring teacher who
would later become president of Spelman and Bennett Colleges in Atlanta,
was deeply inspired by Pearl. When Cole was a student there were very few
role models within academia for black women. Pearl was among the first
to aspire to a PhD even as she was actively pursuing other career goals and
performing to great acclaim throughout the United States and abroad.

Intellectual curiosity had always accompanied Pearl's choreography,
but after the Rosenwald trip to Africa, the dancer, performer, and choreographer merged fully with the developing anthropologist. As a self-described
"artist-investigator" she could be at one with the many peoples she lived
with and learned from, and could also have a formal reason for maintaining
distance. She would regularly remove herself both physically and mentally
to a private, watchful space, the "going in" space, as she called it, where she
could be the observer. In the section of her dissertation on "Ethnography,"
she evoked this psychic space as she described her living conditions:

> The interior was divided into three main areas: (1) a foyer or
> room for receiving visitors, (2) an area that was used by the re-
> searcher as "a not here" section, and (3) a dressing and small
> wash up area for the investigator.
>   . . . "the not here" area . . . was equipped with a large table
> and chair on which was draped blue and white country cloth.

This was the investigator's private area for writing notes, sorting luggage, packing, or just "thinking." When the researcher was in this section, everyone knew she was "not here." The window had a small ledge on which she kept various stones she collected.[1]

"From childhood," she says in a footnote, "the investigator has always created a degree of privacy by closing her eyes and softly saying, 'I am not here.' Everywhere she travels the people enjoy and respect this creative privacy which she is able to achieve even in the most crowded situations." When Pearl emerged from her private space, the artist and anthropologist found unified expression in Pearl as the educator.

Although it is based primarily on her research during the 1948–49 trip to Africa, Pearl's thesis, "An Anthropological Study of Masks as Teaching Aids in the Enculturation of Mano Children," was not completed until 1977. The artist-anthropologist-educator became Doctor Primus, a title she cherished as the rightful signifier of her status. Yet while Pearl's success opened doors for others, she encountered great difficulty opening this door for herself.

After returning from her first trip to Africa, Pearl began graduate studies at Columbia University in 1950. Never one to settle for compliance with existing expectations, she wanted to carve a new space for herself in an academic domain. Her friend Eva recalled that when Pearl returned from Trinidad in 1953, she decided to continue in Columbia's master's program. At the master's degree thesis defense, "they tied her hands so she walked out!" Pearl could not speak without the full expressiveness of her physical body, and Eva remembers her declaring that the only way she would do a PhD was to dance her way to a doctorate.

In a pattern that was repeated throughout her career, particularly in later years, Pearl wanted academia to provide a space for her vision and methods but strongly resisted conforming to conventional expectations. She formally withdrew from the Columbia program in 1956 and transferred to New York University, where she completed her MA in 1958. She was so distinguished, so formidable an artist and educator, she felt that NYU should have allowed her to define her own terms for a doctorate. The nature of her struggle can be seen in Pearl's proposal, in which she used the term "sculpture-danced." In a letter to Joyce McGuiness, assistant to the dean at NYU, she described this as "not merely two words hyphenated but a very important anthropological concept." She continued:

> In my earlier paper I stated: The subject of sculpture-danced implies, at some point, the discussion of masks. Masks imply the hiding of the identity of the wearer. In this study, the emphasis of sculpture-danced is the emphasis given it by the Mano people among whom it functions. This emphasis is not upon the masking of the wearer but upon the projection of the specific ancestral or spirit force, the identification of it and the understanding of the message it brings to the living.
>
> In my present paper I further clarify: The great masks of Africa are costumes created to bring into visibility the spirit forces of the ancestors. Dramatic movement, mostly dance, is the medium through which the manipulator of the mask expresses the language of the spirit force. This dramatic movement animates the fabricated structure of the mask and its meaning is interpreted by specialists within the specific culture.
>
> The change in the title came in answer to continued requests on the part of two members of my committee and, finally, Dean Mayher. This change, I must admit, wrought havoc with my emotional and psychological attitude towards the dissertation. It seemed as if the whole paper was changing because sculpture-danced had appeared on almost every page as a concept of life.

Pearl's resistance focused on this demand, which entailed nothing less than the abandonment of her whole conception of the integrity of African culture and dance as "a concept of life." This concept fused motion and emotion, dance and expression of meaning, and art and the value of life in society. The African mask was decidedly not the African American mask of the oppressed, whether humble or enraged.

At NYU, renowned anthropologist Ethel Alpenfels was eager to have

Pearl study with her. Alpenfels had encouraged Pearl's transfer in the late 1950s and came out of retirement in the late 1970s to help her complete the doctorate. She sought to help Pearl "dance the doctorate." Although her initial proposal to design programs and curriculum for twenty-five schools in Brooklyn had not been accepted in lieu of a written dissertation, Pearl thought that one of her great accomplishments was convincing her committee at NYU to accept the concept of dance and movement as a language. In the end, however, she was not allowed to "dance" her dissertation but had to produce a written document in order to be awarded the degree. Finally, both of Pearl's advanced degrees were awarded in educational psychology and anthropology.

In her narrative resume, Pearl says of her teachers, "Not only were these pioneers her professors at Columbia University and New York University, they were also her special friends." Among these distinguished professors were Ruth Benedict, Franz Boas, Margaret Mead, Ethel Alpenfels, Dan Dodson, and Patricia Rowe.

Along with Ethel Alpenfels, David Julian Hodges, professor of anthropology at Hunter College, was instrumental in Pearl's progress to the PhD. David's mother, Dr. Ruth Hall Hodges, was on the art faculty of Morris Brown and Atlanta Universities, and it was through her that Hodges met Pearl and Alpenfels. Starting in the postwar years, many students and teachers from southern black colleges came to New York to study, and in the summers between 1958 and 1966 Hodge's mother and Pearl's friend Mozel Spriggs would go to New York from Atlanta, Mozel to study dance, Hodge's mother to study art and religious education. In 1971, Hodges attended one of Ethel Alpenfels's classes at NYU in which Pearl conducted a lecture demonstration on African dance. Alpenfels, by then a legendary teacher of anthropology, welcomed the young man and his brother from the South to her classes, and, inspired by her, they both became anthropologists.

Alpenfels and her colleague Dan Dodson were race relations experts and champions of racial equality. In fact, the National Organization for Negro Women gave Alpenfels the Woman of the Year Award in 1955. Dodson was close to Branch Rickey, the visionary general manager of the Brooklyn Dodgers whose thoughtful and strategic efforts to hire Jackie Robinson led to the

integration of major league baseball in 1947. (At Dodson's retirement from
NYU in 1972, in a hall called Brotherhood in Action, Alpenfels introduced
Pearl, who danced and then introduced Jackie Robinson.) Pearl was looking
for mentors who shared her passions and her commitment to equal rights
for blacks. Perhaps this was why she withdrew from Columbia and headed
downtown to NYU.

With encouragement from Hodges and Alpenfels, Pearl became a candidate for the doctoral degree, but many years passed and Alpenfels just
about gave up on her. In casual conversation, she told Hodges, "Pearl's not
going to do it. But I do want to get you and one other student through and
then I'll retire." By the time she did retire in 1972, Pearl no longer felt she
could "do the ritual of getting this," but when Hodges insisted that all she
needed was a dissertation, Pearl said she would be willing to write a "sculptured dance dissertation."

Pearl was exempted from additional classes on the condition that Professor Alpenfels return from retirement to form and supervise a doctoral
committee. The actual writing process was a trial. In spite of having done
all the fieldwork and supplemental research, "She didn't want to do it and
was not disciplined to do it," Hodges said. He and Pearl worked together,
but when there was a crisis Hodges would not be able to reach her. He
would call Joyce Knight, Pearl's companion and amanuensis for many years,
who would make excuses like, "She's got a cold and can't talk now." When
Hodges would say she needed to turn in material by an agreed-upon date,
Joyce would reply, "You're so coldhearted!" But eventually, Hodges said, "I
pushed her and pushed her and over time, it occurred."

On August 11, 1975, years after she began the program, Pearl received
a letter from John S. Mayher, for the Research Proposals Committee of the
Division of Education, accepting her proposal, with minor questions, for
"A Study of Sculpture-Danced as a Factor in the Enculturation of the Mano
People of Liberia, West Africa, Between 1948 and 1963." On October 5,
Hodges wrote to Pearl, outlining what he saw as "profound" implications
of her research for contemporary American education. He saw in Pearl's
writing an affirmation of the view that "any culturally patterned behavior,

however bizarre it may appear at first, at bottom makes plausible sense, is believable and fully human," and he believed that the thesis would expand cultural awareness. "Indeed, a student cannot see his own society until he has begun to see others adequately," he wrote.

Despite her resistance to completing the writing, Pearl's thesis is a treasure—well researched, organized, and documented, tremendously informative about her time among the Mano and the role of the spirit masks in their culture. It also reveals much about Pearl herself, the development of her passions, the depth of her connection to the people she studied, her methodology, and, tangentially, her upbringing. Because her initial research was conducted in 1948-49 and continued through three additional trips to Liberia (1952, 1959-61, and 1962-63), the thesis contains a perspective that comes with time and age. It is a mature statement regarding the spirit masks in particular, the ways of African culture in general, and the implications for education and curriculum development in the United States.

The thesis is dedicated to "My Mother—Emily Albertha, the unexcelled dancer of Adowa, and to My Father, Edward Onwin, the greatest of storytellers," both "Now in the royal court of the Ancestors."[2] It grows out of her years of living among and studying the following groups:

> The Bushongo and the Bapende of Zaire, the Yoruba, Ibibio, Ijaw and Ibo of Nigeria, the Baoule and Senufo of the Ivory Coast, the Mende of Sierra Leone, the Bambara and Dogon of the Sudan, the Gola, Kpelle, Gio, Bassa, Dan, Vai, Kra and Grebo of Liberia, the Mohawk Indians of Northeastern United States, the Trinidadians and Tobagonians of the West Indies.[3]

After first outlining the geopolitics of Africa at a pivotal time in its history, when many colonized countries were becoming independent and when tribal life was changing as urban areas developed, the thesis centers on the Mano people, who lived in the hinterlands of Liberia. Pearl reveals a keen understanding of "village-level Africa" and of the integration of the arts with the culture and the daily life of its peoples. Alluding to the shift from the bush to urban life, she writes in the preface:

In all is the memory of the villages. In all is the sweet echo of their traditional music. Whether it is in the school yard or the factory compound, the mine, the backyard, the living room, the night club, or the street, the traditional dance claims them and for the time they have never left the villages. . . .

Africa is a challenge. The challenge is to understand this mighty giant of antiquity. In order to do so, it is necessary to know her past, her ancient laws, her customs. It is necessary to hear the singing of her people as they cradle their babies, to feel the music of her musicians, to listen to the old, old folk tales around the evening fires, to visit the places of sacred prayer, to witness the dancing, to thrill before the magic of the great ancestor masks.[4]

The thesis is intended to be both a reclaiming of the ancient traditions of the masked dances and a celebration of the emerging Africa in contrast to the conditions of slavery and the oppressions of contemporary America. A footnote on the second page points to an additional motive, a mastery of childhood fear. "It is very possible that the Carnival masks [of Trinidad] did influence the investigator from childhood," she says. "One of her earliest recollections of Carnival in Trinidad is one of fear experienced by her when a huge mask leaped the fence of her yard, danced before her and chased her into the house."[5]

Later she writes of herself in the third person:

One factor which has been most significant in her development and interest as an anthropologist is that she, herself, is a product of multi-cultures. Her mother was the daughter of one of the greatest African priests and musicians of the Ancestral Cult, Peoples of the Orishas in Trinidad, West Indies. The investigator was raised by this proud African mother in a strictly West Indian home within an American community. Cultural differences were very obvious between life outside and inside the home.

She became involved in the study of ancestral masks

through identification with African sculpture in order to better understand herself and the heritage of peoples of African
ancestry.

For her the study of anthropology and the faithful interpretation of a culture through its art forms have become inseparable.[6]

Beginning in the 1960s there were growing concerns about the effectiveness of American education. By 1983 the nation was considered "At Risk,"
but awareness that the arts could play a significant role in bringing about
social and educational change had emerged earlier. Pearl's thesis provided
a response to this moral crisis by presenting a form of arts education that
is fully integrated into a society's understanding of its place in the human
world and the cosmos. "Thus a profile of Mano culture will isolate important strands of the culture, which masks manipulated reenact to remind the
people of their responsibility to their ancestors as well as in the upbringing
of their children in the family," she wrote.[7]

Pearl's chapter on the ancestors opens with a description of life crises
from birth through adolescence and adulthood to death, as taught to her by
the chief counselor of the king, the high priest of the Bushongo people at
Mushenge, Zaire, in July 1949. She then explains how the dancing of the spirit
masks reveals the ancestors and teaches ancestral laws, and she analyzes the
specific role of each mask, describing in detail how it looked, how it entered
a village, the sacred space in which it was stored, who was allowed to handle
it, how to manipulate and move within it, how these rules were developed,
and what they indicated about the social groups in which they were obeyed.
She also discusses how a person is selected to become the manipulator,
the one who dances a particular mask. "The manipulator is a dancer in
spirit's dress, [whose] identity is unknown to the uninitiated. The musician
is also considered a 'chosen' person. Personal anecdote: The investigator
remembers her biological mother's constantly saying with great pride, 'When
Lasseydo touched the drums, the spirits danced.' She was referring to her
father [Pearl's grandfather] who was a great musician of the Ashanti people."[8]

The dissertation contains many examples of Pearl's talent for scholarly observation, but its most original feature is the stories she tells of experiencing the dancing masks themselves. These stories, "Through the Eyes of the Investigator," create striking images of the dance of each mask. For example, the "African Diaries" record an encounter with "Long Ge (Vianje)," as Pearl is awakened from a nap in the early afternoon heat:

> Great laughter suddenly penetrated my ears. Laughter, drumming and chanting!! . . . The drummers' hands gave a sharp command and I jumped out of the cot and flew to the door. . . .
>
> There he sat on the sloping palm branch-covered roof of the house.
>
> Towering into the sunlight, Vianje, "the long one," spread his arms and seemed to fly like a bird from the housetop. Incredibly agile, he swung his legs through the air, turned and dipped gracefully. As he spun around swinging first the right foot then the left over my house, his appreciative audience gasped loudly. Then he would run away rapidly, fly back with dips and turns and suddenly sit on the roof of the house again.
>
> Sense slowly began returning to me as I joined the laughing, cheering audience. "The Long One" had been called by the Paramount Chief to make me very happy.

Two days later, Pearl's teacher, her "Zo Ma," explained, "When you laugh, we see inside you . . . laughing not only is good for the one who laughs but helps others understand there is no pain for them."[9]

A second story involves "Gbetu," a devil who eats children at night. Accompanied by two dancers, one with a "huge curved horn," the other violently waving a fan, Gbetu dances before a huge central fire.

> Gbetu danced on the huge stage of night. He swirled and stopped but his tremendous raffia dress kept turning. Then he turned rapidly the other way. All of a sudden he began to tremble and shrink. Down he went to almost twenty inches. Like a mass of pulsing life he seemed to breathe under the heavy darkness of the

night. Then, like an apparition, he began to grow. The drumming broke into the heavens, the voice of the horn shouted and Gbetu grew, his body filling out and sucking in all the while. A giant!! He swung his heavy head rhythmically in wide circles and began to spin again. The whole world seemed to be filled with Gbetu. Gbetu danced!!

A child appears, and then "he pounced. It was all over. Gbetu shrank and rose twirling. The boy was gone. Gbetu danced triumphantly . . . the mighty 'devil,' had eaten well . . . and he disappeared behind the houses."[10]

"Zo Bundu" is danced by a group of women "dressed in lappas of dark blue and white striped country cloth . . . their heads . . . wrapped, thick braids curved out sideways like wide horns." They dance in a circle to clear the area of evil.

Then I saw her. Zo Bundu came pulsing like a million hearts and arteries beneath the calm discipline of feminine strength. The patina of her sculptured head and headdress created strange shadows around her austere eyes. The carved rolls around her neck seemed to move softly like ocean swells.

Beside her to the left walked her speaker and behind her came the dancing, chanting women. Every fiber of Bundu's garments was quivering, vibrating like the strings of a guitar. She dipped and swayed and dipped and turned all in time with the chanting and rapid staccato beats of the saa saas. When she came to a dramatic halt, so did all sound.

Then stillness!

I felt myself filling up with indescribable joy and pride—joy in belonging—pride in my own womanhood. Zo Bundu danced around me. Her fibered garments brushing against my arms, my abdomen, my back. The voices seemed to fill the air and wrap us in a cocoon of privacy.

I saw and felt her touch me in my dreams for many nights afterwards.[11]

Finally, Pearl includes a moral instruction entitled "Klua Ge," written for the children in the New York City elementary schools in 1965:

> The ancestors do not say don't be clumsy. The pain you suffer when you fall is punishment enough.
>
> The ancestors do not frown when you have temper tantrums. Usually you bite your tongue or lose the friendship of comrades.
>
> The ancestors do not flog you for putting your hand in Zo Ma's food. Zo Ma might just break it off.
>
> The ancestors do not tell you stop knocking over mortars, bowls of water. Until the water dries in the ground, you had better hide yourself.

But the ancestors, Pearl adds, would not forgive anything that offends a guest. "Therefore, even Klua Ge, the dancer of obnoxious behavior, even he could not visit a village where a guest was staying."[12]

Pearl is transmitting in her own teaching the kinds of lessons that prepared the Mano children for their adult places in society. In the bush school, "they will die as children to be reborn as new people with the ability and knowledge necessary to function unhandicapped in the adult affairs of their people and the totality of life in general."[13] The curriculum in dance, music, and song is intended to infuse aesthetic, moral, and psychological growth. "Then at a specific time . . . [each child] is placed on his own to face fear."[14]

> The newly initiated dance with the pride and power of the conquest. . . . When the initiated has conquered fear, a new dimension is added to his personality. He has lived through this period. He has experienced the terror and the exultation. At the root of his being, he has experienced deep ecstasy. He is a human volcano. The technique, the sequence he has learned become vehicles in which his soul can leap to the heavens. Where before he merely jumped because he should, he now defies the laws of

gravity. He soars through space because he must. Where he was taught the technique of a turn, he now becomes a top, spinning himself into the earth.

A child left the village but a man returns! A child left but a woman returns!¹⁵

Pearl could be describing herself as she portrays the journey of the children. In addition to being initiated into the secret Sande Society, she was declared a man by the head of the Watusi so that she could learn dances that women were forbidden to perform. In these settings she learned the truest meaning of her formidable leaps and powerful technique. While the dissertation represents Pearl's keenness as an observer, she was also a wholehearted participant in the physical and psychic life of the people, finding the voices in Africa that spoke words that echoed her mother's words and actions as she grew, coming home to herself.

After outlining the values taught or reinforced by each of the seven masks that she studied, she concludes with implications for American education. For the Mano, "The great masks were like psychological posts which held up the world, the village and the future." But in "another society where the fabricated form is not a culture trait but remains on the walls of museums and in studios apart from life," the mask assumes negative value. Pearl quotes the famous poem by Paul Laurence Dunbar:

> We wear the mask that grins and lies,
> It hides our cheeks and shades our eyes,—
> This debt we pay to human guile;
> With torn and bleeding hearts we smile,
>   And mouth with myriad subtleties.

Making the mask a metaphor for the condition of African Americans, Pearl says, "During the 1960s the mask began to slip from the face of the Afro-American revealing burning anger where quietude was thought to abide, bitterness and pain where unending Joy was thought to be, abrupt impatience and relentless determination where the smile of patience was once effective.

White Americans shuddered in amazement as the demands of 'equal rights now' pierced through the air."[16]

Pearl pleads for the removal of the mask that hides rather than reveals. "A mask grows heavy . . . unless it is taken off, the manipulator becomes molded to the mask. The mask becomes a dictator." She writes:

> Here in the United States, the psychological mask must also be removed. Unless the manipulator is allowed to be, all growth can be aborted. The mask cannot grow. It is a shell which can be outgrown. The manipulator can become a prisoner inside. Worse yet, the wearer can grow into the structure of the mask, distorting it and at the same time being distorted by it. Soon it becomes too late to struggle. In hiding the self, the self has been destroyed.[17]

She argues for the transformation of American education and the inclusion of masks in myriad ways in order to develop a new curriculum that promotes a more creative, inclusive society where students "become aware of themselves as the key to awareness of others by challenging the understanding of their own culture traits and values."

When, in 1949, Pearl was refusing to leave the hinterlands of Liberia, her Zo Ma, a high priestess among the Mano people, said to her, her voice firm, "You must go. You must go home to your village and tell your people about us." Pearl received her mission:

> That evening in December 1949, the investigator sat in silence on a low wooden stool before her Zo Ma while the master-teacher prepared her hair. When all was done, the researcher leaned her head on the old woman's knees and wept. She knew then she would return to her "village" [America]. She knew, too, the work which lay ahead would not be easy but she had no choice. Her Zo Ma had spoken![18]

EIGHT

The Turn to Teaching and Return to the Stage

She moved in circles, and those circles moved.

—Theodore Roethke

AFTER HER RETURN from Africa in 1963, Pearl continued to mature as an educator and artist. She was fully acknowledged in the dance world, but, living between cultures, and between the stage and educational institutions, she wanted "just folk" around her, her folk, and didn't court celebrity status for its own sake. She felt at home having a ginger ale with an old friend or the mother of a former student, or visiting the director of a community center, or cooking her favorite African recipes. In her public life, she taught in academic settings, restaged work, choreographed, worked with community groups, and dreamed of founding an institute and of completing her lifelong work, "The Woman of Zor." With Percy, she developed the Primus-Borde Earth Theater, planning tours and projects. She graced many stages and received many awards, but she also developed a reputation for being "high maintenance," hard to work with, perpetually late. She could be brusque and go inward. Anyone who knew her would calibrate her mood of the day by the intonation of her "Y——e——e—ss——" as she answered the telephone in the morning.

In the mid-to-late 1960s, Pearl's work focused on education, even as she and Percy continued to perform together. In 1969, Pearl began teaching at Hunter College, and soon after was traveling from New Rochelle, New York, where she bought a big brick house, a former synagogue, on Coligni Avenue, which steadily accumulated a lifetime of records and memorabilia. In 1970, Percy took a position in Binghamton, where he became truly established in the academic life. His performing fame included brilliant renditions of "Impinyuza," which was added to his repertory in the 1950s and became his signature piece until his sudden death following a performance in 1979. It must have been complicated for Pearl to see Percy reaching goals that had been part of her life plan, but which she had not yet realized. Pearl was the more well-known artist, on the way to becoming the PhD in the family, yet Percy had the more secure academic appointment as an associate professor. Pearl would say that she didn't want to move to Binghamton because there was too much snow and it was too cold, but in fact, Percy had a separate life there and shared a house with the playwright Lofton Mitchell and the artist Edward Wilson, and the trio were known on campus as "The Three Caballeros."

Many people recognized Pearl's fierce love for Percy. We know that she was initially Percy's teacher, and that she sponsored his arrival to the States in 1953. They traveled to Africa together for extended periods to perform and teach, and maintained a studio and apartment on West Twenty-fourth Street. They each had special gifts, and they were charismatic in their own ways. Over and over, Percy is described as exceedingly handsome, tall, elegant, and gracious. "A real specimen," said Eva Zirker. "That man had an Adonis look about him," said former student Veleria Ramos. On one occasion, Percy left a dinner party to get drinks and never returned from another engagement. Some of the dancers who were on the scene when Percy arrived and Pearl's first marriage was breaking up were unhappy with their union. But many of them stayed with Pearl and made their accommodation, if not their peace, with it.

Such stresses may have been one reason why Pearl's career slowed in the late 1960s and 1970s. Percy's womanizing and his other family, coupled with Pearl's private, independent nature, caused her to turn increasingly inward. She could erupt with joy, but there was also great seriousness. At times she would sit, lean forward with an arm across her knee, and radiate stillness and quiet thought. Those who knew her well respected those pensive moments.

—◦—

Despite the complexities of marriage and family, teaching and performance, Pearl profoundly affected younger generations of dancers and students. She found her students and transmitted her teaching methods in many ways. When she was a youngster studying with Katherine Dunham, Glory Van

Scott remembers Pearl approaching her as she was coming up the steps of the subway after class and saying, "You're a little dancer, where are you going?" From that moment on, Pearl called Glory "Little One," which ultimately became "Little One Who's Grown Up." As her career developed, "Dr." Glory, as she came to be known, became a producer, performer, educator, and activist.

At times, Pearl could be blunt with students. In the mid-1980s, when "Dr." Glory was having trouble as an artist-in-residence in a high school, she called Pearl for advice. Pearl told her about the time a sixteen-year-old boy stood up and started to walk out of her class. When told to return to his seat, he said, "Shut the fuck up!" Pearl replied, "If you take one more step you'll meet your maker." He returned to his seat. The next day, in dance class, she said, "You're so smart, you think you're so powerful let me see you jump like a warrior would jump. Up, down, up down, up. . . . Oh is that how high as you can get?" By the time she finished with him his tongue was hanging out.

Pearl brought people together, cultivating artists who understood her sense of authenticity, engendering tremendous loyalty based on a deep mutual respect, though she also could make students and colleagues impatient with the challenges she created. Those who loved her felt honored by the relationship, touched by her deep connection to the traditions of her ancestors.

Among those whose creative lives Pearl guided were Yasuko and Emiko Tokunaga. At the Boston Conservatory of the Arts, Yasuko Tokunaga directs the Dance Division and her sister Emiko is artistic director of the Summer Dance Program. Together they have had a great impact on dance in Boston and on programs at the Conservatory since the early 1990s. A Japanese-American, Emiko spent her early years in an internment camp in Arizona, the same camp in which Yuriko, Martha Graham's protégé, was isolated with her family. She came out of the camp as a kindergartener who strongly identified with her Japanese heritage, but she felt that people didn't care about the Japanese-American situation. The Tokunaga parents were very traditional, and both girls trained in classical Japanese dance when they were very young, but Yasuko remembers wanting to deny her background as an adolescent.

The sisters' association with Pearl dates to 1966, when Emiko was working on her master's degree at NYU. Pearl became Emiko's mentor and helped Yasuko confront her struggle over her identity. "I had a Japanese cultural heritage and yet was very much a Western dancer," she recalled. "Pearl would struggle with me, and she saw me through all that. She told me that I could not deny my heritage, that I must go back into it, explore it, and create something with it." Pearl gave them a very specific direction: "You two girls must always stick together. With a name like Tokunaga you cannot escape your heritage. Create a dance company or forget about dancing." Yasuko and Emiko did the former and Pearl encouraged Emiko to weave Eastern philosophy into Western technique. They taught classes in Boston called Zen Ballet, and students loved it. Pearl wasn't looking for clones or disciples; she was interested in teaching others to discover their own identity, and, as they did, she was willing to remain invisible.

In 1970, while working at City College of New York and Hunter College, Pearl regularly invited Yasuko to guest-teach for her. In 1976 the sisters performed at Spelman College in "Life Crises," a dance inspired by rituals of childbirth, childhood, adolescence, engagement, marriage, and death. In 1980 they created a dance to a Haiku, "Red Moon Goes Down Light and the Way Shadows Float Eastward and Vanish." Pearl loved this piece. "It was historical, it was cultural, it was East and West," Yasuko said. They performed it soon after Percy's death at the Riverside Dance Festival, and at the end they heard Pearl's voice say "Amen." Inspired by Pearl and with her help and grants from the Japan-U.S. Friendship Commission in 1983 and 1984 they retraced Pearl's path by performing in twenty-one black colleges and universities throughout the country.

In 1991 Yasuko and Emiko initiated a massive letter-writing campaign to the National Endowment for the Arts that led to Pearl's being awarded the National Medal of the Arts.

⌒

In the 1950s, Pearl configured her lecture demonstration format in various ways, and she continued to use it until her death. While transfixing for many age groups, these presentations were particularly geared to children. An early program was "Dark Rhythms (A Lecture-Demonstration)," at the American

Museum of Natural History on a Thursday afternoon in May 1950. The program note says, "In the lecture part of the program Miss Primus will discuss each number fully." The first half of the program included dances and songs from Africa and Haiti, and the second half presented thematic dances representing initiation, fertility, play, and war, with a "Drum Conversation" and "Fanga" concluding the performance. Pearl notes that the costumes for "African Ceremonial," "Impinyuza," and "Excerpts from an African Journey" were all authentic designs. The dancer Charles Queenan reproduced these costumes for "Impinyuza" for the Ailey reconstruction many years later.

Another typical "Dark Rhythms" presentation was planned for December 31 at the 92nd Street Y. Picture a wintry late afternoon in New York. The children entered the theater in daylight and emerged on New Year's Eve! Tickets cost $1.20. Pearl's arrival was an event in itself. She entered in a great sweep of energy, with her multicolored, tie-dyed patchwork of straw bags, of which she must have had dozens. One bag would have papers, one might have fabrics and jewelry, another might have a drum or sculptural objects. She would rush in, eyes alert, and survey the space—its size and acoustics, the height of the lectern—and then address the audience. After events like this, Pearl was showered with appreciative letters.

After her death in 1994, many in the dance community wondered what had happened to Pearl's career after the '60s and '70s. In addition to spending long periods of time in Africa, Pearl poured much of her energy into groundbreaking educational projects, and she was held in high esteem as a "teacher of teachers." Many of these opportunities came her way from the mid-1960s and into the 1970s. Pearl's gifts as a master teacher were recognized by Dr. Vivienne Anderson, who led a newly formed Humanities and Arts Division within the New York State Department of Education, which was expected to raise standards in response to a perceived national crisis in education. Anderson ran the Artists-in-the-Schools program, and had a strong relationship with the black community in Albany.

Known as "the white tornado," Vivienne Anderson was a commanding figure, a small woman with "big pure white hair," said Joe Trupia, the director of music for the State Education Department. She invited Pearl many times to perform and conduct workshops at an annual conference called "Towards Humanizing Education," which convened for New York State educators at the Concord Hotel in the Catskills. To ensure that Pearl would not only arrive but arrive on time, before the first conference Anderson asked Trupia to drive down to New York to meet Pearl, Percy, and Montego Joe, the percussionist. "It was my job, I got them there and I brought them back," Joe said.

Pearl's participation was always enlivening, but she sometimes made Trupia's job frustrating. Once, when Anderson had invited Pearl to star at a summer arts-in-education conference in Saratoga Springs, for which two thousand people were registered, Trupia was expecting to meet Pearl at the train station, but she didn't arrive. He raced between the bus terminal, the airport, and the train station, where he mistook a lovely black woman for Pearl, only to be confronted by the woman's husband. When Anderson finally reached Pearl, she was in South Carolina, having completely forgotten about the event!

The work was occasionally disrupted by racial tensions as well as personal lapses. At one meeting, Trupia, who was white, was accused of racism when he represented Anderson at a meeting in New York to discuss an exchange between Pearl's group and a London theater group. About three months later, at a "Humanizing Education" conference, Pearl brought him up on the stage to receive a bronze mask as reparation for his humiliation.

In October 1971, Pearl accepted the National Culture Award from the New York State Federation of Foreign Language Teachers at the Concord Hotel. The confirming letter is signed "Viv." They were quite a pair, the White Tornado and the African Queen.

Pearl was involved with many other large educational endeavors in these years, including an intensive commitment to the New York City public schools. She worked closely with Terry Baker, who was co-director of the Hunter College Teacher Corps Arts and Humanities Project and who worked at the highest levels of arts education in the New York public schools.

Baker became a close friend and invited her to participate in an East Harlem project and other school programs whenever possible.

In 1966 Pearl was funded by the United States Office of Education to begin "A Pilot Study Integrating Visual Form and Anthropological Content for Teaching Children Ages Six to Eleven About Cultures and Peoples of the World." This was to have been the "dancing dissertation," involving forty presentations in New York public schools. While it did not ultimately lead to the PhD, it did enable Pearl to reach hundreds of children and scores of teachers.

In 1966 Nat Hentoff described these performances for *American Education*, a journal of the United States Department of Health, Education, and Welfare. Entering the auditorium of P.S. 83 in East Harlem on a bleak winter day, he recounts how the children are "unwittingly" part of the research that reveals how children can absorb more of unfamiliar cultures if "those cultures come to life in front of them."

> Clearly this is no ordinary candidate for a degree and this is no ordinary research. The drums become louder, their tempo accelerates, and as the curtains draw more widely apart the children see three drummers in African robes in a complex but irresistibly blood-quickening trialogue of polyrhythms. Suddenly a compact, dark, smiling woman swirls on stage. She moves in cloths of many colors. Behold the PhD candidate, Pearl Primus.[1]

In his piece for the education journal, Hentoff, who then was a staff writer for the *New Yorker*, evoked the shifting moods and rhythms of Pearl's performance, her "gust of different colors," the immediacy of her affection for the material and the people for whom she is presenting, and the children's delighted, rhythmic responses as she presents the cultures of west and central Africa. He understood that Pearl herself was the core of the lesson and highlighted the way she and her way of dancing were inseparable. "The children look at her as few teachers are ever looked at . . . with wonder and surprise and then understanding." They are learning that "the body can talk."[2] At the end of the program of "dance as a teaching method" the children continued applauding. "The need to make their own rhythms can no longer be repressed, and the applause is in sharp, crisp cadences. The curtain calls go on until the doctoral candidate stills the clapping and thanks the children 'on behalf of all the villages we visited today.'"[3]

For Hentoff, Pearl's work added "a new dimension in teaching children about cultural pluralism," her study being "the first of its kind in the history of American education and in the history of the dance." He grasped the profound implications of Pearl's new approach and anticipated several long-term results, new curriculum material for elementary schools, and new approaches to dance education. Students would understand that "the basic concepts, principles and symbolism of dance apply to all people . . . and will be able to identify with children in other areas of the world through an understanding of creative participation in their dance."[4] Hentoff foresaw implications "far beyond what she herself might have envisioned," as Pearl created a model for transforming American elementary schools that "circle[s] back to the culture of the children themselves."

> There may yet be an awakening in our elementary schools to what Ray Charles and other rhythm and blues singers tell of American culture. And what of dances American children do outside of class? Where do they come from? What are their symbols? And what are the initiation rites out on the street? Need the school be so insular and therefore so removed from what its children know of reality outside of school hours? Aren't the blues capable of being used as "language tools"? And aren't there ways to teach, let us say, arithmetic as well as anthropology through dance? Indigenous urban American dances?

At the end of the morning a teacher exclaimed, "I never thought anything like this . . . would ever happen in my lifetime."[5]

As a passionate advocate for arts in education and the inclusion of African cultures in school curricula, Pearl was in great demand. In 1969 the Public Education Division of the Ford Foundation asked Pearl to evaluate dance programs in the British schools to determine their applicability to the

United States' public schools. In 1970 she was a delegate to the White House as a panelist at a conference on children and youth. In classrooms, gymnasiums, and theaters, she modeled the teaching of children for hundreds of artists and educators, setting the stage for programs that have become a staple of arts education.

In 1971, working with Miller-Brody Productions in New York, Pearl produced a set of records called "AFRICA—In story—Legend—Song—and Thought," which starts with Pearl's voice intoning her African names: "I am Omowale, . . . child returned home." "Adaora, . . . one beloved by all." "Nkuyo, . . . one who seeks the light of knowledge." "Jaibundo, . . . she clears the ground of all evil." This series contains stories, chants, and drum solos, and includes specific curricular instructions for teachers at different grade levels in the areas of drama, dance, arts and crafts, social studies, and science. The records grew out of Pearl's ongoing relationship with Hunter College. David Hodges introduced Pearl to Selma Rich Brody and Claire Miller, both education consultants and Hunter alumnae who were working on a series of recordings and filmstrips called *Man on the Move,* an anthropological journey of human beings across time.

Ethel Alpenfels said, "I have heard the folktales and legends . . . many times. Yet I never tire of listening and watching the faces of students—from pre-school through the university—as they respond to the voice of one of America's great storytellers."[6]

Hunter College remained dear to Pearl. In 1970, she received the award of the Centennial Medal. The President's Medal and awards from the Hunter faculty and alumni association would follow. Pearl was on the faculty there from 1969 to 1974, when she became embroiled in a controversy and ultimately submitted her resignation. Much later, President Donna Shalala brought her back to the college, and in 1991 she was awarded an honorary doctorate.

When Dorothy Vislocky, a former dancer with the Alwin Nikolais Company, developed the dance program at Hunter in 1972, she hired Pearl part-time to teach African dance. Vislocky wanted a strong African program and Pearl wanted a special full-time position, but this proved impossible. A new policy at Hunter required faculty to be evaluated by students, however, but Pearl refused. Jacqueline Wexler, president at the time, tried to persuade her but Pearl "locked down," her colleague David Hodges recalled. He tried to cajole her into it, but she still refused. Pearl also shunned the usual responsibilities of a faculty member, such as committee work, department meetings, and the like. "As a creative spirit, it was difficult for her to conform to regulations," said Vislocky.

Another crisis at Hunter had to do with a theater production in which Pearl had been asked to add choreography. On February 24, 1972, Pearl wrote to Professor Robert Kya-Hill in the Department of Theatre and Cinema, informing her that, having arrived at the Hunter Playhouse for a rehearsal, she was so "shocked and dismayed" by the physical hazards posed by the stage that she was withdrawing from participation. This was four days before the opening. She was also offended that "to her horror" those creating the set had learned only the night before that there would be any dance at all and hadn't been informed that "dance was to be an integral part of the play." "I cannot ask them to work on that set," she wrote. Pearl then notified the professional dancers she had hired and the Hunter students, as well as the press and radio, that she would no longer be with the production. The press release went out the day of the opening, February 28: "Urgent notice: Due to circumstances beyond our control, the dances for the Hunter College theatre production, 'Blackman vs Blackman' will *not* be created by Pearl Primus."

Using a faculty Complaint/Grievance Form, Pearl indignantly enumerated the ways in which she had been misrepresented, misjudged, and denied due process in a college review. She claimed that the college had not utilized her true abilities, experiences, and stature, and, among other things, had failed to accept her "Workshops in Cultural Enrichment." On November 24, 1973, a letter of resignation addressed to Professor Sylvia Fishman, chairman of the Department of Health and Physical Education, and copied to President Jacqueline Wexler, Dean Milton Gold, and Dr. Raymond Welsh followed:

This is to officially inform you that I have decided to resign from the Faculty of Hunter College as of August 31, 1974. . . . The present general atmosphere of rigidity at Hunter is definitely not conducive to my further growth as a professional artist and educator.

She concluded the letter by stating that her "loyalty to Hunter will remain forever unshakable. Both the High School and the College have nurtured in me a fierce love and deep respect for academic freedom. Both have recognized and greatly encouraged my creativity. Both have given me the strength to endure in our society which is dishonest and unkind."

In 1979 Pearl applied for a position in the dance program at Hunter and was not a finalist in the search. It was Hunter president Donna Shalala, understanding that Pearl occupied a unique place in American arts and education, who brought Pearl back into the Hunter fold. While Hunter's president from 1980 to 1987, she recognized Pearl as "a cutting edge person, with a PhD in anthropology and in dance education, an extraordinary figure in American dance and in black studies." Looking for a prominent alumna for special events, she turned to Pearl. "As soon as we invited her back, we were through it," meaning the pain of the rupture. "I remember her having an enormous presence when she walked through the halls. She couldn't get through the halls, because everybody was all over her all the time!"

Shalala regularly invited Pearl to attend alumni events and fund-raising events in elegant New York apartments, occasionally asking her to co-host an evening. Throughout the 1980s, various directors of development at Hunter thanked Pearl for lending her name to these occasions. But when Pearl talked with Shalala about her dream of starting an institute, she was told that resources were lacking.

Pearl also had a long-standing association with Spelman College, the private, independent, liberal arts, historically black college for women, founded in 1881. As part of the Atlanta University Center, Spelman is joined to the largest consortium of historically black institutions of higher learning in the world.

As she tried to find a base for her teaching career, Pearl grew to count on Professor Mozel J. Spriggs and President Johnnetta Cole, who had been an associate provost at the University of Massachusetts Amherst before becoming Spelman's president in 1987. Mozel was Pearl's lifetime "sister-friend" and, like David Hodges, was from a southern black family that prized education and had a strong sense of its roots.

Mozel first saw Pearl perform in 1947 when her company toured the historically black colleges, but they didn't meet for twenty years, until 1967. After that meeting, Mozel, who was then on the Spelman College faculty, invited Pearl for a master class and a performance. Later that year, Mozel invited Pearl back for a monthlong residency, and the invitation was renewed many times between 1969 and 1985. These residencies were always opened to dancers from Atlanta and were coordinated with theater students. Pearl critiqued choreography for concerts, and she would have her students sit for a talk about the dances and cultures of Africa. Occasionally, her presence coincided with Caribbean festivals or a visit from an African dance company. On several occasions she brought percussionist Alphonse Cimber with her, and, in the 1980s, after Percy's death, she would bring Onwin. She was strongly drawn to Spelman, where people celebrated her achievements and attended to her everyday needs. "Pearl loved Spelman and would always say she would like to come here to retire," Mozel recalled.

Mozel was among the few people to whom Pearl extended invitations whenever she was being honored, and they were in close contact over the years, sharing as dancers, educators, and mothers. Whenever Mozel went to New York—on one occasion to see her daughter Linda Spriggs perform with the Ailey Company—she would stay at Pearl's home in New Rochelle. Mozel encouraged Pearl to write her autobiography. "There's all this stuff written about Katherine Dunham," she would say. "Write your story so that it will be accurate."

⁓

In the 1980s, Mozel and Pearl went to stay at the home of a friend of Mozel's on Cranberry Island, Maine, to work on the proposal for the creation of an institute that would embrace the study of dance, drumming, anthropology, and related subjects. What Mozel remembered most vividly was not the writing but Pearl collecting beautiful stones of all colors from the beaches. Just as she used to find stones for the windowsill of her "I'm not here room" in her African hut, "Pearl filled a suitcase, a whole suitcase! She brought them home so that she could create a rock garden in her home."

One of the earliest formulations of this institute was "A Brief Prospectus for the Development of a Department of Anthropology" at Spelman in 1974. The department would embody "new and effective methods" of reaching beyond "the walls to all people." With that in mind, the department would "focus strongly on Man's cultural heritage as expressed through his arts." But even more importantly, "For the first time in the history of American Education a Department of Anthropology will incorporate as one of its main areas an Ethnic Dance Major which will seek to investigate Ethnic Dance as a mirror of human behavior."

Pearl thought that Spelman was the ideal location for this "bold new concept." She suggested the key personnel, including herself as the director and Dr. Ethel Alpenfels, Dr. David Hodges, Professor Pervical Borde, Professor Michael Dei Anang, Emiko Tokunaga, and Tom Two Arrows (Mr. Thomas Dorsey) as professional consultants, and Mozel Spriggs as the Spelman liaison. She proposed a procedure for initiating this project in three phases—planning, developmental, and operational—as well as a timeline for a budget.

This was the first of several institutional models created by Pearl, but she was never able to bring her vision to fruition. "Pearl needed so much materially that I simply could not supply," President Cole lamented. "Her hope and her expectations were much more complex and deep than I could meet. But it was a joy, just to be able to listen to what it was that she wanted to do and to have her on campus," she said. "Long before I met her she was large in my life," the Spelman president remembered. "When I went to Hunter College, I was very aware that Pearl had walked places where I was walking, that she had been a student there." She admired Pearl's ability to move in and among fields of knowledge and dimensions of cultures. "Pearl was so at home in her own Afro-Caribbean-ness that that allowed her to be at home some other place," she observed. "There was no need for her to be threatened by other folk and their culture. She knew her own and could therefore move out." Cole recognized in the proposed institute "an extension of who she was—a place without borders, a place that would be daring and even irreverent enough to raise questions that folk did not ordinarily raise."

Realizing that she was capitulating to academic conservatism, Cole said, "I did not make it a priority. Difficult decisions must be made when funds are limited, physical plants need tending, students need scholarship aid." She did, however, offer an honorary degree to Pearl in 1988, at her first Spelman commencement. The letter of acceptance is Pearl poetics:

> I have just returned from my galaxy far beyond the physical, emotional, mental or spiritual reaches of modern day human beings. There I rejoiced with the Creator and thanked all the ancestors for the magnificent events of my earthly existence. I usually do not make this great journey during college sessions because students really cannot understand and administration cannot tolerate one who is living in a period of supreme inner exultation.
>
> Your voice and your letter sent my unique ever-waiting space ship with me in it on a magnificent journey. I have not as yet investigated the academic consequences of my rejoicing. Whatever they are, they cannot match the excitement and happiness inside me. . . .

The Spelman degree was one of many awards she received in the mid-1980s, and, though she had not fulfilled her dream of a new form of education, Pearl felt secure in the academy. In 1984, she had been appointed a Five College Professor in Amherst, and was living in a little apartment at Smith College overlooking Paradise Pond. But all this success had also accompanied the need to establish a life without Percy, whose own life had ended so abruptly soon after their reunion in 1977.

∽

In the 1960s and into the 1970s Pearl's activities often blurred the boundary between educator and artist. She performed, lectured, and taught throughout the country and abroad, moving from performances in Liverpool, England, and research throughout England in 1969 to an appearance on television on the *Today Show* in 1971; from college campuses to the White House in 1970; and from the Alvin Ailey American Dance Theater to junior high school students in Buffalo. Pearl's and Percy's careers had diverged in this period when he took a position in the Theater Department at State University of New York at Binghamton. In the late 1970s they were encouraged to reunite. In 1979 they re-formed the Earth Theater company and performed to great acclaim at the grand Riverside Church and at the Perry Street Theater in Greenwich Village. Her work in the theater continued into the 1980s and 1990s as she restaged "Excerpts for an African Journey," her signature early solos, and Percy's signature piece, "Impinyuza." The last extended residency was jointly sponsored by Howard and American Universities, where she worked hard to meld two very different groups of students into a community for performance. She included professional dancers in the early work "Negro Speaks of Rivers" and in her last new work, "The Griot."

Many people—dancers, percussionists, students, artistic directors, rehearsal directors—were caught up by Pearl's spirit and her work. Their memories and stories embody vital facets of her aesthetic sensibility and reveal her ways of teaching and translating movement from her body to those of her dancers. We learn about her aesthetic vision through the restaging of the African work and the early modern dances, and about how she dealt with the central question of authenticity. For years, she had been very reluctant to restage the early solos, once going so far as to invite Martina Young, a dancer from the West Coast, to Amherst to restage an early solo and then refusing to meet with her. But a few years later, the dancers to whom she finally did teach the early solos provided insight into what these works meant to Pearl as a performer.

∾

Pearl taught at the Alvin Ailey School over many years, twice set work on the company, and performed her famous "Fanga" at the Lincoln Center State

Theater when she was honored by Alvin Ailey himself in 1978. But transmitting Pearl's "Fanga" to another body proved frustrating. Pearl taught the
dance to Judith Jamison in 1974 for a concert in which she also restaged "The
Wedding" (premier, 1961), a suite of dances given a narrative form, based on
ceremonies and rituals from the country then called Zaire. One of the star
performers in the Ailey company, Jamison became its artistic director after
Ailey's death. "She set 'Fanga' on me and that was very difficult, very, very
difficult to do," Jamison recalled. "I hadn't moved that way in a long time,
since I was little. The dance itself was, on the surface, looking very easy to do.
Dr. Primus had so many nuances going on in her body it was unbelievable."

Jamison's description of her struggle is revealing. "I think most all of
us remember her shoulders and how she didn't do anything with her shoulders. It was the rest of her torso that was making her body move in a certain
way." When Pearl would demonstrate, Jamison would force the movement,
"hoping [she] was imitating what [Pearl] was doing, instead of having it
emanate from internally, from the torso and radiate out." "Then there was the
argument that the movement is ancient. It's been there for centuries. So why
should I put something on it?" she added. "She also gave me advice: 'Stop
moving as if you are dancing on cement!' I thought I was dancing on earth, on
the ground. It's a whole different feeling. Your feet have a different sensation
when you're on the earth as opposed to when you're on something hard."

"The way I approach dance," Jamison said, "is that I have to be totally
understanding and immersed, even on a level that I don't consciously understand. It's very complicated, but I know what I'm talking about. I have to
put the dance on like it's a skin. If I don't feel like it's a skin, like it's another
layer to me, then it feels away from me instead of like I've really embraced
it. I couldn't quite get my arms around 'Fanga.' That really annoyed me.
Therefore my tears came because I was too frustrated trying to do these
triple steps." Jamison felt she needed to recall "blood memories" in order
"to perform specialized movement with the intentions Pearl demanded." She
sought to remember or intuit the experience of having grown up dancing on
the earth. Though Jamison mastered her version of the dance, "To this day,
nobody will do that 'Fanga' the way [Pearl] did it," she concluded.

Jamison also performed in "The Wedding" on "Dance Mobiles," large flatbed trucks that traveled throughout New York City, bringing the arts to people who might not attend the theater. "I had the heaviest headdress on I've ever had in my life, huge and heavy. No entrance, no exits, just step up on the back of the truck with headdresses as wide as my arms," she recalled. Mari Kajiwara danced the lead role of the Bride—Ailey's casting was determined by skill, not race. Frances Herridge, writing in the *New York Post*, described the dancing as an "intriguing combination of tribal and Martha Graham."[7] In the *Village Voice*, Robert J. Pierce offered a more elaborate description:

> "The Wedding" is actually a suite of dances within a narrative form. A beautifully costumed procession escorting the Bride (Mari Kajiwara) to the home of her husband stops to rest and, incidentally to perform a series of fast, slow, serious, and abandoned dances. The clarity and definition are wonderful: bold, heavy, strong big body movements with rhythmic footwork and demi-pointe bourees, heads whipping back, abdomens thrusting forward, backs arching powerfully: all contrasted with more tranquil, restrained, elegant movements.

The critic praised the efficient expression of emotions, as the Demon of Evil (Dudley Williams) attacked the wedding party, provoking "a struggling or frenzied dance and eventual trance-like writhings on the floor," and the Healer (Jamison) arrived "just in time" to subdue the Demon, as "the forces of good triumph, and everyone lives happily ever after."

"Problem is," Pierce continued, "I don't know if the story line is a Primus or a Congolese contrivance. I'm told the dance is authentic, but theatricalized, and that can mean anything. Ultimately, I guess I really don't care who contrived what. The movement is real and exciting, and that's what's significant."[8] In their African settings, the dances varied from village to village. Pearl's "theatricalization" was the inevitable result of transposing these dances to the stage, but her focus always remained on the symbolic and communicative function of each movement, especially in the dancers' contact with the earth.

In her preview article for this Ailey season, Anna Kisselgoff, then the chief dance critic for the *New York Times,* allowed Pearl to speak for herself:

> Her efforts in the early forties encountered "great resistance from the black community here," she said. "I was laughed at." "People are part of their society. It took the present thrust into black dignity to even begin to understand what I was saying. The American black man had been taught that the African mask was childlike, stupid. With the emergence of the countries of Africa, there has come a great awareness," Miss Primus said.

Noting that the American Academy of Psychotherapists had published Pearl's monograph entitled *Dreams and the Dance,* Kisselgoff gave Pearl the final word: "'These things were also brought to me in dreams and African people understand this. I hesitate to say this, as I am aware of how it sounds. But I am taught in my dreams.'"[9]

When the Ailey company honored Pearl in 1978 for her lifetime achievements at an opening concert, everyone in the sold-out house seemed to know that they were sharing a singular event. Pearl had just emerged from a period of seclusion, a "going in," and she radiated confidence. "It was a phenomenal evening," Donald Washington, a member of Earth Theater, remembered. "She said what she had to say and all of a sudden the drums started and we really didn't know what she was going to do. This lady—you don't know whether she's retired from dance or whether she still moves. All of a sudden the drummers started and she began 'Fanga.'"

> This lady connected to the drum, the movement, the music, the culture, all of this, like no one else I had ever seen. That little tiny lady, she worked that whole stage. Every part of her body moved—her hands—they had a whole pattern of movement going on. The isolations in her body—there were the shoulders, there were the hips, and her feet. All of that. . . . and the eyes. Her eyes danced. She had a whole ballet going on with her eyes. She gave a finale to "Fanga" that was one of the unique finales to a

ballet that I had ever seen. She transported everyone from sitting in those seats in that theater to across the ocean, as she would say.

When Pearl next worked with the Ailey company in 1990, the experience was less gratifying. Judith Jamison commissioned her to stage "Impinyuza," with David St. Charles as the soloist, but the dancers struggled to align themselves with Pearl's instruction. This dance had not been performed since Percy's death in 1979. Jamison acknowledged that her expectations were influenced by the remarkable opening sequence of the film *King Solomon's Mines,* where we see the "Royal Dance for the King," which is based on the dances of the Watusi people. Jamison had fallen in love with the power and grace in the movement and felt the men tried to take it as far as they could. "It is sometimes thought that African dance is something that you just roll off the log," she said. "It's not. It's repetition, it's hypnotic, it's difficult. It's about subtlety of movement. It's about nuance." Jamison continued: "Pearl had artistic license to do whatever she wanted to do, but I was looking for some of the movement I had recognized from the film. She did do some but then she'd theatricalize some of it. But she has a right to do that." In fact, the producers of *King Solomon's Mines* had wanted Pearl to be in the movie, but she declined, telling Eva Zirker that "it was going to be inauthentic."

Pearl exercised her "right" in her distinctive working process with the twelve men upon whom she set the work. She talked half the time and worked physically the other half. "It is very difficult, however, to sit dancers down for long periods of time and then have them get up and move," Jamison recalled. Dudley Williams, who galvanized audiences with the Ailey company from 1964 until 2005, felt that the difficulty went deeper. "Some of the dancers don't have a clue. It's not about technique. It's something else. It's so hard to teach that something else," he said. "She gave us all these images, the different clays that we walk on. In one part of Africa you have red clay or it's very dusty, but not many people got it. You had to listen." Teaching "Impinyuza" was complicated for Pearl, too, he suggested insightfully, because Percy had died after performing it, and Pearl was trying to forge a place for Onwin, who had designed the lights and arranged the music and who was drumming with the great drummers Ladji Camera and Montego Joe. Dudley felt that she never developed an ending and it simply petered out. "Quite possibly she wasn't giving and they weren't giving," he reflected. "It was a tough summer."

Sylvia Waters, former member of the Ailey company and the artistic director of Ailey II, the junior company of the Alvin Ailey organization that acts as a bridge between the Ailey school and the professional world of dance, shared Dudley's view of the mismatch between Pearl and the men. "There was a communication problem where they couldn't come into her world. She wasn't having it. I think it had to do with Percy. I think with the solos, it's different because that's woman-to-woman," she observed. Ironically, the women dancers wanted more of Pearl. Deborah Manning St. Charles, the wife of the lead dancer David St. Charles and also a member of the Ailey company, said the women would sit in the doorway, watching on their own time. They were jealous that the men were getting to work with Pearl.

Jamison brought in Charles Queenan, one of the original dancers in "Impinyuza," but Sylvia felt it "just didn't flow together." Part of the problem may have been Pearl's belief that the current training style and repertory nature of companies made it impossible for young dancers to "get" her work. Sylvia believed the disjunction had to do with the fundamentally different eras and frames of reference from which the dancers and Pearl were coming. "Life has gotten much faster, not only the technique of the dancers. It's a technological era. Everything is, 'I want it yesterday.' That's where I felt the communication gap was," Sylvia thought. Chuck Davis, founder and artistic director of the African American Dance Ensemble and the DanceAfrica Festival at Brooklyn Academy of Music said, "I saw 'Impinyuza' and cried. They became theater as opposed to being real. Mama didn't have time to teach the essence."

Yet David St. Charles was at the top of his career when he performed the lead in "Impinyuza." He had performed with Dayton Contemporary Dance Theater and Philadanco, and he spent a few years in Paris and in Broadway shows, but his long-term dream was to perform with Ailey, whose company he was a member of from 1984 to 1993. David was prepared for the African work by his training with the Philadelphia Dance Company, especially by his participation in a major work by Harold Pierson, which journeyed through various eras of black dancers. With Pierson, who had reconstructed works of Asadata Dafora, David had learned Watusi movement, especially the arch of the back, the proud carriage. When Pearl auditioned the Ailey men, he was the only one in the company who had done Watusi, and she knew immediately that he could embody the dance. "I right away knew what she was talking about," he remembered. "Also, I'm six feet two inches and she wanted the tallest guys. At the audition, I did what I knew and she went berserk! When she put me in the lead, a lot of the guys who thought they should have been the lead were not happy."

David was shocked, and a little frightened, when Pearl said he looked like Percy. "I honestly believed that when the drums started, it was where her husband came from," he said. "When the drums played, the music just got into your body. We wanted to honor him. It was so close to her heart. The fact that Ailey let her do it was big. You could picture yourself in the circle, in the tribe, the dance for your wife, being a warrior. It was awesome." David felt a responsibility to coax the group of technical superstars to the place where they could experience tribalness. He wanted the Ailey dancers to understand how personal and intimate, even sacred, this dance was for Pearl. "It had to be exactly right," he realized. "No matter how tired you were, no matter how unfocused you may have been, you respected this ballet as you have never respected a ballet before, because this was her husband's ballet, and spiritually she kept Percy with her, always."

Reading Anna Kisselgoff's review in the *New York Times,* one would never know that Pearl had difficulty teaching this piece. "The stage fills with warriors, their proud carriage broken by a sudden swift rotation of the huge white manes they wear on their heads," she wrote. "Miss Primus has staged African-inspired works for the Ailey troupe in the past. But this time she has outdone herself . . . the Ailey troupe now has one of the largest groups of first-rank male dancers in its history, and they have taken to this intriguing ceremonial suite with passion and conviction."

She continued with background about Pearl's career and then described the dance:

"Impinyuza" . . . is a creative view of a dance in Rwanda by the
Ishyaka royal dancers. Impinyuza means the incomparable, and
in praising their king's powers the dancers also praise the deity
he represents. There is munificence about the entire composi-
tion onstage. David St. Charles, raising a curved bow (the men
will later pick up arrows), stands initially like a sculptured figure
amid his hunters. . . . The picture comes to life in what could be
called a suite with a ritualistic logic.

The energy of the dancers is directed upward in constant
jumps, with knees raised and turns in the air. There is a lot of
stamping, but with an unexpected lightness that does not inhibit
the men from running lyrically about the stage on half toe.

And throughout there is a steady rhythm of the bells on the
ankles of the dancers and the outbursts of vigorous head rotation,
as they fling their white manes through the air.[10]

"Impinyuza" had its final performances in the December 1990–91 season.

Reviewers appreciated both Pearl's work and Ailey's commitment. In
the *New York Post,* Clive Barnes wrote, "Miss Primus showed all the charm,
grace and intensity we have always associated with her."[11] Don McDonagh
of the *New York Times* wrote, "The scope of Pearl Primus's contribution to
black dance has yet to be fully assessed, but Alvin Ailey's decision to include
her works in his repertory can blessedly spur the process."[12]

The Ailey company provided Pearl with a professional base, contact
with many dancers, and, to a degree, a sense of belonging. They brought her
back to be honored and to teach, lecture, and restage work from 1974 until
her death in 1994. In 1980 she received a letter from the Alvin Ailey American
Dance Theater thanking her for her participation and contribution to the
"School's Dance History from a Black Perspective" course. "Your artistry,
knowledge and experience have been an inspiration to the students as well
as to the entire administration. You have been a source of encouragement
that will enrich the futures of these aspiring students for years to come. We
hope that a mutual and lasting artistic bond has been established, and we

look forward to working with you again in the near future," it said. Pearl's teaching played an important role in the development of the full-scale education program, headed by Denise Jefferson.

∽

In the mid-1970s, after she left Hunter, Pearl was offering workshops. In 1974 she set work on Ailey, but had not yet renewed her own performance career. In 1977 Pearl was teaching at the New Rochelle Community Center. John "Tunisi" Davis, a percussionist who had known her and Percy since 1968 when he was coordinator of the arts for the Connecticut Commission on the Arts, began to talk to her about performing again. When he started playing for her she said, "John-John, you play for my feet. Not everybody can play for my feet." "That's my legacy. That's my honor," Tunisi said. "I played for her feet."

Pearl's friend Ossie Davis would come down to the center, Tunisi remembered, and he would say, "Mna, how come you're not performing?" Tunisi encouraged her to create a performance with a group of girls she was working with and arranged for two weekends in Bridgeport at a dinner theater called the Wagon Wheel. He invited some of the people from the local board of education to attend. "Come in, do your performing and we can expose Onwin," Tunisi said to Pearl. At this time, Onwin had a band called Thrust. Pearl enjoyed a terrific reception and "she was awestruck. She came back out, like the Queen Mother," Tunisi said.

Earlier, Pearl had become concerned for Tunisi's development and "decided" that he would go to Africa during the summer of 1971 with Percy and a group of students from Binghamton. "Take care of Percy, stick with Percy, look out for Percy," she said to him at the airport. The group was to base itself in Liberia and travel to seven other countries. In Africa, Tunisi "began to understand who this lady really was." He attended a graduation ceremony from the Zoe's, the women's secret society that Pearl describes in her PhD thesis. Theirs was the first group of men in twenty-five years to see the young women's graduation. They traveled to the traditional societies that had ruled before and during the slave trade. Because of Pearl's connection to the Ashanti, when the group went up to Kumasi (the capital city of the

Ashanti region and an important cultural and historical center in Ghana), "The red carpet was out." There they met the Asantehene, the Ashanti king. Tunisi's trip with Percy continued to Elmina Castle, one of the slave-trading castles on the coast of Ghana, and then to Nigeria, where they stayed with Chief Fagbemi Ajanakuhis, the Araba of Lagos, who later became head of the Yoruba spiritual hierarchy. In Nigeria they met the Oni of Ife, the one who had given Pearl the name "Omowale." Ife is the center of many religious cults among the Yoruba people, and Oni means king, the "chief of chiefs."

After his trip to Africa, Tunisi and Pearl became close, and he drove her everywhere. "I was her adopted son," he said. "It was like me and Miss Daisy." She taught him to be fiercely proud of his blackness, telling him about her experience with Paul Robeson, about his struggle and his contribution, and about Langston Hughes. They would sometimes go to see Ossie Davis. Through this process, Tunisi sensed that she was regaining confidence and preparing herself to "come out." They began talking ideas and Percy became part of the discussions. The separate paths she and Percy had taken when he was at Binghamton, coupled with her embattled period at Hunter, had set Pearl back, but the work in New Rochelle became serious preparation for a professional resurgence. Percy starting coming down from Binghamton more and more frequently, and Tunisi's wish to see them reunited was fulfilled by 1977, when they began to prepare for performances at the Theatre of the Riverside Church, which led to performances at the Perry Street Theater in 1979.

⁓

By the late 1970s, Pearl had not been seen in performance for almost a decade. She told Donald Washington, who would perform with her when she ultimately emerged, that one day she looked in a mirror and said to herself, "Primus! How can you criticize these people, bastardizing 'Fanga' and many of the other dances you brought here in a traditional way. . . . How can you criticize these people, when you are in your house, and will not come out?" So she decided to go back out and show them how it should be done.

That was Donald's understanding of the beginning of the Riverside Church and Perry Street era. Mary Waithe, one of the loyal friends who provided a sense of safety when Pearl needed to withdraw, also encouraged

Pearl's reemergence. She and Pearl used to use the All Boys School, the old Hetcher Foundation between 110th and 111th Streets and Central Park West, for classes in the mid-1970s. Many Ailey people were coming to take her high-energy classes. "The Ailey people ate her up. 'Ma, we'll do anything for you.' Ma, this, Ma, that," Mary remembered. Then, when Pearl auditioned for the Riverside series, "those dancers flew to her like nobody's business. She used a couple of them, not all of them, and started building up again." Pearl looked for strong male dancers for these performances. Mary recalled that she would say, "I want a man on my dance floor." "'Whatever you are outside,'" she'd tell them straight, 'Don't come in here with this kind of foolishness. I want a man to dance and that's what I need to see coming through.'"

"Her reputation as a pioneer in this field, particularly in re-creating the dances of Africa from authentic sources, has obviously stood strong despite her own absence as a concert performer for many years," Anna Kisselgoff wrote. The theater in the church was packed for "Earth Theater," with Pearl as narrator and dancer, Percy as guest artist, "a new young company," and Alphonse Cimber, "a great musician," according to Kisselgoff. She was particularly impressed by former Ailey dancer Elbert Watson, whom she said was "nothing short of terrific."

The program opened with an Invocation, followed by "Fanga." "Changing costumes for every appearance," wrote Kisselgoff, "Miss Primus had no trouble projecting her celebrated presence, as seen again in a fertility dance in which the strength of her arm gestures was as pronounced as the facial expression she showed later as a cloven-foot sorceress in the Antilles who bewitches and kills her male victim in 'La Jablesse.'" In this rendition, the dance enfolded "Limbo," but the seductive game came to an abrupt halt when La Jablesse reappeared. A duel of two men with long sticks followed, until one vanquished the other and the narrative of La Jablesse continued.

African based dances were followed by a Caribbean suite and then a section called "Afro-American Scenes," which included "Wade in the Water" and "Michael Row the Boat Ashore." "Miss Primus comes out of modern dance's psychological era—and the theme here was catharsis and resolution," Kisselgoff observed.[13]

Mixing art and education, Pearl came to the stage between dances in colors and jewelry appropriate to the location and content of each piece, and her narrations would also link the allegorical meaning of a dance with particular recent experience. As she entered for "Michael Row the Boat Ashore," for example, she said:

> In our struggles as human beings on this side of the ocean so many things have happened and so much will happen. Two little girls were killed in a church. The newspapers . . . said that one of the mothers did not weep. We know that sometimes tears are too deep. . . . We also know that mother was searching across the boundary of life and death for that child . . . that through the singing and the dancing we had to draw her back . . . to reality.

The dance then enacts the mother's immobile grief and its transformation, as she rises to throw herself across the bridge between life and death, which is formed by the dancers, and is drawn back into their arms, while tambourines and the song "Fare thee well, fare thee well" celebrate the release of the child's spirit into the world beyond.

"Pearl Primus and her dance company, with guest artist Percival Borde, have made me fall in love all over again with dance," wrote the dance critic and playwright Jean Nuchtern. "She's like a tree whose roots extend deep into the earth. Her second position is extraordinary. She makes me understand the richness of that position, how, when executed with such gravity-connected strength, it evokes all earthly images, images such as birth, womanhood, or the forces of nature. Her works bring me back to the origins of movement."[14]

Part of this program was repeated on July 3 at Carnegie Hall, at an Independence Eve Celebration that was part of a New York Ethnic Dance Festival '79 production. Pearl was given top billing. Her company included Mary Waithe, Andree Valentine, Diane Gary, Lydia Payne, and Larry Ferrell. The musicians were Alphonse Cimber, Onwin Borde, John (Tunisi) Davis, Earl Thorne (Earl Robinson, aka Ayan Layo), Harryson Buster, and Koli Atigbi, and the Haitian singer Gessy Lewis. Members of the Alvin Ailey American Dance Theater and eleven students from the Harbor Junior

High School of Performing Arts Dance Company augmented the small company.

~

The performances at Riverside Church led to an engagement at the Perry Street Theater in Greenwich Village. A flyer for the August 17, 1979, opening read, "Earth Theater—presenting a dynamic program of authentic and creative dances of Africa, the Caribbean and America." The program was also scheduled to be part of the Lincoln Center Out-of-Doors Festival in Damrosch Park. Evenings were for concerts and Wednesday afternoons she planned to present "The Inner Being of African Sculpture," which consisted of "dances created to exhibit the mask or the staff or the drum or the fabric."

"A lot of people thought I was still in Africa," Pearl told Jennifer Dunning, who appreciated the company's "family quality." Percy was performing, Onwin was playing, Mary Waithe was dancing—having been with Pearl for thirty-five years—and Alphonse Cimber, the noted percussionist, had been an associate since the 1940s. Dunning mentions that Percy was described by one of his students "with awed affection as a 'wild man.'"[15] The proceeds from the concerts were directed to the Pearl Primus Dance Language Institute, not the Primus-Borde School of Dance or Earth Theater, an indication that Pearl was seeking to fund her unfulfilled aspiration.

After rave reviews, Pearl had had ambition to bring the Perry Street show to Broadway. But then, in a shock that would echo through the rest of her life, Percy died of a heart attack. Donald Washington described the awful moment:

> He had just completed "Impinyuza," at the end of the first act. He came downstairs to the dressing rooms to get ready for the second act. Then all of a sudden we heard this awful crashing sound off the dressing room table. We knew something horrible had happened, for everything, bottles, makeup, everything that would normally be on a dressing room table for a performer all just hit the floor. In a panic, everyone ran to Percy's dressing room. That was the beginning of his passage. He never recovered from that.

Tunisi Davis witnessed Percy's last performance.

Percy did his dance, "Impinyuza," just before intermission. Before the show Mna had come to me and told me, "John-John, don't play fast. Percy isn't feeling that well." When he started dancing I was playing it slow. He danced up to me and scolded me. Scolded me! While he was dancing! So we took it up and he was flying. I mean he was flying. Also, every time he finished his dance I went down before him, going down the steps to the dressing rooms. He put his hands on my shoulder to come down every performance. Coming down the steps after that performance I turned around and I said to him, I said, "Pa, you can't say that you didn't dance the dance tonight and that they didn't love you. They loved you tonight." "Yeah," he said, "But after this a younger man than me will have to do this dance." That's the last he spoke to anybody, those were his last words. He went to his dressing table. They were changing him and I was around in the back when they were calling me, "John-John! John-John!" I ran around there and he fell out of his chair and he died like that. He was 57. After Percy died, Pearl just shut down completely. Nobody here knew how to heal her spirit.

At Percy's funeral and memorial service, which were held on the same day, Pearl explained the meaning of each part of the ritual and how it would help Percy's spirit to transition. In the Limbo, for instance, the pole was symbolic of pushing the person's spirit from one side of life to a new life. Lavinia Williams spoke, and Ossie Davis praised Percy's talent as a drummer and dancer, emphasizing "his great love for his wife and the work they did," and Percy's "ability to dazzle any crown with his eloquence, charm and pretty smile." Jean-Leon Destine led the libation that would help the soul's passage to the ancestral world, as Louis Ramos stood behind the casket in a white robe "looking like an angel or a black Jesus," Tunisi remembered. Pearl told Donald Washington that Percy had selected him as his protégé and that she wanted to continue Percy's art. She always referred to him as "the last protégé of Percival Borde."

After Percy's death, Pearl had to decide how to proceed with the Primus-Borde Earth Theater, for which Percy had been in charge of the business side. Pearl did not want to become the administrator. Throughout her career, people often tried to involve her in the business aspect of things, but "she was such a purist when it came to all of her time going into her research. She saw other things as pulling her away," Donald said.

Montego Joe, one of the drummers in her innermost circle, said that he and others felt that Pearl should have gone back to Africa, to be among the Yoruba people, for a year of mourning, for certain rituals to be performed, and for her own spirit to heal. She would have been housed and taken care of. "Spiritual things would have been done for her . . . to regain her balance." But she did not go.

Pearl did cope with her loss, in part, by incorporating Percy's memory into the staging of "Impinyuza." Three women in the background used to start the dance with libations. Then they would leave and Percy would be onstage by himself in the Warrior portion. Now she placed a spotlight on the stage, symbolizing Percy's spirit, and the drummers would drum to the light.

Donald Washington was a bridge for Pearl between the excitement of the Perry Street performances and her later work with Ailey, when she restaged "Impinyuza." He became the general manager of the Alvin Ailey American Dance Theater. He first met Pearl in 1977 when he was enrolled in New York University, pursuing graduate studies in dance education and working as an intern in the dance office. He was typing letters and memos, students were coming and going, and in she walked. "There is the most regal woman you've ever seen, walking through the door. . . . She was always in a whirlwind of some kind and you just wanted to help her in whatever way you could," he recalled.

Soon after, Donald went down to the Perry Street Theater hoping to meet Pearl in a setting other than the office, never dreaming that he would eventually work with her as closely as he did. He was in a workshop with Percy when Pearl came in to observe the dancers working on highlights from a Caribbean sequence. Knowing that Pearl was watching him, he sensed that this was his audition for the production she was preparing. After the workshop Pearl told him to prepare something for the next day. At home that night, he choreographed something of an "ethnic" nature, and, "She liked it!" As she was going out the door, she told Mary Waithe, "He's fine, but watch him, he's a pelvis kid."

Pearl had an idiosyncratic way of teaching. She would tell stories in the studio and say things like, "I give you the spirit of the people. Don't lose this." Then she might digress from the technical aspect of the rehearsal to tell a story about the royal dancers of the Watusi. Donald remembered how she talked about the use of the foot in relationship to the earth for a particular dance. "The toes are the only things that touch the floor in a certain movement, because the earth is so pristine, you should not defile it by putting your whole foot on it." She would often give anthropological disquisitions that she then expected to see embodied in the movement.

"The Wedding" in particular brought together Pearl's experience as a performer, anthropologist, scholar, and dancer. She would start out by telling the story of the young woman traveling from one compound to another to get married. "There's a whole belief system that is very foreign to us as Westerners," Donald recalled. "Before even attempting a hand movement or a gesture or placing a foot, you asked, 'Why are the hands like this?' You are looking up to God but yet at the same time, you have to acknowledge the sacredness of the Earth. . . . She would go off on mini-lectures and then we would go back to the movement. 'Now let me see it,' she would say."

One highlight of the Perry Street concert was Pearl's performance of "Fanga." As would happen later with the Ailey company the dancers would stand in the wings and try to do the movements, and Pearl would watch them sidelong. "'Fanga' was taught directly only to those Pearl chose. That was an extremely personal thing with her," Donald said.

⌇

After Perry Street, the company briefly toured in California, with a performance at the Masonic Temple in San Francisco, and in Midwestern states, performing for audiences that had not seen the richness of black cultures as Pearl could present them, but the company never knew from one day to the next where they would be going. One stop stood out clearly for Donald—a performance at what he thought was a nuclear plant! "Somebody's pulling somebody's leg here," he mused. But then in the distance, in this no-man's-land, "all of a sudden a dome appears, just one building, the only thing around." They were taken into an elevator that seemed to go hundreds of yards down. "We were buried. Everywhere we looked was concrete, two to three feet deep." Donald vividly remembered the evening of February 9, 1980:

> With that evening's performance, for scientists from all over the world, this grand lady along with us, we transformed that concrete, cold, sterile atmosphere into people seeing and feeling the energy of the earth. People were freed from that environment for a two-hour performance. They didn't leave that compound very often, because their work was all consuming. So artists would be brought to them. That's why they built the stage there. Dr. Primus took them from where they were, into her life, into her experiences, as she would say, "across the ocean.". . . Only Dr. Primus could have pulled that off.

What Donald thought of as a nuclear plant was the world-famous Fermilab, a center for research in high-energy physics, known for bringing the arts to scientists.

Despite such experiences, Pearl sometimes felt inwardly unmoored, even with a full schedule and national honors and awards. "Then she would say, 'I'm going into my house, and I'm not coming out. Because I can't, I can't fight the system any more,' and she would give you those eyes that said everything," Donald remembered. There were obstacles for a woman of color struggling to perform in theaters operated by white impresarios. But, in fact, Pearl did resist the racism, lack of money, political opposition, and the social conditions of dance. She would always turn her negative feelings into positive action, and find the energy to say, "I'll dance!"

NINE

Academic Trials and Triumphs

Two loves I have of comfort and despair.

—Shakespeare

AFTER PERCY DIED, Pearl was asked to complete his contract at the State University of New York (SUNY) at Binghamton for the 1979–80 academic year. In an interview tied to an upcoming performance at Avery Fisher Hall, "Afro-Brazilian-Haitian Dance Explosion!" Pearl expressed her desire for a firm academic appointment as a base for her work, and she alluded to "plans she hopes to implement in her husband's program at SUNY/Binghamton." She would bring "insights which have persistently eluded many of her colleagues—dancers and academicians." "Her approach to dance strikes a delicate balance between scholarly methodology and performance," the interviewer wrote, as Pearl emphasized her desire to present African dance as a manifestation of "the fabric of life . . . —the pulse—of the heartbeat of a people."[1]

But Percy's contract was not renewed for Pearl. Louis and Veleria Ramos, her friends and strong supporters, felt that the Binghamton administrators didn't understand Pearl's conception of African arts. "The majesty of Pearl Primus was so evident that these white men could not deal with it," said Louis. "Percy was all jovial and he'd get along and was one of the boys, that kind of thing. Mna wasn't like that. Mna was very regal, very majestic in her stature."

Louis was proud that he and Pearl had managed to convince the university to name a dance studio for Percy. "Finally, I got my 'A' from Mna," he said. After Pearl died, the name of the studio was changed to the Primus-Borde Dance Studio. Onwin came from Florida for the ceremony, students danced, Lofton Mitchell, Edward Wilson, and Louis spoke, and the ribbon was cut. Pearl would have appreciated the irony of another honor without the much-needed support for her work behind it.

200

For the academic year 1981–82, Pearl was offered a one-year Visiting Artist-In-Residence appointment at Spelman College, where she was asked to serve as the director of dance during a sabbatical year for Mozel Spriggs. Pearl approached Donald Stewart, Spelman's president at the time, about housing an institute, but without success. She also did some teaching in the Department of African and Afro-American Studies at SUNY/Albany in 1982, and at the same time was proposing work in public school education. She clearly was trying to establish a footing for herself.

—⁓—

In 1980, while finishing out Percy's contract at Binghamton, Pearl applied unsuccessfully for the directorship of the Leonard Davis Center for the Arts of the City College of New York, which was providing programming in the arts for young people of all ages. Despite eloquent letters sent to well-known individuals such as Yoko Ono and Jacqueline Kennedy Onassis, requesting "an audience . . . to explain in person a very beautiful project ('The Dancing Griot')," no sponsorship emerged. She also sought, but did not find, funding to document her work with Percy. Then a very fortuitous convergence of interests occurred in Buffalo, New York.

In the fall of 1981, a nascent college of Afro-American studies in "The Colleges," an experimental enclave within the larger State University of New York at Buffalo, was in need of a headmaster. The Cora P. Maloney College was one of eleven small, mostly residential programs of three hundred to five hundred students each. The Colleges were conceived in the 1960s during a burst of growth and creativity in public higher education nationally. They were designed as interdisciplinary, thematic educational communities, living and learning environments, alternatives to standard academic departments. For instance, Rachel Carson College focused on the environment, while Black Mountain College II, founded by the poet Robert Creeley and Murray Schwartz, encompassed literature and the arts. Cora P. Maloney College, named for the first black city councilwoman in Buffalo, would focus on minority achievement and cultural awareness.

In 1979 Murray Schwartz was appointed dean of The Colleges, and he set out to revive what by then was a flagging experiment, with the support of the Acting Vice President for Academic Affairs Robert Rossberg. In 1981, when the Cora P. Maloney College was searching for a leader, Murray came home one day and said, "I received a thirty page resume from a dancer named Pearl Primus. Have you heard of her?" "Hire her!" said Peggy without a moment's equivocation. "We need her in Buffalo!" Serendipitously, Robert Rossberg had grown up in New York in the 1940s and 1950s, hung around the Apollo Theater in Harlem, and carried instruments for the musicians as a way of getting into the theater. He had seen Pearl dance in her prime, knew her work, and supported Murray in this unexpected hire, providing an extra $10,000 to meet her salary requirement.

Both the city and the University at Buffalo welcomed Pearl. The *Challenger*, a newspaper serving the Afro-American community, ran a front-page photograph and called Pearl a "towering figure in the world of dance." A university publication captioned a photo "Educational Coup," as it announced Pearl's appointment both to Cora P., as it was known, and as an associate professor of theater.[2]

The journalist for the campus newspaper didn't quite know what to make of Pearl, with her gele, a traditional head wrap, and colorful African dress, bracelets, pins, and rings. He said she looked "slightly out of place in the stony Ellicott Complex," and when he asked Pearl if she would explain the meaning of her costume, she answered wryly, "I'll tell you the meaning of mine if you tell me the meaning of yours." One of the major roles of her college, Primus announced, would be to strengthen students emotionally and psychologically, and inspire confidence in those who felt lost or confused at the university. "The minority student might withdraw," she explained. "He might be lonesome, afraid of being hurt or insulted. Other students are so innocently blind." The college would not limit itself to black students but would focus on other minorities as well. She also set out to coordinate with other departments, notably Afro-American studies, women's studies, anthropology, and theater and dance, and began to bring her worlds together that way. For a Martin Luther King celebration, she brought David Hodges from Hunter College as the featured speaker and enlisted junior high school students from the Buffalo Academy for Visual and Performing Arts to dance under her direction. She insisted on formal table settings. "There'll be no plastic knives or paper cups. I want it proper," she announced.[3]

Pearl proved an inspired administrator, and Cora P. Maloney College had a thriving social and academic life under her direction. She thought she would be lonely living off-campus and so she moved into a dormitory apartment, where she enjoyed being surrounded by student life. "I'm seeing, feeling and hearing what happens on campus," she said, and she hoped to stay at the university as long as she could be "of service . . . for a good stretch. I felt lost, but I feel a lot of love here now."[4] The *Challenger* gave a banner headline, "Star-Studded Black History Month in Buffalo," to the efforts of the Cora P. Maloney College and others for bringing in a "host of national and local headliners, as the city's Black community prepares to celebrate its heritage!"[5] These included such luminaries as Ossie Davis, Ruby Dee, Sonia Sanchez, Andrew Young, and Shirley Chisholm.

When Pearl visited the Buffalo Arts Academy to teach a group of seventh-graders a suite of dances to be performed at The Colleges and at the Buffalo Convention Center as part of Black History Month, she explained the slave origins of a certain song and step, the celebrational aspect of another dance, and the polyrhythms of the body. Before long, this group of dark- and fair-skinned children were glowing in their long, white skirts as they danced "Hi-Life." Dancing as meaningfully as professionals, but with raw adolescent energy, they became the dance, the slaves, and the celebrants, because she treated them with the seriousness she ascribed to all dancers. No budget for costumes? Show the older students how to make brilliantly colored necklaces out of tin foil, paints, elastic, and large needles—necklaces of all colors, worthy of the originals.

Ironically, at about the same time that Pearl was settling into her life in Buffalo, the interdisciplinary colleges were increasingly jeopardized by a tightening economy and a reactionary tide in higher education that involved a reversion to traditional department structures.

In 1983, we left Buffalo so that Murray could serve as dean of humanities and fine arts at the University of Massachusetts Amherst. Pearl, whose life had become increasingly entwined with our own, followed one year later.

When Pearl first arrived in Amherst and was staying with Molefi Asante, then a professor in the Department of Black Studies, she called Peggy and said, "I'm ill. I need soup." Pearl would describe how "in the bush, the meal would be left outside my door." Her self-image as respected elder mixed curiously with a childlike expectation to be cared for.

In the Pioneer Valley of western Massachusetts, the University of Massachusetts Amherst (UMass) had itself been a pioneer in minority appointments to the faculty. The Afro-American Studies Department was one of the strongest in the country by the 1980s, and distinguished black artists were teaching in several fields. Murray took full advantage of "Special Opportunity Appointments" to add women and minority faculty to many disciplines. Music was already rich in distinction, with Horace Boyer, Max Roach, Billy Taylor, and Fred Tillis on the faculty, and Murray added the jazz musician Yusef Lateef through deft budgetary maneuvering. He brought John Edgar Wideman to the English Department, the painter Richard Yarde to Art, Madeleine Blaise to Journalism, among others. Soon after we moved to Amherst, James Baldwin and Chinua Achebe arrived with special faculty status, and the intellectual soil was ready for Pearl's appointment.

Murray saw in the "Five Colleges" consortium of Amherst, Hampshire, Mount Holyoke, and Smith Colleges and the University of Massachusetts Amherst a vehicle for creative programs and appointments, and he convinced provost Loren Baritz to appoint him as the university spokesperson. E. Jefferson "Pat" Murphy, coordinator of Five Colleges, Inc., viewed Pearl's situation from his vantage point as an Africanist, and he and Murray became allies. Murphy had come to the area in 1975 and developed an African studies course at UMass with art historian Josephus (Femi) Richards, a Ghanaian faculty member, African history specialist Dovi Afesi, and anthropologist Johnnetta Cole. When Pearl arrived she was invited into this course to lecture on the arts.

Through Five Colleges, Inc., it was possible to create faculty appointments based at one college or at the university. Ever the diplomat, Murphy was able to embrace positive intentions, harness cooperative desires, and bring disparate groups together. Several colleges would contribute, and teaching would take place on more than one campus. In October 1983, Murray asked the Five College Dance Department (FCDD) to host a lecture and master class for Pearl, and chancellor Joseph Duffey to host a dinner for members of the FCDD and the Afro-American Studies Departments. Guests arrived at Hillside, the chancellor's house, enjoying drinks and hors d'oeuvres, but no Pearl. Finally, she descended the staircase, bedecked and bejeweled in her African dress, glowing and smiling. Joe Duffey was as charmed by her as she was by him. But the Five College Dance Department initially declined Pearl's appointment, in part because she was known to be "high maintenance."

Pursuing an alternate route, in the spring of 1984 Murray invited Pearl to participate in a conference on "The Future of the Humanities, the Humanities of the Future," along with nationally recognized figures such as Tom Wicker of the *New York Times,* and he gathered support from four campuses for a five-college position. In August, Pearl was appointed Five College Professor in the areas of black studies, anthropology, and dance for the 1984–85 year, but the Dance Department made no direct commitment. Her position was housed in the W. E. B. DuBois Department of Afro-American Studies at UMass, and Smith College provided an office.

Marjorie Senechal, a professor of mathematics at Smith College, witnessed Pearl's arrival. She was walking on the campus when she saw a big convertible, top down, driven by a young African American man with "huge spiky bracelets on," and sitting in the passenger seat was this "African queen, with a brilliant blue turban, enormous rings and colorful robes." "Dr. Primus," she said to herself. "This place will never be the same!" Not many people in the Pioneer Valley knew that Pearl was actually returning to Smith, having been hailed as "one of the most competent and inspired dancers of this age" when she performed in John M. Greene Hall during one of her many visits to Smith in the early 1950s.[6]

Murray and Peggy hosted a dinner for about fifty people shortly after Pearl's arrival. Upon learning that we hadn't planned to have it catered, Pearl said, "You'll need help." The morning of the dinner our kitchen filled up with people we had never met. One began washing salad greens, someone else created a tasty rice dish, another rearranged furniture in the living room. A huge banner was strung around the dining room saying, "Welcome Pearl Primus!" We don't know how she found these helpers, but by then nothing surprised us.

The reappointment process in the Five Colleges became a recurring issue. Pearl counted on Murray to maintain a position for her, and though Murray had Pat Murphy's full support, he did not want to negotiate annually in order to keep her employed. It was a hard process, one that created strains during his eight years at UMass. Pearl's reputation for marching to the beat of her own drummer preceded her and then plagued her, but she loved the Five Colleges and wanted to stay.

Despite tortuous academic procedural pathways, previous distinguished Five College appointments had been improvised for James Baldwin, Anthony Lake, and Joseph Brodsky, but in Pearl's case Pat was anxious not to proceed "without full consultation with certain departments at several of the colleges."[7] He created a Pearl Primus Support Committee and clarified the procedures to be followed. Everyone agreed that Pearl was a major figure in American culture and was making important contributions to the Five Colleges, but it remained difficult to navigate an ongoing appointment in the face of some petty, self-righteous, and territorial attitudes. Marjorie Senechal recalled one unusually turf-conscious professor of anthropology at Smith who saw Africa as her sole teaching domain. "She took this to such an extreme that she tried to prevent the biologists from teaching Darwin because she taught a course on the evolution of the human race out of Africa."

Finally, Jill Ker Conway, president of Smith College, came fully on board and offered to house an appointment at Smith. It was agreed that Pearl would be given the title Distinguished Professor of Ethnic Studies. Conway admired Pearl and wanted a more permanent senior professorship for her but found "opposition to a permanent appointment from a number of different quarters including dance and theatre. I think she was too large a figure for easy acceptance in a liberal arts college with fairly traditional faculty attitudes," she said.

What happened then was particularly painful. The dance faculty at

Smith College had worked closely with Five Colleges, Inc., to create a new five-college position in African and Diaspora dances studies, to be housed at Smith. If Pearl applied and was offered this regular appointment, it would have stabilized her situation. But to her great distress, she received a call from a member of the search committee "inviting me not to apply." Ironically, by that time the FCDD chair, Hannah Wiley, had expressed concern that Pearl was being kept from them.

Of course, Pearl wasn't the only "high maintenance" celebrity. Marjorie commented that "there were other difficult characters around" and told stories about James Baldwin, who once took a taxi from Boston to Amherst and billed the president of Smith College, and, on another occasion, having been drinking, appeared at the wrong classroom yet managed to deliver a brilliant lecture. But there wasn't any question about Baldwin's field—it was literature—and "he didn't step on other people's toes," observed Stan Sherer, Marjorie's husband. Besides, Baldwin's significance was widely known, and *The Fire Next Time,* which was hugely popular on campuses, validated the political tenor of the times. Although Pearl and "Jimmie" had known each other for decades, her radical history was not prominently remembered, and she was also a woman. In other words, there was strong support at Smith, as well as strong opposition. At UMass, the Afro-American Studies Department did all it could to accommodate her classes and lecture-demonstrations, but some faculty members who professed support for Pearl kept their distance, perhaps because she didn't approve of their womanizing ways. "They didn't need Mna Pearl around pointing her finger at them," one administrator commented.

The saga continued year-by-year, and Pearl remained on temporary contracts. Her presence on the five campuses was valued, especially her interaction with students, but "the curricular needs of the institutions were not sufficiently clear . . . to warrant continuation of a full-time teaching appointment."[8] In 1987, the deans came up with a compromise offer of a half-time appointment for two years as a Five College artist-in-residence, "in recognition of her specialized skills and talent."[9] Pearl found this offer demeaning and responded to Murphy with a one-page list of her conditions for accepting an appointment, including a reasonable teaching load, housing, office space, and benefits. She requested a three-year contract, but finally accepted a two-year arrangement. In a gesture of support, Murphy penciled in an allowance to cover "a small overrun" for drummers.[10]

Murphy was Pearl's strong supporter, but he too was caught in a bind. In his position, he was eligible for housing at Smith and he received a note from the president, now Mary Maples Dunn, to the effect that she was thinking of offering him the campus apartment currently inhabited by Pearl. Knowing that Pearl attached deep emotional significance to her cozy apartment above the Faculty Club, and that it seemed to symbolize her place in the community, he preferred that Pearl be allowed to stay, even if her Five College teaching responsibilities did not take place at Smith.

From year to year, Pearl's titles, assignments, salary, and teaching load kept changing, and by 1990 the university budget had begun a free fall, a symptom of the collapse of the "Massachusetts Miracle" that became fully visible when Michael Dukakis lost the presidential election to George H. W. Bush. Pearl's needs were now out of sync with both the academic world and the world beyond.

Then came the final blow. Though Pearl maintained her Five College appointment housed at Smith, she was compelled to retire at the end of the 1991–92 academic year, as she had turned seventy, then the mandatory retirement age at Smith. She asked that she be allowed to keep the apartment that she loved for one more year but was turned down. Reflecting on these years, one close friend commented, "No gem is polished without friction. She went through refining fires."

�—∽—

Despite the administrative permutations of her appointments in the Five Colleges, however, Pearl's teaching utilized her rare breadth of knowledge. Peoples and Cultures of Africa examined "the philosophy, culture-traits and values of African peoples such as Ashanti, Berber, Egyptian, Bambara, Vai, Fon, Ibo, Hausa, Pygmies, Watusi, Yoruba, Bakuba, Zulu, Xhosa, Dinka and Masai." Dance Ritual and Myth in African Societies emphasized the function and use of dance in African communities, and Legacy: African Culture in the New World presented the African Diaspora in "the fields, streets and cities of the United States and the Caribbean from 1600–1987." Yet when she first came to the Afro-American Studies Department at UMass, there was nothing the department could offer her to teach. Then-professor Femi Richards agreed to let her teach his Introduction to African Studies, whereupon she changed the curriculum, introducing new and significant readings. She taught this course several times with enrollments of two to three hundred students and ironically became a stabilizing force for the department, enhancing student interest in African studies.

Pearl also taught many dance classes in the Crew House on the Smith College campus, a beautiful studio overlooking Paradise Pond, just up the street from her Faculty Club apartment, an idyllic New England campus setting if ever there was one. For her Anthropology of Art course, people came from as far away as New Haven, Albany, and Brattleboro. The large classroom was always packed as she lectured on the prehistoric paintings in the caves of Lascaux, the exquisite sculptures of Benin, and the masks, rituals, and dances of the Yoruba. As she recited her stories, Pearl, though in her sixties, would move in ways that revealed a youthful energy, and she sought the dancer in every student. For a final assignment, students created art projects and conducted anthropological research that connected to their own cultures.

Another project, this one theatrical, reunited Pearl with one of the most prominent black actors of her generation, Gordon Heath. Heath had been directed by Elia Kazan in *Deep Are the Roots* on Broadway in 1945, and had played Othello as early as 1950, before leaving for Paris to escape American racial and social prejudices. There he pursued a successful career as an actor, musician, and producer of classical and modern theater. Their collaboration at UMass was made possible by another creative union, between the Theater Department and a brilliant young faculty member, Roberta Uno.

Roberta Uno had a complex history within the Five Colleges. She graduated from Hampshire College in 1978 and completed a master's degree in the Theater Department at UMass in 1994. In 1979 she founded an ensemble called the New World Theater, at first a performance group composed of people from the Five Colleges and the community and, in time, a nationally renowned presenter of new dramas. Her vision was to bring plays by artists of color to the region and involve students and community people of diverse ethnicities and backgrounds in performances. She led New World Theater until 2002, when she left for a position at the Ford Foundation.

Roberta's story is important, because, like the Tokunaga sisters, she carried Pearl's influence into the next generation of women of color who were seeking to establish their place in American institutions. She felt that she and Pearl were in similar situations as people of color. Whatever their primary discipline, they were "offered" to the Afro-American Studies Department as faculty. Roberta found this humiliating, but she also felt it was much worse for Pearl, given her stature and her age. "We were joining the faculty without costing a department anything yet were still treated as not really qualified, as a 'multi-cultural add-on.'" Yet in a certain way she felt vindicated by Pearl's struggle. "If they can treat Pearl like this, then it really isn't personal, about me," she thought.

Roberta persisted and, as a junior faculty member, she proposed to direct a production of *The Lion and the Jewel,* by Wole Soyinka. Because she hadn't been hired into the Theater Department as a director, the faculty would not let her direct, but she was permitted to assist Richard Trousdell. Although the first question she heard was, "Who is Soyinka?" she felt vindicated when Soyinka was awarded the 1986 Nobel Prize in literature later that year.

The performances of *The Lion and the Jewel* in April 1987 featured Gordon Heath in a professional venue with Pearl for the first time since the 1940s. He and Pearl revived an old and deep friendship—he had been a reader of "Strange Fruit" during Pearl's performances in the 1940s. The presence of Heath in the role of the Lion grew out of a chance meeting between Heath and Ekwueme Michael Thelwell, professor of Afro-American studies. Thelwell had gone to Paris to attend a ceremony honoring James Baldwin, who was being awarded the Commander of the Legion of Honor. A mutual friend put him in touch with Heath, and Thelwell arranged for Heath and Richard Trousdell to be in touch. "There was in Gordon Heath not a hint of the isolated, alienated black artist who felt victimized and embittered by the stifling of his talent and career by 'racism,'" Thelwell later wrote. "There was nothing deracinated about him. Co-existing with the urbanity of the sophisticated Parisian was the calm, unpretentious self-acceptance of a conscious, deeply rooted black American."[11]

When Heath arrived in the theater for the first rehearsal, at a signal from Pearl, the members of the cast began to play a welcoming rhythm and perform a dance of welcome. "For Gordon, it was as if the whole African village was greeting their king. It was touching to see these two legends in their latter vulnerable years and to see their younger selves shining through," Roberta said. At first Heath seemed surprised, "but not for long," wrote Richard Trousdell:

> Quickly and lightly he picked up the beat, and stepping his way between the corridor of swaying dancers, he moved toward Pearl Primus herself, each beaming at the other with delight and pride. Moments later, we all sat together for a first reading of the play. When Gordon spoke the old king's first lines, the quiet manner of a bemused professor was completely gone. In its place were the ringing tones and full emotion of an accomplished actor in engaged performance. The waking lion roared, and we all felt his power.[12]

Pearl's rehearsal process had a deep impact on Roberta as a director. She talked about the cosmology of the play and its world as she saw it, about the relationship of African dance to the ground and what it meant to be in contact with the earth, what the drum meant and what it meant to invoke the ancestors. But most poignant was Pearl's talk about their feet and how to care for them. Roberta loved learning the African concept of the organic connection between the feet and the earth, but the lesson was also practical. "You'll get cracks or blisters," she said. "As a woman director I feel like I'm being stereotyped as either the dragon lady bitch or the earth mother cooking chili for everyone," Roberta said. Pearl gave her another way to perceive her role, and she took note as Pearl welcomed the children of cast members or faculty at rehearsals, or asked a dancer to tie a toddler on her back and dance with her. Roberta's own children loved to go through Pearl's jewelry, and Pearl told them that she would be buried covered head to toe in her jewelry and nothing else.

Pearl nurtured the gifts of other students as well. Jeffrey Wright, for example, then a student at Amherst College, played the part of Lakunle in *The Lion and the Jewel.* Although not a theater major in college, he went on to win a Tony Award for best featured actor for his role in Tony Kushner's Pulitzer Prize–winning play, *Angels in America.* Another student Pearl inspired was Jerry Lavine, the first visitor in an exchange she had started between the Barbados Dance Theatre Company and the Five College Dance Department. Jerry was in residence during the spring semester 1987. After his performance with Rebecca Nordstrom in an excerpt from *The Wedding* at a Smith College commencement concert, he appeared in Roberta's production of *The Lion and the Jewel.* Eager to share his experiences, Jerry returned to Barbados, but, tragically, he was attacked by a robber and died in the early fall of 1987 at the age of twenty-six. The exchange was not continued.

When the performances of *The Lion and the Jewel* were over and there was a moment for reflection, Roberta wrote a note to Pearl: "I feel we have broken a barrier and with your guidance have done so with pride and dignity intact. I am very pleased with the profound and proud images I have seen resounding from the Rand Stage and I attribute this to you. You have given the students and myself inspiration and instruction that we will remember all our lives."

— ❧ —

While she lived in the Pioneer Valley, Pearl's vitality was enormous. She maintained intimate friendships even as she engaged in an astonishing range of teachings and performances. She would find time to be a witness at the wedding of her close friends Marjorie Senechal and Stan Sherer. They shared a background in radical politics, and Pearl found in their friendship another connection to the Jewish world. Marjorie remembered how "she gave us a mezuzah that had belonged to her father, unadorned ivory except for a tiny metal plaque with a Hebrew letter on it. We nailed it to the door frame in our living room." Another close friend, Dovi Afesi, connected to Pearl's African identity, as Dovi belongs to the Ewe people of the Volta region in eastern Ghana. Pearl eventually took him on "as a son." Dovi would visit her, cook for them, and they would eat "African style," with their right hands.

Through her friends and many collegial relations, Pearl was continuously sought after for events in the Valley. Her presence always lent an air of theatricality, whether at an informal gathering at the home of Amherst College dean of faculty Richard Fink, or at a more formal event, a luncheon hosted by Chancellor Duffey for Robert Mugabe, then in his progressive years as president of Zimbabwe, who was being honored at the University Fall Convocation in 1986. At a full-day workshop on African arts for educators, Pearl led a processional throughout the campus of elementary school teachers from around New England who had become a tribe-for-a-day. She also responded to many invitations to appear at dance classes, and organized performances and exhibits at the Augusta Savage Gallery in the New Africa House, the home of the Afro-American Studies Department.

Pearl gave freely of herself to community groups. In Amherst, beginning in 1985, she participated each year in an "International Sunday" ceremony, an event organized by a friend, Lynn Vendien, who had published a book of songs, games, and dances from around the world. A news article described the audience as people talking quietly in Spanish and in Vietnamese, "men in business suits, black women with hair beaded and braided . . . women in Indian saris, men in yarmulkes." A UMass physics professor from India offered a Hindu meditation on peace, a Pakistani woman read from the Koran, a woman from the Soviet Union recited a passage from Revelations, and "a man from Israel . . . read from the Book of Micah in the rich, lilting music of Hebrew." Pearl talked about and performed "Fanga" for the packed church.[13]

Pearl also found time to take part in another of Roberta Uno's productions, *Shango De Ima*. Michael Thelwell played a deity and Pearl danced and acted the other leading role. She said of her part, "My character, Obatala, is very important in the Yoruba religion. My research into that culture, and how the ancient religion of the ancestral spirits became translated in Cuba and Haiti by people who were cut off from them by slavery, has all come into helping me analyze the character."[14] As always, she wanted to show how authentic archaic expression could be reintegrated into the lives of black people of the Diaspora and offered to a diverse audience.

∞

Another organization Pearl came to treasure was the Hamilton Hill Arts and Craft Center (HHACC), which was founded in 1968 in inner-city Schenectady, New York. Schenectady had lost its manufacturing base many years earlier and struggled to provide educational opportunities for its youth. Initially a drop-in arts center for neighborhood children, mostly black, the center grew to include a range of art activities designed to build self-esteem and enrich the cultural education of the children. From 1983, when she met Margaret Cunningham, then the director, until her death in 1994, Pearl always found time to devote to this much admired group.

Shortly after meeting Margaret, Pearl was invited to be a guest speaker at an annual dinner. Margaret remembered that "she refused to use a microphone. She never stood still and her entrancing, personal magnetism and distinctive attire, coupled with her rich West Indian accent, charmed her audience as she moved back and forth across the stage." In late 1983 she conducted a series of African dance workshops for the Burundi dance group (adult black females) as well as area dance teachers and advanced adult dancers. This attracted people from nearby cities and towns.

One day, Margaret unexpectedly received a phone call from Pearl, telling her to meet her train as it passed through Schenectady. Margaret rushed down to the train station at the appointed time, and when the doors opened Pearl jumped off, thrust a small package into her hand and hopped back on the train. As the doors closed she called out, "This is what they're wearing in Nigeria!" Margaret tore open the wrapping paper to find a beautiful necklace.

In 1984 she commuted from Amherst several times to prepare a children's dance group for an Urban League dinner. By late that year she was committed to going to Schenectady several weekends each year before Kwanzaa to help prepare for this celebration. "Her energy and enthusiasm were boundless," Margaret said. "Her voice was like music. When we weren't working, we just visited. She was a wonderful houseguest. Those weekends always went too fast, because we bonded as a family." Eventually, the Kwanzaa celebrations grew so much they needed to move to larger quarters, and ultimately Pearl was presented with the keys to the city for her contributions.

In a letter to Jacquelyn Hawkins at HHACC, Pearl wrote that the center was helping people "find the crystal of creativity in a world which tends to stifle the individual." With Pearl's support and participation the HHACC received funding from the Urban League of the Albany area for performances as well as considerable news coverage in the local press. As always, her work did not have to take place on a well-known theater stage. Although she sometimes seemed to have disappeared from the dance profession, she was actually busier than ever.

Pearl was forever receiving invitations for speaking engagements and lectures, causing disgruntlement among some colleagues. "How can she keep up if she's always out and doing?" On November 1, 1988, for example, the Association of Black Storytellers wrote, "We need your stories and essay on the role of the Griot as soon as possible." On November 15, the Hampshire College Humanities and Art secretary wrote, "It has come to my attention that you never turned in course evaluations for Creative Dance Vocabulary, which you taught at Hampshire College last spring." Although assistants often filled in for her, these small lapses were Pearl's way of announcing a larger message: that she was to be treated as exceptional, and deserving of special consideration. She took her time so that others would recognize her stature.

But when special status is conferred on a faculty member, envy vies with celebration, and honors kept flowing her way. In 1985 she received a Distinguished Service Award from the American Anthropological Association, and she taught and spoke at large and small campuses around the country. In 1986 she received the Ernest O. Melby Distinguished Alumni Award (along with Dr. Jonas Salk), on behalf of New York University, for "attaining prominence and distinction in her chosen vocation." In 1988 she received an honorary doctorate from Spelman College, along with Marion Wright Edelman. In January 1988, New York governor Mario Cuomo informed her that she would be part of that state's celebration of Black History Month.

In June of that year, Pearl was honored at the Caribbean Cultural Center's "Osun Festival." In 1990, the Smithsonian Institute Museum of American History honored Pearl along with Katherine Dunham. By this time Pearl was complaining about all the awards, suggesting that they were no help with the difficulties that plagued her for the rest of her life. "All these awards, but they don't pay the bills," Pearl said many times.

In Washington, D.C., Dr. Elgie Gaynell Sherrod, who had known Pearl as a young dancer in Buffalo, asked Pearl what her generation should do to continue Pearl's work, and Pearl replied, "Stop honoring us." Pearl was sitting in the front row with Katharine Dunham but she had Gaynell go up to the stage to accept the award for her. Gaynell simply said, "She didn't feel like it." "Stop honoring us for the things we did fifty, sixty years ago," Pearl said. "Build on it. A greater honor would be to build on what we've done, take it to another level."

In 1991 Pearl was awarded the National Medal of the Arts for her "exceptional contributions to the cultural life of the nation." She received the National Endowment for the Arts Teacher/Mentor Award in the fall of 1994, just before her death. Ironically, this award, received posthumously, covered the costs of her funeral.

One last major award received posthumously was the Samuel H. Scripps American Dance Festival Award. The $25,000 was used to provide scholarships for students in the ADF summer program. Kim Bears performed "Negro Speaks of Rivers," and Joe Nash spoke, praising "Ms. Primus' desire to share the beauty and majesty of African Culture."

⤫

Neither the protection and freedom of academic tenure, nor the predictable income of an academic appointment, were available to her after 1992. The problem was not simply that Smith College still had a mandatory retirement age. The Five College consortium could have made other arrangements to keep her on, at least for an extended period. The most stable alternative would have been to move her appointment to the university, since mandatory retirement was no longer legal in public universities by then. But this did not happen. To be sure, there was a severe financial crisis in Massachusetts public funding during the early 1990s, but the Five College consortium was designed for creative arrangements. In the Afro-American Studies Department the desire was not strong enough at the time. Instead there was a mix of attitudes, a respect bordering on reverence, which was undercut by the political construct that put racial struggle at the forefront of identity. Pearl no longer fit that mold. Her allegiances were not defined or bound by the racial politics of the time. Her worldview had become thoroughly egalitarian and cosmopolitan.

But to some extent, Pearl was also the creator of her situation, for it was always her style to expect her place in the world to be conferred on her, as it was when her name "Omowale," "child returned home," had been given by the tribal authorities. When it was not, she was deeply disappointed. "She thought she had found peace here," Dove Afesi said. "It was a real heartbreak." One of her key advocates in Afro-American Studies, Michael Thelwell, spoke of his "tremendous regret" that she wasn't kept on. "She was as important as Robeson and the others," he said.

Pearl got by on temporary teaching appointments and grants for the rest of her life, but it was a struggle.

TEN

Transmitting the Work

UPON HER ARRIVAL IN AMHERST to take up her appointment in the Five Colleges in September 1984, Pearl assembled a cast for a new version of "Excerpts from an African Journey," the concert and lecture-demonstration format she had developed many years earlier. Pearl took dancers of mixed abilities, mostly white, few of whom had had any experience with African dance, and created a village atmosphere. Her training of these students was important far beyond the performance itself, as she was teaching them to transcend categorizations by race, and the work itself was stellar.

At the beginning of the second half of the concert, Pearl emerged from the wings in all her finery to graciously introduce her work and then step aside. The dancers entered, pouring libation, chanting, and flowing in and out of many of her classic African works, before concluding the concert with "Hi Life," a social dance that originated in Ghana. Various groups appeared in the costumes of the piece they had last performed, creating a swirl of masks, flowing fabrics, skirts, robes, and the like. The first group of women spun their way across the stage and then formed a semicircle within which each dancer created her own solo. One group after another was drawn from the wings until the whole cast assembled for a last, joyous dance. After all the drummers took their bows, they brought a smiling Pearl to center stage to be greeted enthusiastically by her village. As the drumming reached a crescendo, everyone joined in the Creole chant from Sierra Leone, "Mahmba, Mahmba, Jolly Mahmba," with which the dance began.

When she danced "Fanga" that night, Pearl was on fire, clearly thrilled to be back on stage. The audience was electrified, as was the cast when they all reappeared to dance spontaneously with her. The teacher, the dancer, the

218

choreographer, the lecturer, the storyteller, the village elder, the matriarch—they were all present as one.

The dancers came from all over the region. Among them were Lynn Frederiksen, whose family was from Saint Croix and who was then a graduate student at Smith College, and Elizabeth Fernandez O'Brien, who had studied with Percy in Binghamton, had conducted research in Trinidad, and was teaching physical education in the Amherst public schools. Ivor Miller was an undergraduate at Hampshire College. Lynn and Elizabeth remembered the challenge Pearl confronted in creating a village out of her assorted cast. "She maneuvered everyone around somehow so that she could get something from everyone," Lynn said. People brought fruit and candles, and Lynn brought an orange from her father's tree in Saint Croix. Elizabeth, knowing that Percy used to give Pearl yellow roses, brought a yellow rose and also a red one. Pearl was continually reinforcing the village nature of the group.

At one point, Pearl told Lynn about an experience at a funeral she attended while doing research in the South. Apparently, she struck up a conversation with a white man who had invited her to come to dinner the next day. After learning that he was one of the grand wizards of the Klan, she still insisted on keeping the appointment, because the man had felt connected to her as a person and decided that she was not black! This perception could also work in reverse. Pearl once told Terry Baker, New York arts educator and longtime friend, that she believed he had black ancestry, because she felt a strong spiritual connection with him.

For Lynn, Pearl was "not just a conduit but a transformer of the heritages," though she taught her students to "keep the essence" of their own cultural traditions. Lynn felt an aura of mystery about Pearl; she seemed connected to something much larger that herself.

Ivor Miller, now a respected cultural and dance anthropologist, had a similarly empowering experience performing "Bushasche." In 1984, when he was an undergraduate at Hampshire College and passionate about African dance, he found that as a white man he was often not welcome in black dance circles. By featuring him in the Five Colleges concert, Pearl strengthened his resolve to continue his studies and to commit himself wholeheartedly to dance. Because "Bushasche" was danced only once every twenty years, it spoke to the generational passage from the elders to the young. Ivor said, "Pearl's way as a teacher was to universalize ideas so dancers could relate them to their own lives." The universal in "Bushasche" was about combating evil, a concept as relevant for a white, middle-class young man from Amherst as it was for an African tribesman.

In 1988, Pearl asked Rebecca Nordstrom, professor of dance at Hampshire College, to work with her on excerpts from "The Wedding" for a Smith College commencement concert. Pearl felt that Becky, whom Onwin called "the whitest little black bride I ever saw," had the African spirit. Sitting at Pearl's feet for hours, Becky felt like a young student or supplicant. "I'd ask myself, 'How is it that I'm getting the full attention of this amazing person?'" she recalled. Pearl had invited Jerry Lavine, a young man from Barbados, to partner with Becky.

The work was demanding, as Pearl was not rechoreographing but working from memory, and she didn't demonstrate but clapped the rhythms to get a frantic yet free-flowing yet fast quality. They spent a lot of time on locomotor patterns, coordinating the pelvis and legs, being very specific in counts, directions, and body coordination, with continual attention to the soles of the feet and her particular way of stepping. She wanted her subtlety to become second nature, engrained in muscle memory. If Pearl got exasperated she might joke, "Girl, I should take you into the bush and show you a thing or two," or "Honey, when you get home, do this for your man!" Pearl would close her eyes while telling stories, as if going into a trance, with her head tilted, eyes narrowed to slits.

Becky and Pearl were not only dancer and choreographer; they were also friends and colleagues. When Becky was engaged to marry the photographer Jerome Leibling, Pearl slipped her V-shaped silver bracelet off her arm and onto Becky's, a gift from spiritual mother to daughter. At Jerry's retirement dinner in 1990, Pearl first honored Becky's parents, then told the assembled party that she was Becky's "black mother." Pearl also loved

Jerry, with whom she shared New York radical left-wing roots and connections. She was always teaching to a larger vision.

~

In her mid-sixties Pearl began grappling in earnest with a growing desire to influence her legacy, but she struggled when it came to restaging her early solos, knowing that these were a priceless part of modern dance heritage, yet reluctant to adapt such intensely personal statements. What dancers of today could possibly perform them? In time the need to document them became more urgent than the despair she occasionally expressed about whether they could actually be reinterpreted and performed anew. Then, in 1988, the American Dance Festival (ADF) developed a three-year project funded by the National Endowment for the Humanities and the Ford Foundation to revive "'lost' or little-performed works and record them on videotape, [and foster] scholarship through seminars and the publication of a collection of essays." This provided the framework she needed.

Pearl was invited by Charles Reinhart, director of ADF, to revisit "Hard Time Blues," "Negro Speaks of Rivers," and "Strange Fruit" for the first summer of performances. The program was also to include Talley Beatty's "Congo Tango Palace," Donald McKayle's "Rainbow Round My Shoulder" and "Games," and Eleo Pomare's "House of Bernarda Alba." Entitled "The Black Tradition in American Dance," the plan was to present artists "who draw upon the black experience" as "creative artists within American modern dance, not as exponents of an ethnic form." Describing a panel on the "past, present and future of The Black Presence in American Modern Dance," Anna Kisselgoff wrote that "nobody in this series would seem to embody that presence so symbolically as Pearl Primus."[1]

Pearl's early solos, in particular "Strange Fruit," "Negro Speaks of Rivers," and "Hard Time Blues"—the three that were newly performed—are a holy grail of sorts as much because of her legendary performances as for the choreography and subject matter itself. She spoke of being not only a dancer when she performed these works, but a concept. When introducing "Negro Speaks of Rivers," for example, she evoked "the rivers of sharks that followed the ships across the ocean, the rivers of tears as we were torn from our homes, the rivers of blood as the whips cut across our backs." This was the challenge she had to convey to the two young dancers selected from the Philadelphia Dance Company to perform them.

Kim Bears and Warren P. Miller II first met Pearl as performers with Philadanco in 1986. She chose a man to perform "Hard Time Blues," as she said there were no women strong enough to do the jumps that the choreography demanded, and there was no one dancer strong enough to maintain the level of performance for all three works in one concert. Pearl had been setting "The Wedding" on Philadanco, and though they never performed it, this working period allowed her the time to identify the two dancers to whom she would ultimately teach the early solos. Kim was in her early twenties and Warren near thirty when they were given these works to learn.

The emotional work involved in "Strange Fruit" was so difficult for Kim that it challenged her sense of herself as a dancer. "When I got an opportunity to work with Dr. Primus, it was evident that her way of movement had to come from somewhere deep down in your soul," Kim said. "Technically it wasn't something I felt that I couldn't achieve. But emotionally, spiritually and of its essence—that was the hardest. I had to re-educate myself as to how I approached dance."

Rehearsing at Hampshire College, Kim and Warren had little contact with the outside world. Frustrated with the pace of the work, Pearl asked Peggy Schwartz to rehearse Kim in "Strange Fruit," and Peggy met with her to explain how hard it was for Pearl to release these dances. This comment proved helpful to Kim. In a later rehearsal, Pearl had Kim run in the studio for three hours in order to get her to the right state of emotional and physical exhaustion. At the end of "Strange Fruit," when the woman holds a scream that she wants to let out at the top of her throat, she starts to run, and her frenzy has to be intensely vibrant. At first Kim didn't understand why she had to keep running, but once she got to her limit, Pearl said, "There it is!" and then Kim knew where she had to go.

Pearl told Kim of talks with Langston Hughes about "Negro Speaks of Rivers," and of her own struggles to have her voice heard through her art. Afraid that her ability might not live up to this history, Kim called her mother to say she was quitting. "At twenty-three, I didn't have a hard shell," she recalled, but her labor paid off. "Every time I went on that stage, it had to be honest. That was the greatest thing she brought me back to: you just don't do the movement for the sake of movement." Integrating the dances with music was also complicated, as Pearl's commitment to precise rhythmic phrasing was total. Sometimes the musicians would be in the studio from nine in the morning until ten at night.

Warren's version of the nerve-wracking rehearsal process echoed Kim's. "It was like going to a different country without knowing anything about it," he recalled. He had started dancing as a sophomore at Western Michigan University, which he attended on a track scholarship. Perhaps this resonated for Pearl, who also was a track star in high school. "Ma Pearl would say to me, 'The ancestors will take care of you. Trust the ancestors.' Once, spinning at top speed in the studio at Smith, I thought I'd go right out the window into the nasty water of Paradise Pond. She said, 'The ancestors would have gotten you.'" Warren said the piece caused him so much anxiety that he never wanted to perform it again.

To prepare for the actual performances at ADF, Pearl went to a separate room and insisted that Kim and Warren have a room to themselves so they could work their way into their roles, reimagining the era in which they were first performed, undistracted by other dancers. Before each performance they would form a small circle and call on the ancestors to support them, as in a prayer ritual.

Kim worked with Pearl directly on an American Dance Guild Gala, which celebrated the work of the New Dance Group, and performed "Negro Speaks of Rivers" in concert and for a videotape documenting the solo. She also worked closely with Jawole Willa Jo Zollar to restore Pearl's work to performance, and taught "Strange Fruit" to Dawn Marie Watson, a principal dancer at Philadanco for the film "Free to Dance" when she felt that knee surgery would prevent her from performing it with full integrity.

After Pearl's death, when Kim was asked to perform or teach "Negro Speaks of Rivers," she called Joe Nash and asked, "Do I have the right?" Joe replied that she had been given the right when Pearl chose her. Pearl had given Kim the costume she made as well as a gift of a piece of the cloth used for the original costume, which had become a kind of talisman. "She gave me a piece of her—and that's something that I'll always have."

In 1989, after the three solos were performed at ADF, Pearl proposed to reconstruct "Our Spring Will Come" for the 1991 Festival. She had choreographed this dance in the mid-1940s to a poem by Langston Hughes, with music by John Cage. She wrote to Charles Reinhart at ADF that she had the music in a trunk, complete with Cage's directions for preparing the piano, but that dance wasn't taken on tour "because pianists tossed up their hands and flatly refused to play his music." Pearl described this piece as "an ultra modern and sculptress dance," the theme of which was a line from the poem, "Like the melting snows, Our Spring Will Come!" She proposed either Kim Bears or Linda Spriggs as the performers. "Charles, I really want to see this dance alive again. It is still so timely . . . and would be a fine addition to your archives," she wrote, clearly desiring that her legacy include work as an abstract modern dancer, though this piece was never restaged or documented.

─◇─

In October 1988, Pearl received word that she had received a $10,000 National Endowment for the Arts Choreography Fellowship to create a new work. She asked Linda Spriggs, faculty member at the University of Michigan and former member of the Alvin Ailey company, as well as daughter of her friend Mozel, to come to Amherst for three weeks to develop it. The work would premier in Ann Arbor in December 1989. When Pearl told Linda she had clear ideas for the piece, Linda replied, "Fine as long as you don't ask me to do that walking-on-air-Primus-thing!" Linda's experience with Pearl took them to the heart of Pearl's creative process, the place where the new creation evokes the archaic African spirit world in ritual performance.

Pearl began by sitting her down and talking with great specificity about her intentions in creating "Shango," and the nature of the movement, yet did all of this without generating any demonstration other than arm gestures. They performed libations and the rituals to pay respects to the ancestors and to ensure protection from going into a trance, working for a long time without music.

Linda had to enact two roles, the Griot and his transformation into Shango, the god of thunder and lightning. "The Griot contains the history of the village. He's a revered person, usually a man," she explained. "The character that I would manifest into was also a man. Pearl talked about how all aspects of the self are important to bring this forward. When the Griot makes a transition into Shango, he allows the Orisha to mount him. Then I am both the Griot and Shango. The Griot is of the earth, but is also Shango." Expressing both love and arrogance, Shango walked with long legs and stretched and flexed feet. His gaze provoked fear, and his anger could flare out of control. "I couldn't believe how much energy I expended standing and emoting, how psychological the whole thing was," Linda continued. "Spiritually, you have to go there with the mind of Shango. Pearl did lots of talking about what this energy was like." To bring this energy out, Pearl worked on arm strength, giving Linda pails that the Griot would use and a gourd she made to pour libations. "I'm a practicing Buddhist," Linda said. "Pearl encouraged me to secure myself and anchor myself to my own religious beliefs, to continue with my chants, my practice."

As the Griot, Linda was recounting how Shango, the god of thunder, takes over a village and sets fire to the huts. Pearl had in her possession a hammer from Shango from one of her many trips to Africa. At first, she had Linda use a prop for the hammer, for fear that the true hammer of Shango would bring too much of the Orisha to her. Finally, Pearl did let Linda use the true hammer, with dramatic consequences. Shango jumps and turns, swinging the hammer around high overhead. He gets all wound up in the power and lightning and control, and hears a voice ring out. Then he realizes that in the heat of passion he has lit the fire, burned his own village, and killed his wife. He goes mad.

This was Pearl's version of the dance, and she made it clear to Linda that there are other versions. The psychological key was Shango's realization that he has destroyed himself by not being able to control his destructive impulses. He goes mad and kills himself. The Griot loses himself in the story, and struggles so as not to be immersed in it and taken over by the Orisha, but he emerges only to get pulled back into fusion with the god. Linda explained:

Repetition. Repetition: burning of the village. The Griot is fused with the Orisha. The Orisha's life overtakes it. I had to do this physically, again and again—"Pearl I'm not you." "Yes you can. You're a good little dancer." It was incredibly challenging to keep up the stamina, the physical and emotional strength. To do the dance justice, you have to go there, must understand the psyches of the individuals you are representing. Madness and loss of control. The heart of the dance. I understood her admonishment to keep myself strong.

This dance was being premiered at Ann Arbor with a professional company of faculty, Ann Arbor Dance Works, on December 1, 1989, the very day Alvin Ailey died. The costumes and props were set. Pearl had made Linda's costume using materials from her collection, her lappas, a warrior costume, with wristlet and bracelet. They had found someone who could braid Linda's hair in the style Shango would have worn, like a blade across her head. Wanting it to stand high, Pearl used extensions, and the woman doing her hair would spray them and use a flame to lightly catch the ends, but this time when she lit the match, Linda's whole head went on fire. Linda recalled the moment:

> Here's the story of the god of thunder and fire and lightning. My whole head was on fire. . . . She put the flame out, but even just for that moment, to see myself in the mirror with my hair on fire—it was really shocking. I told Pearl about this and she said, "Be very careful, Linda, he's here."
>
> Then before the dress rehearsal, she gave me the staff. "Be careful, I think you are strong enough to handle it. I was wary of giving it to you to use. The staff has a life of its own." She was concerned because I had the life of the Griot and of Shango and the staff, which might bring Shango even more fully to me. I'm in these jump turns swinging the staff over my head. In other rehearsals, I used papier-mâché, something light. Now, I'm swinging the staff over head, my arm way overhead, and the

staff hits me in the face. Broke my nose between my eyes. I could have sworn I swung it overhead. "I told you to control the staff." Thankfully it wasn't a big break, I could put it into place. But I had a scar for a while, a cut. It was as if the staff jumped up and hit me in the face!

Just before the show, Pearl told Linda that Alvin Ailey had passed away, and they talked about how Shango went mad when he realized that his loved one was dead. Pearl encouraged Linda to use the sadness and love she felt for Ailey, one of her mentors. "Now I'm representing Alvin and truly doing this for him, as a father figure, someone who taught me and raised me. . . . It was also difficult thinking of living up to the dance and doing it for Pearl. It was even more emotional, an incredible mix of emotions," Linda recalled.

The second time Linda performed in Michigan, she felt that Shango overtook her. "It was really scary. People could see it. Afterwards, people couldn't come near me for a while." She performed it again in Washington, D.C., and in Atlanta as part of a Black Arts Festival, but she always found it draining. "I survived it," she said.

Through her experience of Shango, Linda felt she understood the fight that had been Pearl's fight. "Everyone now says 'dance is a language,'" she observed, "but Pearl said it with a particular meaning about the way the intensity of movement telegraphs people and culture." Linda identified strongly with that quality:

> If you are a revolutionary you have to break through the wall
> . . . and it's not graceful. Not female. Pearl was very specific and
> direct, and those qualities were not considered feminine. I un-
> derstood that, and every now and then find someone I can share
> that with, and they can then take it to another level . . . that pushes
> us forward, so that knowledge of these things can continue. She
> must have felt some jealousies and some resentments and was
> not able to share her entire legacy.

Pearl wanted to teach Linda "Hard Time Blues" but there wasn't enough time.

―◯◯―

Pearl had left Smith College and the Five Colleges in the spring of 1992. In March, Sherrill Berryman-Miller (who became Berryman-Johnson) and Naima Prevots of Howard and American Universities, respectively, submitted a grant to the Lila Wallace-Reader's Digest Arts Partners Program that was being coordinated by the Association of Performing Arts Presenters. One of their goals was the documentation of Pearl's work for artistic and educational purposes. Pearl welcomed the challenge of creating a new "village" with students and colleagues at the two universities, and also wanted to use the opportunity to prepare for a fiftieth anniversary celebration of her 1943 debut at the 92nd Street Y. This was to be the final instance of her navigation between worlds, black and white, artistic and academic, the theater and the lecture hall.

The scope of activities was ambitious. Over a period of twelve weeks, Pearl was going to set her work on students of all levels in preparation for two performances, one at Howard University and the other at the Kennedy Center. She was to give master classes and lecture demonstrations throughout the greater Washington, D.C., area and deliver four lectures in surrounding venues on "Arts of Africa," "Legacy: African Culture in the New World," "Dance Is My Language," and "Life Crisis." These activities were to be videotaped and shaped into a documentary intended for "outreach and awareness of Primus and her legacy." The opportunity had come none too soon, for Pearl's health and physical stamina were beginning to fail, and others began to notice alarming changes in her appearance.

Participants in the residency give very different, even contradictory, accounts of the experience. April Cantor, an American University freshman of Filipino descent, enjoyed "the earthiness" of her participation and described it as "finding home," but she also identified a fault line between the two academic groups. "Most of the rehearsals were at Howard, so we always felt we were going to their turf. They had a certain territorialism. They were very strong in their own culture." Pearl's Barbadian assistant, Sheron

Trotman, who combined "spiritedness with forcefulness," encouraged April to resist this division. "For a little bit we really broke down some barriers," said April. "Whatever things we came in with, whatever walls, brick by brick we were taking them down." April particularly remembered the powerful dancing of Hope Boykin, the leading dancer at Howard University, who became a leading dancer with the Alvin Ailey American Dance Theater and a choreographer in her own right. But despite April's best hopes, tensions emerged between Sherrill Berryman-Johnson at Howard and Naima Prevots, the lead American faculty member.

Pearl was not sure that she could successfully integrate the two groups, and thought of retreating. Naima felt that Pearl, for health reasons, did not exert sufficient artistic control over the event. Pearl had created a central role for Onwin, but this led to excessively long solos, and April and the dancers felt uncomfortable and even embarrassed about Onwin's performance at the Howard University concert. Pearl had also added dance movements that they never really mastered.

Information to the press was misleading about the nature and the sponsorship of the residency. An article in the *Capital Spotlight*, a free newspaper distributed in Washington's African American neighborhoods, announced that the Anacostia Museum of the Smithsonian Institute will present "An Afternoon with Pearl Primus" on Sunday, November 5. The article states that Pearl was "currently in the midst of a six-week residency at Howard University in Washington, D.C.," and never mentions the joint nature of the work.[2] Other material was skewed in acknowledging the collaborative nature of the grant. Pearl disliked being used in this way. She eschewed separatist impulses.

The Kennedy Center performance did turn out to be thrilling for the performers, however, and Pearl put the best face on the whole experience. When it was all over, April remembered exclaiming, "Pearl, you're a true survivor!" "We are ALL survivors!" Pearl replied, then she paused and said with a smile, "But you're right, I am the best survivor of them all."

Toward the end of the residency Pearl, now seventy-three, was using a cane or a walking stick, "hobbling around." At times, she would summon her energy and the students could glimpse the dancer in her prime, but she looked drawn, there were new lines in her face, and she clearly had lost a lot of weight. She would talk about regaining weight but also about medical tests, though never specifically, and she had been in touch with an old friend and colleague, Spider Kedelsky, for a referral to a physician. "She was ill but she would never let you know," Kim Bears recalled. She and Sheron Trotman would bring Pearl home-cooked meals and help with whatever needed doing.

Howard University never submitted a final report to the Lila Wallace-Reader's Digest Foundation, and the promised video documentation of the residency is still not available.

∽

Pearl's final important restaging was the teaching of "Strange Fruit" to Michele Simmons, former Ailey dancer, in California, her last "creative exchange," as Michele described it. The project began in the fall of 1993 when Bonnie Oda Homsey, artistic director of the American Repertory Dance Company (ARDC) in Los Angeles, with Janet Eilber, of the Martha Graham Company, planned a dance and theater program in conjunction with an exhibit, "Picasso and the Weeping Women," for the Los Angeles County Museum of Art. Bonnie knew that she would want Martha Graham's "Lamentation" on the program and, as a former soloist with the Graham company, called Martha, who recommended "Strange Fruit" for the concert as well.

Thus began Bonnie's "bumpy ride with Mna Pearl." Pearl made it clear that "Strange Fruit" was so personal that she would rather withhold rights to the dance than see it performed badly. "She was not talking about technique," Bonnie reflected. "She was referring to the artist's capability to transmit the infinite and critical nuances of intention and meaning so the solo could rightly illuminate its fundamental question and response: How has mankind allowed such injustice? All such acts of cruelty must never occur again! The breadth and scope of Pearl's artistic, cultural, political, and anthropological beliefs merged within the accusations lodged in this dance."

It took over five months of long-distance phone conversations plus Donald McKayle's recommendation of Michele Simmons before Pearl gave the ARDC permission to perform the dance. Pearl was so identified with it that returning to it stirred up painful feelings, as she took Michele into "a deeply interior space," guiding her into the rhythms of the dance, which was done in silence. In fact, the rhythms had to be so internalized that as they erupted kinesthetically, the power of the text would not take precedence over the movement. Over and over again, Pearl worked with Michele to help her keep her concentration and not react to the text.

Bonnie Oda Homsey's description of the collaborative process provides a valuable record of this seminal work in the canon of American modern dance:

> Pearl described the setting as an outdoor gathering. The woman is leaving, following the group in an offstage right direction when something behind her catches the periphery of her attention. The woman hesitates in an open stride stance, then, she turns to face the off-stage right area where a lynching has occurred.
>
> Pearl worked with Michele on that opening stance for almost two hours. It was NOT a pose of physical design. Yes the feet were apart. Yes the weight was tipped on the right front foot. Yes the facing was off-stage right. Yes the arms were relaxed by the side. But these body components did not inform the stance. The form emerged from reality of circumstance.
>
> Over and over as Michele struggled to discover essence of form, Pearl would call out another descriptive comment. . . . At one point Pearl said that the stance was like one of those carvings of someone caught in the act of throwing a spear; the inanimate becomes utterly alive.
>
> The second rehearsal Pearl began working on the spiral turn, collapse and reaching movement motif. She reiterated focus on the catalyst predicating the spiral and collapse to the floor. And how the repetitive reaching sourced from the duality of curiosity and repulsion initiating from the legs up the back and out to the reach of the right arm. The motif must not manifest merely with the head turning toward the "forbidden zone," the area of the tree and lynched body. The following serpentine rise

from the floor made physical the twisting trunk and boughs of the tree.

Pearl was noticeably thinner and expressed weariness in conversations, but she was fully present in the studio, and they worked for hours as Michele learned to master the reaching motion from the crumpled position, "from the legs up through the spine and then through the head." When the dancer's arms come together and reach overhead, it's as if she replicates the body swaying in the breeze. "As Michele started to own that movement I had the image of the body trying to stamp air to levitate out of that position," Bonnie said.

Bonnie observed that Pearl would correct Michele and say, "It's too big," or some such, but she wanted Michele to plumb her own imagination to make the movement real:

> It was not immediately evident, but about the end of the second rehearsal I suddenly realized another purpose in Pearl's deliberateness. Without impinging or influencing Michele's interpretation of the movement, she was pushing Michele to self-discovery of the inner rhythms of the choreography that could then frame the secondary layering of the spoken poem . . .
>
> There is a point following . . . an arcing pathway of thrashing on the floor, punctuated by thrusts of leg and arm, when the woman rises to face the forbidden zone. Pearl gave an image of standing in the Congo that informs the movement. As the hands clasp overhead, she described the feet clenched in imitation of deer hooves. Pearl described those rapid bourrées of the feet as a frantic attempt to escape.
>
> The spiral turn and serpentine rise occurs for the third time to text, "Pastoral scene of the gallant south." Pearl wanted Michele to find a way to convey the irony of the words juxtaposed on the movement motif that also propels her into the next phrase of frantic traveling turns across the stage ending in the body collapsed prone on the floor. The motif should not evoke the same

physical rendering as in the prior repetitions; the challenge—to elicit the truth of that moment. . . .

After another series of crawls and high arch falls, Michele sits up suddenly as the narrator speaks, "Scent of magnolias sweet and fresh." Again, Pearl made the point about physically manifesting the irony of the text against the reality of the smell of burning flesh. The clarity of intention sets up the final arch—fall, and deliberate rise for the great circling of runs. . . . I recall Pearl describing the run as gathering the consciousness of mankind to this act of cruelty and injustice. The ensuing circling that ultimately becomes a staggering self-revolution marks the unbearable weight of the act, until the woman succumbs and falls to the ground.

The woman rolls onto her right side, her gaze turning to the lynching. I get chills remembering the way that Pearl kept throwing out descriptive images and emotional impulses, coaching Michele through these movements . . . the tentative, right-left pacing toward the forbidden zone/lynching emerges from the context of full recognition. The final fist gesture after the words "bitter crop" embodies, without judgmental emotion, the pure statement that acts of such cruelty and injustice to mankind must not happen again.

Bonnie observed Pearl as closely as possible in order to see how she moved while watching the dance. "There would be a kind of inner trigger and all of a sudden Pearl's body would jerk. I could see that there were physical memories occurring for her as she was going through the dance. They were so real, involuntary, sometimes rhythmic, sometimes a surging of energy as she watched what Michele was doing." This helped Bonnie in her work with Michele after Pearl left.

Bonnie arranged for dance anthropologist David Gere to interview Pearl and prepare a story for the *Los Angeles Times.* Pearl agreed, but then at the last minute said, "I don't want to do the interview. Share the things with him that I sent you." David drove from one end of Los Angeles County to the other, from Malibu to Claremont, not knowing if Pearl would meet with him. In the end she relented, and Gere's article contained a vivid description of her appearance and method:

> At 74, Primus appears so energized in rehearsal that it is easy to imagine her dancing "Strange Fruit" again, right now, on command. At the side of the rehearsal studio at Scripps College in Altadena [*sic*], she sits squarely in the folding chair, shoes off, her body wrapped in volumes of green and maroon African textiles that make her small form seem larger than it is. Only the gnarled hands with which she directs dancer Michele Simmons convey any sense of age or infirmity.
>
> "You have to 'earth' that run more," she exhorts Simmons, who is struggling not only to learn the steps from a videotaped performance by Kim Y. Bears, a dancer with the Philadelphia-based Philadanco dance company, but to anchor them with the firm grounded quality Primus prefers. (Etymologists take note: Primus may be the only choreographer in America to use earth as a verb.). . . .
>
> "I didn't create 'Strange Fruit' for a dancer," she explains. "I created it to make a statement within our society, within our world. And therefore, it was made with my body. When I danced it, I wasn't a male or female. I wasn't the wind. I wasn't a tree. I was a concept."[3]

For Pearl, art needed to come from the place where the song, the history, the movement, the dance all become one. Of the final last circling run in "Strange Fruit," Pearl told Michele, "As you come up, it's not just flinging the arms up as the run begins, it's almost as if you're gathering the consciousness of mankind. You're gathering up everything in order to make that last final pull down gesture that this injustice must never be repeated."

Pearl told Michele that in the last, excruciating run at the end, "You are saying to the audience, 'This is on you, this is on me and, what have we done?'" Michele said:

So when I went to perform it downstage left and made that run, at that point it was a lynching, but Bosnia and Herzegovina was there, the Holocaust was there, every horrible thing that human beings have done to each other on this planet. . . . It bothered me terribly that Muslim women were being raped. . . . Buchenwald, the death camps, all of that. Lynching, too. . . . That's what made it become so deeply, deeply, deeply real to me.

At the end of the rehearsal period Pearl asked Bonnie to work with Michele and send her a tape. When she sent it in March, Pearl called and blew up, saying that she couldn't let them perform it because what Michele was doing was "not it," but after speaking with them and Donald McKayle she calmed down and allowed them to continue. Michele thought Pearl was like Martha Graham in her "specialness and profundity . . . cut from the same oak." "These artists created work on and through their own bodies, not imagining that other dancers would perform them," she observed.

Michele taught "Strange Fruit" to one other dancer, Lorraine Fields, transmitting the energy of the dance as Pearl had given it to her. As she taught, she felt Pearl's presence, "one of the queens, the queen of black modern dance."

ELEVEN

Barbados: Return to the Sea

IN HER LAST DECADE concern for her legacy was only one level of Pearl's consciousness. Just before the start of her 1984 teaching appointment in Amherst, she made her first trip to Barbados, a journey that signified a return to her roots, for in the practices of the Spiritual Baptist Church she rediscovered elements of her West Indian heritage, and in the Barbados Dance Theatre Company she revitalized her link to Caribbean and African dance traditions. As her journey to Africa embodied a first transformational experience, the immersion in the Spiritual Baptist Church provided a final location, more important to her than a literal return to Trinidad, for her experience of authenticity. Barbados, the church, and the archbishop Granville Williams—place, practice, and exalted person—converged to offer her a sense of wholeness and peace.

Mary Waithe was a bridge for Pearl between New York and Barbados. Although Mary had moved back to Barbados in 1982, she and Pearl had stayed in close touch and spoke often. In the early 1980s, Mary had returned to New York annually to perform with Pearl, and she presented Pearl's work at the dedication of the Errol Barrow Centre for Creative Imagination at the University of the West Indies, lecturing and teaching "Fanga." Later, in 1993, Mary restaged "The Wedding" for the Barbados Dance Theatre Company's twenty-fifth anniversary. After Pearl died, she worked in Brooklyn with Trinidadian Cheryl Byron, another of Pearl's spiritual and artistic heirs, and Michael Manswell, and their African-Caribbean company, Something Positive, with its unique blend of poetry, storytelling, theater, music, and dance, to create a celebration of Pearl's life and work.

Mary planned and coordinated Pearl's first trip to Barbados in association with the Barbados Dance Theatre Company. Hetty Atkinson, the artistic director, encouraged the visit to the church and a meeting with Bishop Williams. Pearl's encounter with the bishop and his church was as powerful an experience as any she had had when she first went to Africa. The sense of revelation is evident in an article she wrote for a thirtieth anniversary magazine celebrating the Spiritual Baptist Church.

> No one had prepared me. I was without any knowledge of what my eyes would see . . . my ears hear . . . my inner being feel. That Sunday night in August 1984 I did not go as the professor or the researcher not even the visitor. I arrived prepared to merely show my respect by honouring an invitation. I had reluctantly planned to stay just ten minutes. . . .
>
> The vehicle carrying us stopped a little past the side of the church. The voices lifted in chant bridged the space between earth and sky . . . bridged across the roaring ocean. Suddenly I was in Africa!!
>
> The chanting drew us in. Like a magnet of majestic sound it drew us in. I thought I had returned to a specific church in western Nigeria near the boundary of the Republic of Benin [Dahomey]. The worshippers were testifying with great emotional intensity, reaffirming their belief in the power of prayer, crying out their dreams and visions. They were telling of their perilous soul journey.
>
> Image upon image crowded the retina of my eyes but clear in my vision was the Leader of the people, a man of tremendous spiritual strength. I accused myself of dreaming. Was this not my brother, Chief Ajanaku, Araba of Lagos? Was this not one of my uncles, the Timi of Ede or Akensua of Benin, Nigeria? Bishop Granville Williams sat in a chair down from the altar. His flowing garments reminded me of descriptions of the great kings of Africa.[1]

Pearl idealized the bishop, and found in him someone who would dignify her in return during her later years. They were swept up in mutual admiration, and in her typical way, Pearl immediately sought to transmit a profound personal discovery to her other worlds, "to explain this church to scholars, to believers and non-believers." Her spiritual quest also became an anthropological project.

Pearl returned again to Barbados four times between 1984 and 1993. On her first trip, she was accompanied by Joyce Knight, her personal assistant, Ethel Allen, a close friend from Buffalo days, the photographer Stan Sherer, and Onwin. She had asked Mary to arrange for her to meet the famous Barbadian writer and kindred spirit George Lamming at the Atlantis Hotel. But most of her time was spent tutoring those who would be the ultimate inheritors of her mantle, neither famous writers nor superstars of the dance world, nor the luminaries of academia, but students who would honor and continue her work. In Barbados she taught Louis and Veleria Ramos, who had been Percy's students, and she encouraged Cheryl Byron, fellow Trinidadian and spiritual daughter, to participate in the Mourning Ground, a ceremony of symbolic death and rebirth, at the church. She sat by the sea with her beloved Baba, the archbishop, who became her spiritual guide and teacher, brother and father, dear friend. Barbados was a place of nourishment and ease where she found community and was well cared for, loved, and respected.

Veleria and Louis Ramos became Pearl's "children" and accompanied her to Barbados in 1985 and 1993. On their first trip, Louis and Veleria, Ethel Allen, a woman named Michele from the Five College area, and Regina Bruckner composed the Barbados Study Group. They lived together at the Banyan Court complex, where Barbadians prepared their meals and drove them from place to place. They would go to the church daily, staying for several hours at a time, getting to know congregants. They visited community centers to watch dances and became involved with community projects. Immersed in the culture, they were taught to observe and participate from an anthropologist's as well a dancer's perspective. At the church, Pearl would say, "Do you see that?" and "she would move just a little bit and we would all just move," Valeria remembered. The next time they visited they would see it again, as their eyes and bodies were entrained to the movement.

They met with Pearl daily for a dance class and lecture, and then had another class with a member of the Barbados Dance Theatre, where Pearl also taught a two-week workshop that was attended by people from different parts of the world. Onwin held percussion workshops, as did other prominent drummers on the island. Sheron Trotman, a young dancer in this workshop, remembers that "it wasn't just about the dance, but about the full experience of life." She recalled how Pearl responded to the African aspects of life in Barbados, the "calm yet vibrant energy, the layout of the land, and the weather patterns." Pearl's teaching coincided with the increasingly strong Pan-African Movement in the West Indies. Almost sixty years after Pearl's first trip to Africa, her student Sheron would be praised for having "assimilated the reconnection to the Motherland" at the Season of Emancipation 2006 at Queen's Park, Barbados. Sheron continues to carry on Pearl's work in her studio, Dance Strides Barbados.

Each day, Pearl would have Veleria and Louis working on different dances or meeting people in different places. She taught them her technique but, equally importantly, she recounted in great detail how to teach it, "how to study a dance that people may not think of as dance." By this time, the Spiritual Baptist Church (also called the "Shouters") had begun to embrace its Africanness more fully, and Pearl included the rhythmic movements of the congregation in her teaching. She also saw to it that the members of the group were guests of the Barbadian government, which meant invitations to theater, dinners, and meetings with dignitaries from the British Consulate.

The August 1985 trip overlapped with the fourth New World Festival of African Diaspora Conference, organized by Richard Long, professor emeritus at Emory University, author of *The Black Tradition in American Dance*,[2] and one of the most important historians of African American culture in the Americas. Pearl was setting "The Wedding" on the Barbados Dance Theatre Company, and Long was able to schedule a performance and a lecture demonstration at the conference, where many distinguished artists and educators were in attendance, including John Ross, who was from the Elma Lewis School of Fine Arts in Roxbury (a section of Boston), and Mattiwilda Dobbs, an internationally renowned opera star. There were local dances and exhibits at local galleries. The New World Festival coincided with Cropover, Barbados's arts festival and its answer to the Carnival celebrations of other Caribbean islands. Long thought that Pearl would have felt more comfortable with the Barbadian celebration than with the more unruly Trinidadian Carnival. "Carnival is very raucous," he said. "Cropover is in no sense a carnival where everyone participates. For Cropover, people sit in a stadium and observe."

Richard Long and Pearl had met long ago in 1947, but this trip to Barbados was the first time they were frequently together, seeing each other every day and taking trips to the countryside. From then on, they would see each other regularly, and during her trips to Spelman College Pearl would often visit Richard.

On the third trip to Barbados, in 1987, there was a still more familial atmosphere, and "she was always the mother, very giving, playful—like a little girl," said Valeria. One beautiful day, when they were in the car, "I Want to Know What Love Is" came on the radio, and Pearl was "really into this song, singing and smiling, looking out the window, looking out and up at the sky. It was so lovely. We just knew it was a precious moment, and I felt then that the sadness and the mourning had lifted from her life." Then Pearl said, "Let's go get ice cream!" Louis recalled. This was the "just folk" side of Pearl, the side that got gossipy news from the tabloids at the grocery checkout and that could cry as she sang along to soft rock.

Rejuvenating visits to Barbados were only one facet of Pearl's quest in the 1980s and early 1990s. As always when she was most at peace with herself, she was busily interweaving her worlds of recent years—Buffalo, Amherst, Barbados, and, always, New York. She wanted to develop an exchange between the Five College Dance Department and the Barbados Dance Theatre Company, and to host the bishop on his first trip to the United States. She was exuberant about bringing Murray Schwartz and the bishop together, and one heard in many conversations that "the bishop, the bishop, the bishop, is coming!"

Pearl planned thoroughly for the bishop's visit. Once she had support from the Five Colleges' black studies departments and had added nominal support from the Pearl Primus Dance Language Institute, she convinced American Airlines to provide a plane ticket between Barbados and New

York. The bishop arrived on April 8, 1986, and was welcomed by "family"— Onwin, Ethel Allen, and Joyce Knight. It seemed to her close friends that, at some level, Pearl was also seeking to unify the black and white in her ancestry, the Ashanti and German-Jewish grandfathers. She was an African queen, yet she had often sought the support of Jewish men. In these years, Pearl's African self lived most fully in the Barbadian church, where the religious practice was Africanist in nature, but one of her happiest moments was when she finally brought Granville Williams to our living room. Her inner world was at one.

The bishop stayed in the States until May 26, a detailed itinerary mapped out each day, with classes and lectures, receptions, visits to historical sites, church services, dinners, radio interviews, tours, theater performances, and shopping excursions filling his days. The first few days were spent in the Five College area, where he attended a lecture at UMass on "African History" by Dr. Femi Richards and Pearl, and then was honored at the New Africa House Augusta Savage Gallery, where he spoke on Barbadian folklore. He spoke on the Cropover Festival at Smith College in the President's Lecture Series, his talk titled, "Bridges to Pluralism." Marjorie Senechal said he "told Bible stories as if these things were taking place right there in the fields of Barbados. He made those stories come alive. He was a great preacher."

Pearl introduced the handsome, self-possessed, and courtly bishop to many faculty members and administrators, and from Amherst he was taken to Boston, where he attended services at the Pillar of Fire Church in Roxbury, and was scheduled to meet Maya Angelou. The whirlwind continued in New York, where he visited cultural, historical, and educational sites throughout the city, including the Bronx Zoo. Then on to Buffalo and Niagara Falls, and back to Boston and the Five Colleges. He met Drs. Molefi Asante and Kariamu Asante of Temple University, friends from Pearl's Buffalo days, and went on to Washington, D.C., where he visited the White House, various memorials, and Howard University. Pearl worked hard to help him establish a base of support for his Africanist spiritual practice in the northeast, an outgrowth of her interweaving of elements of African, West Indian, and American black cultures.

The bishop returned to the Valley a second time in the fall of 1988 and stayed with Pearl's friends Stan Sherer and Marjorie Senechal for a month. His followers took care of him, and Marjorie said they "took over the house." Her daughter came in one day and asked, "Mom, who are those people singing hymns to Jesus in the kitchen?" His followers, who came from New York and Boston, called him "My lord, my lord." For the bishop's part, he told Pearl that he was convinced Marjorie and Pearl were men, because professional women had to be men.

Pearl told Marjorie that the bishop felt he had "proprietary rights on all the women in his congregation, and that he exercised them, too." Meanwhile, Pearl became a "Mother of the Church," and it was clear to others that she and the bishop loved and respected each other. Valeria Ramos observed that one time when they went out to dinner, underneath all her African clothing, "Mna had on black stockings with a leopard on them! What kind of love, who can say. We never saw any disrespect for his wife, but obviously they were simpatico."

In March 1988 Pearl tried to organize the summer travels for Barbados yet again. She invited sixteen people to accompany her from July 29 to August 12. But money was short and this trip did not happen. On August 14, Pearl wrote the archbishop, addressing him as "My dear Brother Granville" and expressing great sadness. "The butterfly is grounded this summer but at least I can spend time with Marjorie, Joyce and my dogs and birds and plants. I am writing a great deal and am trying to get myself together for this coming semester." She wrote that she looks forward to seeing him in the fall at the opening of Stan Sherer's photography exhibit at UMass of his photos of the bishop's elevation to archbishop. In a sentence that is in retrospect a bit eerie, she wrote, "Folks up here are worried that I'll die because I cannot get to Barbados for the Ceremony of Mourning this year [the first time in five years]. Only your presence up here in October will save me. . . ." She finished by saying, "Excuse me for not being my bubbly self. I am seriously trying to wean my heart from a certain tiny island in the Caribbean Sea. Love, Omowale." At the bottom of the page is a drawing of a crying face with a halo and tears.

Pearl next turned her prodigious energy to organizing the photo exhibit at the Augusta Savage Art Gallery, in the New Africa House. Stan proceeded to print, mat and frame photos, and Pearl went into overdrive to bring people up from Barbados for the opening. Pearl invited Dr. Ezra Griffith of Yale University to speak and extended a formal invitation to the archbishop. On September 29, 1988, a press release announced the archbishop's visit and the opening of the exhibit, "Journey into the Soul: The Spiritual Baptists of Barbados, West Indies."

Pearl kept up her pace of teaching and planning for several more years, but by December 1993 she was rapidly losing weight, and by the summer of 1994 she was losing her energy, too. On July 29 she wrote to Douglas Sontag, then head of the National Endowment for the Arts, to explain why she had to postpone a videotaped interview with James Murray at the Schomburg Library, telling him that she had fallen while in California at UC Davis. "I thought my right knee, hip and elbow were going to crumble," she wrote. Apparently some members of the audience didn't realize she was falling, as "they had never seen anything so graceful." But back in New York, she realized how traumatic the fall was and she spent June and July in bed, unable to complete the project. She asked Sontag for an extension until the end of August, and told him how anxious she was to finish the oral history project. James Murray offered to film it at her home, wherever and whenever she could manage to be available. The first long interview is comprehensive, covering her early years and her start in dance, but the second interview, about the Africa years and beyond, never took place.

While in Davis, California, Pearl visited with her old friend Eva Koonan Zirker and her husband, Joe, and, back home on August 5, 1994, she dictated a letter describing her condition. The letter ends, "May the ancestors help us." It is signed by Joyce as Pearl's secretary, giving Pearl's title, adjunct professor of dance, on NYU letterhead. How Pearl cherished her academic appointments!

In the fall of 1994 Pearl was teaching a course at NYU, and she asked Cheryl Byron and Michael Manswell to bring members of Something Positive to perform "Ancestral Chant" for her class. Pearl had tried to keep her illness and decline hidden from close friends, but the word had begun to spread. Cheryl and Michael were distressed by her condition; she was weak and thin. After the class she had difficulty standing, and her student assistant's husband carried her to the door of the room, where she leaned on Michael as he led her to a waiting car. Cheryl saw her once more after this, when she went to New Rochelle to visit and braid Pearl's hair. She described Pearl's state as one of "lassitude." Pearl said to Cheryl, "Daughter, your Mna is really tired and I don't have the strength to plow another field. I want you to lay down a bank of prayers for me."

Pearl developed excruciating pain in her feet at the end, ironic for one so connected to the earth. On Peggy's last visit, Pearl had said, "Don't watch me come down the stairs. Go outside. See Percy's peonies." She came down the stairs, leaning heavily on the railing, and sat on a small bench, looking tiny, but never old. When she arrived home, Peggy called her mother and said, "Mom, she's going to lose her feet!" Her mother sagely replied, "She'll never let that happen." Two weeks later she died, on October 29, 1994.

The day before, when Peggy called from New York, Pearl had said, "Yes, call the doctor." But that morning the doctor replied, "Nothing is life-threatening." By Friday at noon she was gone. Pearl died at home in New Rochelle with her trusted companion, Joyce Knight.

We arrived soon after. Joyce had tried to keep us downstairs until Arthur Bart, an old friend and drummer affiliated with the Spiritual Baptists, arrived to cleanse the body and release the spirit, but, unable to wait, we went to her room to find this small being lifeless in her bed, her home overflowing with instruments, costumes, props, plants, stage sets, letters, programs—the backstage to the life she lived in the world. Water Witch—"Doggie," as she called him—was going crazy in the bathroom. Peggy put her hand on Pearl's heart, praying to feel a beat, and then closed her eyes. EMTs arrived and absurdly tried to restart the heart in the little body of this once robust woman. We called Onwin in Florida, and there were a few people he wanted called right away. But we did not want to jeopardize payment of the National Mentor teacher award she had received just that week. That check, cut just a few days before she died, was sent to Onwin.

At the New Rochelle hospital, the doctor said the cause of death was cardiac arrest. Privately, he told us of the appointments she had cancelled with him and her neurologist, refusing further care. We remembered the message from him on our answering machine earlier that fall: "Diabetes. Nothing life threatening for a woman her age." Diabetes. She had never uttered the word.

We had arranged for Onwin to fly to New York from Florida. Ethel Allen had come down from Amherst. Joyce Knight, of course, was there, along with Cheryl Byron. Peggy stayed in the kitchen and, at Onwin's request, made phone calls. First she called Chuck Davis. "The drums will sound tonight," he said. Then Jennifer Dunning at the *New York Times* and Sally Ann Kriegsman at the National Endowment for the Arts, who were stunned by the news. Joyce and Cheryl informed the West Indian community of dancers and drummers. When we returned to Amherst, Peggy called Ethel Allen, Femi Richards, and dance colleagues. The word quickly reached Pearl's many communities.

The funeral was held in Harlem at the Bentha Funeral Home and was presided over by the archbishop Granville Williams, who flew up from Barbados. The small chapel was packed with people who paused before the open casket, where Pearl was laid out bedecked and bejeweled. Then we waited for what seemed like forever until Onwin arrived wearing his boots with jangling spurs and the T-shirt Pearl loved from her last residency at Howard and American Universities: "Pearl Primus—celebrating 50 years." "Everyone leave the chapel," Onwin boomed. We filed out amid lots of murmuring and talking, and were then invited back in. The casket now was closed. Apparently Onwin had wanted the casket closed before the ceremony began, but there had been confusion about whether the casket should be open or closed.

Then the service began. The archbishop spoke, as did Femi Richards on behalf of the University of Massachusetts, and Patricia Rowe, one of Pearl's PhD advisers from NYU. Donald Washington, then general manager of the Alvin Ailey American Dance Theater, a kente cloth scarf thrown around his shoulders, was dashing and articulate. As he evoked Pearl's presence on various occasions, he elaborated the refrain "When Pearl entered, heads turned." Onwin spoke and was quite moving in what he chose to share—how fun-loving his mother was, how she enjoyed going out with friends and laughing, eating, and sipping her ginger ale. She enjoyed just hanging out, "limin'," in good Trinidadian fashion.

Finally, Cheryl Byron's dancers and drummers entered from the rear, circling the chapel before taking their places on the small stage. As they continued to drum, the dancers encouraged everyone present to dance around the perimeter of the chapel and pay their respects one last time. As the energy built up, this became an ecstatic moment, the drums uniting the assembly in support of Pearl's spiritual transition.

At a reception after the service David Hodges and the archbishop implored Onwin not to sell Pearl's priceless collection of artifacts, masks, sculptures, fabrics, and instruments.

The first night after her death, Peggy felt Pearl's presence intensely. The next day, it seemed as if her spirit lingered, and then transitioned through our home in Amherst. Our bedroom light inexplicably became blindingly bright and three telephone lines went dead. The next night two large hanging fuchsias spun wildly on the porch on a windless night. Each time Peggy entered the bedroom, the light was still blindingly bright. In Barbados, years later, in 2003, Peggy sat by the sea with the archbishop and shared her memories with him as best she could. When she got to the part about the plants spinning on the side porch, he said, "They became active?" Peggy described them spinning on that windless night. He said, "These things happen," and nodded, listening intently, hands clasped in his lap. When Peggy finished her story, he said, "She called you as an ancestor." And he told her about his profound sadness when receiving the phone call that Pearl had passed and about his departure for New York, where members of the church in Brooklyn came to comfort him. Then he sat lost in thought.

The following year Onwin called his friend Margaret Goodfellow to tell her he wanted her and Joyce to go to Barbados with him to scatter Pearl's ashes. Cheryl had wanted the ashes scattered close to the water's edge. She had a vivid memory from her last trip with Pearl, who bathed with a calabash, just at the edge, where the land meets the sea. Pearl's Orisha was Yemenja, Yoruba goddess of the ocean. She had a healthy respect for the power of the sea and would bathe close to the shore. "Why so far out?" she would say when Louis and Onwin would go out into the water. Cheryl wanted the ashes scattered where the water meets the earth to honor what she perceived as Pearl's duality, an earthiness balancing her water self.

But Pearl's ashes were actually scattered at sea by the archbishop, at the easternmost tip of the island. The archbishop knew that there is a place out at sea on the Atlantic side of the island where the currents cross from the Caribbean to the ocean and go east to Africa. The small group piled into a boat and motored about three miles out. He said, "This is the place." The ashes were released and formed themselves in a straight line—pointing straight to Africa.

Acknowledgments

This book could not have been written without the cooperation and support of very many people who loved Pearl Primus and cared about her legacy. First and foremost are the scores of her relatives, friends, and colleagues who agreed to be interviewed by Peggy. We are grateful to each of them for their willingness to share memories, personal experiences, documents, photos, and videos. All of those interviewed are listed separately, but a few deserve our special gratitude. The late and beloved Joe Nash always had a new story to tell, a photo to share, a book with information in it, or someone else for Peggy to meet. Others who have passed—Onwin Borde, Virginia Primus, and Yael Woll—contributed essential accounts of aspects of Pearl's life that would otherwise be lost to time. Cheryl Borde, Bob Henry, and Mary Waithe facilitated important interviews in Trinidad and Barbados and provided generous guidance and support on those important trips. Many of Pearl's students and close friends gave selflessly of their time and energy, often responding to urgent e-mail requests for details and fact checks. Among them, we want to give special thanks to Rashida Ismaili AbuBakr, Kim Bears-Bailey, "Baba" Chuck Davis, John "Tunisi" Davis, Lynn Frederiksen, Louis and Valeria Ramos, Mozel Spriggs, Eva Zirker, and, again, Mary Waithe. Thanks to Tunisi Davis for making available precious films of Pearl in performance at Riverside Church, and to Eric Charry and G. "Sule" Wilson for sharing their knowledge of drummer lineage. Thanks also to Davis Lacey for sharing his research as he prepared *Free to Dance* for PBS.

We thank Debra Elfenbein, former archivist at the American Dance Festival Archives, for her instruction in the mysterious ways of libraries and archives, and Dean Jeffrey, the current archivist, for his readiness to search for materials, and especially for his help in locating photos. Thanks also to Steve Siegal at the 92nd Street Y archive, Alison Quammie at the Schomburg Center for Research in Black Culture, and Pam Juengling, Music Librarian at the University of Massachusetts Amherst for their ready assistance in finding reviews.

Thanks to Pearl's friends Marjorie and Stan Sherer for their wise advice, and a very special thank-you to Stan for devoting endless hours to the preparation of a photo essay that brings Pearl's life into visual focus. We are grateful to our daughter Larissa Schwartz for helping to select photos and for wrestling the chronology of Pearl's work into a logical format. A special thanks also to Jerome Leibling for his keen opinions of the photos. Thanks to Jawole Willa Jo Zollar for celebrating Pearl's life and bringing it back to the concert stage, to Ade Bayou (aka William Middleton) for his dedication to the residencies in the Five College Dance Department and at New York State Summer School of the Arts, and to Carolyn Adams and Julie Strandberg for their vision in bringing Pearl's work back into schools through the American Dance Legacy Institute's Etude Project. Thank you to Marilyn and Sekou Sylla for creating an exuberant presence of West African dance in the Five College Dance Department and for all colleagues in the FCDD for their belief in the vitality of this work. Marcy Thorne and her crew at A Better Type spent endless hours transcribing interviews. Jack Begleiter saved critical material from a crashed computer. Gemze de Lappe and Vickie Hamilton graciously allowed Peggy to use their lovely apartments for interviews, and Bonnie Oda Homsey hosted us while interviewing in Los Angeles. Karen Hildebrand at "Dance Teacher" helped with citations. Bobby Shepard encouraged us to ask difficult questions about race. Kane Stewart provided photos and scanning. Each of them deserves our heartfelt thanks.

Friends and colleagues offered valuable advice, insight, and support at every step of the way, especially Billbob Brown, Jacquie Davis, Paul Dennis, Jennifer Glossop, Constance Valis Hill, Cathy Hutchinson, Mary Lou Laurenza, Becky Nordstrom, Naima Prevots, Darwin Prioleau, Amilcar Shabazz, Dawn Skorczewski, Ekwueme Michael Thelwell, Betty Thurston, Tom Vacanti, Missy Vineyard and Tom Ehrghood, Judy Wideman, and Wendy Woodson and Eric Poggenpohl.

We thank David Kerr and Leslie Mason for introducing us to the lovely island of Vieques, where so much of the writing happened, and for the keys to Casa Alta Mira and their trusty Trooper.

We are grateful to the University of Massachusetts Amherst and to Emerson College for approving simultaneous sabbatical leaves during the spring of 2008, and Peggy thanks the UMass Book Subvention Award Program for a grant in 2010 to help with photo publication. Peggy thanks Dean of Humanities and Fine Arts Lee Edwards and Music and Dance Chair T. Dennis "Denny" Brown for time assigned to writing in 2005–2006, and Dean of Humanities and Fine Arts Joel Martin and Chair of Music and Dance Jeff Cox for continued support. Murray thanks Chair of Writing, Literature and Publishing Daniel Tobin and his colleagues Pamela Painter, Ladette Randolph, and Frederick Reiken for their encouragement and counsel. For belief in the importance of this work and for support for research, Peggy extends a special thank-you to Jody Arnhold and Diane Troderman.

We are very grateful to Ileene Smith for her expert editorial guidance. She improved our text immeasurably from beginning to end. We also thank Sarah Miller, associate editor, for fielding our many questions throughout the production process, and Jeffrey Schier, senior manuscript editor, for his detailed and thoughtful line-by-line text edit.

Throughout the long journey that led to this biography, we have had the loving support and enduring faith of our family, Larissa Schwartz, Joanna and Clay Ballantine, and Jena and Greg Strong, grandchildren Hannah, Caleb, Aviva, and Pearl, and extended families, all cheering us on.

Sustained collaborations are rarely easy, even when they are built on the solid foundation of a long marriage. The most vital force has been our faith in one another, and we each thank the other for hanging in through thick and thin—for our long morning walks talking about Pearl, for the long days facing each other from behind our computers, writing, editing, and passing files up and back, and for sharing a quiet space of deepest concentration for hours and days on end, a gift of Pearl to us.

1919

Pearl Eileene Primus was born in Port of Spain, Trinidad, to Emily Albertha and Edward Onwin. Her mother's heritage was Ashanti. She had a German-Jewish grandfather on her father's side.

1921

With her mother and her brother Edward, Primus moved to the United States to join her father, who had already emigrated to New York.

1920s–early 1930s

Primus attended Public Schools 94 and 136 in New York City.

1933–1937

Primus attended Hunter College High School.

1937–1940

Primus attended Hunter College and received a BA in biology and pre-medicine. She aspired to be a physician.

1940–42

Primus did graduate work in health education at New York University, and in May 1941 transferred to the Hunter College graduate psychology program. In 1941, she was also employed by the National Youth Administration, a Works Progress Administration (WPA) project, and understudied for a part in "American Dances," which was performed at the World's Fair. It was during this period that she met Joe Nash. During 1941 and 1942 she was a scholarship student at the New Dance Group and a counselor at Camp Wo-Chi-Ca. In addition to studying with dance pioneers Martha Graham, Doris Humphrey, Hanya Holm, and Charles Weidman, she was trained in classical and preclassical dance forms by Louis Horst. The teachers she credits with shaping her destiny as a dancer were Jane Dudley, Sophie Maslow, Nona Schurman, Eve Gentry, Margo Mayo, Beryl McBurnie, and Olga Kubitsky. On May 11, 1941, she performed in "Authentic Dances" and "First Shine" in a New Dance Group Festival Program of American Dances at the Heckscher Theater. In 1942 she first performed in Beryl McBurnie's (aka Belle Rosette) *Antilliana.* She created a new choreography, "Hear the Lamb A-Crying," based on a spiritual.

1943

On January 8 and 9 Primus performed again in *Antilliana,* at the Baltimore Museum of Art. *Antilliana* addresses the history of the West Indies and the

253

mix of cultures in the region from 1492 onward, including Spanish, French, English, and African. The program said, "The Shango, Voodoo, Plavoodoo, Rhada, and Bongo are the best known among the African dances, and are practiced in the backwoods of the country, away from the cynical eye. They are danced to the accompaniment of drums and generally take the form of rituals, expressing long suffering and sacrifice. The Beguine, Belle Air, Meringue and Rondo are popular among the French. In a lighter vein than the African, they are more on the order of country dances, expressing a delightful light-heartedness and gaiety. Spanish waltzes and the Bomba are best known among the Spaniards. The Calypso as an art form is an excellent example of the fusion of racial elements that is so typical of the West Indies." In addition to Pearl Primus and Beryl McBurnie, dancers included Clementine Blunt and Freida McBurnie. Alphonse Cimber and Norman Coco (Coker) were listed as the drummers, and Lionel Belasco as the pianist. Coker was later to become one of Primus's drummers with whom she refined her knowledge of African rhythms.

On February 14 she had her professional premiere at the 92nd Street YMHA (typically shortened to "92nd Street Y") in New York. Her part of this shared concert included, "A Man Has Just Been Lynched," set to the poem "Strange Fruit," by Lewis Allan; "Greetings from South America," with native Brazilian music recorded by Regionale Orchestra under the direction of Leopold Stokowski; "African Ceremonial," with the music "Conga Kongo," recorded by Thurston Knudson; "Hard Time Blues," with Josh White on the guitar, and "Rock! Daniel," with Sister Rosetta Tharpe, the vocalist with the Lucky Millinder band. Mary Ann Cousins was the percussionist for this concert and Horton Foote the narrator. Also on the program were Nona Schurman, Iris Mabry, Julia Levien, and Gertrude Prokosch.

In the spring Primus was performing at the Stage Door Canteen and Music Box Canteen, nightclubs for members of the armed forces. On May 2 she appeared at a "Labor for Victory Rally" at Yankee Stadium, at which Paul Robeson sang. On June 7, she performed at the first Negro Freedom Rally at Madison Square Garden, which included Paul Robeson, Canada Lee, and Duke Ellington, among others. On August 1, she received the Dance Laurel Award No. 2, presented by John Martin of the *New York Times*. In October she performed at the "All Star Victory Rally" in the Golden Gate Ballroom, New York, organized by the African American bandleader Teddy Wilson. Participants included Coleman Hawkins, Hazel Scott, Billie Holliday, Mary Lou Williams, and Ella Fitzgerald. On December 12 she performed as a soloist at Carnegie

Hall with Asadata Dafora in an "African Dance Festival," sponsored by African Academy of Arts and Research and attended by the First Lady, Eleanor Roosevelt. She performed at the Ziegfeld Theatre in a benefit performance for the Spanish Relief Appeal and, in April, began a nine-month run at Café Society Downtown, the first dancer to be hired at this location. Her acclaim was such that a photograph appeared in *Life* magazine. At this time she was also working toward a master's degree in psychology at Hunter College and studying pedagogy as well as creative writing. In New York City she received the Alpha Kappa Alpha scholarship award for original poetry. Other dances performed in 1943 included: "Jim Crow Train" (alternately titled "Freedom Train"), to a Langston Hughes work titled "Freedom Train," with music by Woody Guthrie; "Motherless Child" to a spiritual; "Folk Dance"; "Bambare"; "Conga"; "Calypso"; and "Chamber of Tears" to a poem of her own.

1944

Primus continued to perform at Café Society through January and February.

On January 23 she performed at the 92nd Street Y, sharing a concert with Valerie Bettis. She used the format of this concert for the next few years. The first section was called "Primitives," and included "African Ceremonial," a drum solo, and "Yanvaloo," described in a program note as an "Interpretation of Haitian Voodoo Ritual in honor of Dambala, Chief of Gods. His symbol is the snake. Worshippers possessed with this spirit take on the movements of a serpent." Also "Drum Interlude" and "Haitian Play Dance." The next untitled grouping included "The Negro Speaks of Rivers" (quoting Langston Hughes's poem: "I have known rivers—ancient as the world and deeper than the flow of human blood in human veins. My soul has grown deep like the rivers . . ."), "Study in Blues," with music by Mary Lou Williams, and "Strange Fruit." Gordon Heath read for "Rivers" and "Strange Fruit." The last grouping, also untitled, included ""Rock Daniel" (to which she added a program note, "A lesson in jazz"), "Hard Time Blues," and "Our Spring Will Come," accompanied by John Cage. She included a quote from a Langston Hughes poem: "The pent up snows of all the brutal years are melting beneath the rising sun of Freedom." The drummers were Alphonse Cimber and Norman Koker (Coker); costumes for "Ceremonial" and "Study in Blues" were created by I. Eisenstot, and for "Yanvaloo" by Charlotte Trowbridge. "Negro Speaks of Rivers" and "Our Spring Will Come"—Sylvia Thumin, designer, executed by Mrs. Hatfield.

In February her photo appeared on the cover of *Dance Observer*. Additional performances included an April 22 solo at the Y, with familiar pieces, and her first appearance in Chicago on May 29 at the Americans All Rally for Victory and Security, presented by the Midwest District of the International Workers Order and which included Matija Gubec Choral Society; "Partizanka," song of the Yugoslav partisans; Jewish Peoples Choral Society; and the Monumental Baptist Church Choir. She performed at Hunter College on June 1, a concert billed as "Dance Recital, Pearl Primus, American's Foremost Negro Dancer," and at New York Times Hall on June 14–16 in a New Dance Group Festival, in which she performed "Shouters."

In the summer of 1944 she visited rural black communities in southern states, including Georgia, Alabama, and South Carolina, to research African traditions in black church services as well as the conditions of black American farm workers. Her political activism continued with an appearance on September 28 at a Madison Square Garden rally celebrating the twenty-fifth anniversary of the Communist movement in America, at which Earl Browder was the featured speaker.

On October 4–14 she made her Broadway debut at the Belasco Theater on Forty-fourth Street. Presented by Max J. Jelin, the program was similar to the January 23 program. It included: "African Ceremonial"; "Afro-Haitian Play Dance," with Thomas Bell; "Drum Conversation," with Alphonse Cimber and Norman Koker (elsewhere spelled "Coker"); "Agu—Dance of Strength," performed by soloist Prince Camadea with Thomas Bell, Albert Popwell, and James Alexander; and "Yanvaloo," with singer Leon Destine. Charlotte Trowbridge created the costumes for "Yanvaloo." The second act included "Negro Speaks of Rivers," with pianist Sarah Malament; "Slave Market," with a poem read by Owen Dodson; and the song "Steal Away," sung by Alice Moss. The program read, "On my back they've written history, Lord/In my back they've lashed out hell." "Strange Fruit," with costumes by Edythe Gilfond, closed act II. Act III included "Our Spring Will Come," with costumes by Sylvia Thumin; "Study in Nothing," with John Cage performing percussion; "Improvisation," with music by Frankie Newton and his band; "Mischievous Interlude," performed by Primus and Albert Popwell; "Hard Time Blues"; and "Rock Daniel," with Luckie Millinder's music played by Frankie Newton. Gordon Heath was the narrator for this concert.

Later that fall, November 29–December 23, "Pearl Primus and Company" performed at the Roxy Theatre. Primus rechoreographed "African Ceremonial" for fourteen dancers. Additionally, the Dance Teachers Advisory Committee presented "Pearl Primus in Concert," her first solo concert (Louis Horst was chairman of the committee, which included Bessie Schoenburg,

Murial Stuart, Anita Zahn, Barbara Page, Eugene Schein, May O'Donnell, and Ruth Jones). Owen Dodson published a piece in the December issue of *Theatre Arts* entitled, "Pearl Primus." She received a Certificate of Merit from the USO for dancing in army camps, hospitals, and at ports of embarkation, and she was presented by the Citizens Committee of Upper West Side in "Pearl Primus in Concert." The title "Dark Rhythms" was introduced and used sometimes for lecture-demonstrations, sometimes for parts of concerts, and sometimes to describe a whole concert.

Other dances performed in 1944 included: "Slave Market," "The Hypocrite," "Good Night Irene," "Take This Hammer," "Mischievous Interlude," "Wade in the Water," "Gonna Tell God All My Troubles," "Americana Suite," "'Tis me, 'Tis me, Oh Lord," "Bala Conga," and "Great Getting Up Mornin'."

1945

The year began with Primus performing on January 11 at Times Hall with the dancer Hadassah and Haitian singer Josephine Premice. She performed "African Ceremonial," "Yanvaloo," and "Play Dance." On January 23, she performed at the Soldiers & Sailors' War Memorial Building in Trenton, New Jersey. Pieces not listed on earlier concert programs included: (Act I) "Primitives," "Dance of Thanksgiving," "Hawaiian Duet," "AfroHaitian Conga," and "Play Dance"; (Act II) Spirituals and "Songs of Protest" included "Lost," a solo for herself. The program note read, "A new slave in a new country—always groping—always trying to find a way out." "Certainly Lord" was performed by Thomas Bell, Edith Hurd, Alma Robinson, and Remitha Spurlock. The program note read, "Religion becomes the outlet of the slave's frustrations." The program note for "Steal Away" was "Tribute to clear thinking leadership of slave revolts who cleverly used religious songs as protective covering for their real messages." "Wade in the Water" was performed by Thomas Bell, Alma Forrest, Edith Hurd, Curtis James, Richard James, Albert Popwell, Alma Robinson, Remitha Spurlock, and Alma Sutton. Program note read, "Depicting strength of unity against surging waves of discrimination, abated only by group action." Act III included "American Folk Dance," performed by Thomas Bell, Alma Forrest, Edith Hurd, Curtis James, Richard James, Albert Popwell, Alma Robinson, and Remitha Spurlock, with music by Woody Guthrie. It also included "Strange Fruit" and "Freedom Train." Woody Guthrie sang, Gordon Heath narrated, Herbert Haris was the percussionist, and musical arrangements were by Hershey Kay. Costumes were executed by Nellie Hatfield, and lighting design was by Jane Rosenthal.

Other concerts in this year included several at the Central High School of Needle Trades, one in February with Charles Weidman and others on March 24, November 4, and November 17. On March 24 the piece called "Lost" was performed. The program note read, "Confusion—a new slave in a new country." The November 4 program was a benefit performance for the ORT Federation, with Charles Weidman at the Central High School of Needle Trades, and included a piece not seen on other programs, "Spinster's Hop," which was part of a Mary Lou Williams/Josh White suite. Also performed were "African Crying Song," "African Stick Song," "Songs of Africa," "Soleil Malade (The Sun Is Sick)," and "Dja oh rele dja." The program note said, "Ceremonial work song which accompanies rhythmic pounding of pestles in the mortar," sung by Helen Tinsley and drums by Alphonse Cimber and Norman Coker.

Primus performed on February 25 at the 92nd Street Y. The program included a piece called "I Know a Secret," which was performed again on November 10.

Pearl's involvement with the New Dance Group grew in scope. She became an instructor at the school, developed an Ethnic Dance Studies course with Jean Erdman and Hadassah, an East and West Indian Dance Program with Hadassah and Josephine Premice, and a lecture-demonstration on African dance and its influence in Haiti and the U.S. South. On June 14–16 she participated in a New Dance Group Festival at New York Times Hall along with Jane Dudley, Sophie Maslow, William Bales Trio, Eva Desca, Jean Erdman, Hadassah, and Lili Mann.

Additional performances and lecture demonstrations took place at the American Museum of Natural History, Irvine Auditorium in Philadelphia, North Carolina College, Settlement Theatre in Pittsburgh, and West Virginia State College. Pearl performed at Hunter College, toured New Jersey and Connecticut under the management of Max Jelin, and launched the Primus Company Cross Country Tour, under the management of Austin Wilder.

She performed a "Zodiac Suite," which included "Twinsome Two Minds," "Just Born," and "Scorpio," as well as a piece called "Mean and Evil."

Her academic interests continued to deepen and she took graduate courses at Columbia University in the PhD program in anthropology, where she studied the folklore and arts of Africa, North and South American Indians, Oceania and the Middle East, and techniques of scientific research. The teachers who influenced her at Columbia and later at New York University included Ruth Benedict, Franz Boas, Ralph Linton, George Herzog, Margaret Mead, Duncan Strong, Paul Wingert, William Sears, Ethel Alpenfels, Dan

Dodson, Gene Weltfish, Charles Wagley, Harry Shapiro, Joseph Greenberg, Elsie Hug, Marion Smith, and Patricia Rowe.

1946

Primus was the featured dancer as Sal and the Dahomey Queen in the revival of *Show Boat* at the Ziegfeld Theatre, which opened on January 5. *Show Boat* featured original choreography of Helen Tamiris, who was assisted by Daniel Nagrin and dance captain Paula Kaye. It closed on January 4, 1947. *Show Boat* was produced by Jerome Kern and Oscar Hammerstein II, with music by Jerome Kern and lyrics by Oscar Hammerstein II. It was staged by Hassard Short, with set design by Howard Bay and costume design by Lucinda Ballard. Additional dancers included Talley Beatty, Marta Becket, Janice Bodenhoff, Eleanor Boleyn, Vivian Cherry, Terry Dawson, Andrea Downing, LaVerne French, Betty Jane Geiskopf, Carol Harriton, Vickie Henderson, Eddie Howland, Elmira Jones-Bey, Paula Kaye, Audrey Keane, Ora Leak, Gerard Leavitt, Olga Lunick, Claude Marchant, William Miller, Nick Nadeau, Joe Nash, Jeanne Reeves, Stanley Simmons, Alma Sutton, Viola Taylor, Yvonne Tibor, William Weber, Henry Wessel, and Francisco Xavier.

On April 14 a performance at the 92nd Street Y included "Chamber of Tears," "No—There Is No Music," "Just a Throbbing in My Veins," "Even Like the Ticking of a Clock," with words by Pearl Primus. From October 4–11 she was featured as the Witch Doctor in "Emperor Jones" at the Chicago Civic Opera at the invitation of Ruth Page, the director of ballet at the Chicago Civic Opera.

A national tour with Joe Nash and Jacqueline Hairston took Primus to the American Museum of Natural History (with Hadassah) (October 17 and November 3, New York), Jordan Hall (November 3, Boston debut), 92nd Street Y (November 10 and 13, New York), Irene Kaufmann Settlement Auditorium (November 13, Pittsburgh), North Carolina College for Negroes (November 15, Durham), West Virginia State College (November 17, Charleston), Winston State Teachers College, (November 18, North Carolina), Irvine Auditorium (November 20, Philadelphia), 92nd Street Y (June 16, New York), Detroit Music Hall (December 29, Michigan), and Cleveland (December 31, Ohio).

The first half of the April 14 program at the Y, "Dark Rhythms," included "African Ceremonial," "Te Moana—The Deep," "Study in African Rhythms," and "Dance of Beauty." Program note: "In the hills of the Belgian Congo lives a tribe of seven-foot people. Their dignity and beauty bespeak an elegant past." "Dance of Strength" followed. Program note: "The dancer beats his muscles to show power. Common in the Sierra Leone region of Africa." Then came "Afro-Haitian Play Dance," Caribbean Conga," "Afro-Cuban Rhythms," and "Myth." Program note: "To-Kabinana dances before the figure he has carved. His passionate intensity brings it to life. Interpretation of the Melanesian Myth of the creation." "Shouters of Sobo" followed. Program note: "The priest appears in the street and by the ringing of a bell, summons the people to the ritual feast prepared in the forest. Chant: Trinidadian." Part II of the program included "To One Dead." Program note: "'Soldier, autumn is here/and in the country/The hills are trembling with color,' with words by Pearl Primus." Then came "Folk Song," "Strange Fruit," "Study in Nothing," "Trio (Statement, Counterstatement, Conflict)," "Mischievous Interlude," and "Hard Time Blues." All choreography was Primus's, and the singers were Helen Tinsley and Gregory Pascal; dancers were Jacqueline Hairston and Joseph Nash; the pianist-composer was Camilla De Leon; narrator was Gregory Pascal; drummers were Frank Aulet, and Harold Azvedo. The lighting design was by Doris Einstein; stage manager was Sturge Steinhert; costume designers were Charles Sebree and Charlotte Trowbridge; and costume execution was by Nellie Hatfield. The technical Director for YM and YWHA was Jock Stockwell.

Other dances performed in this period included "Initiation," "War Dance," "Michael Row the Boat Ashore," "Dance of Beauty," "Legend: Onishagen, Two Women, and Kaito," "Spring Fever," "Witch Dance," "Passage," "Cacao," and "Dance with Rattles."

Primus continued to study at Columbia University in the anthropology PhD program and to teach at the New Dance Group studio. She was also listed in "Who's Who in America."

1947

Primus opened the Pearl Primus School of Primal Dance at 17 West Twenty-fourth Street in New York, and continued her graduate studies at Columbia. She continued to tour with Joe Nash and Jacqueline Hairston, which now took them to Western College (January 8, Oxford, Ohio), Practical Arts High School (January 13, Portland, Maine), Rhode Island School of Design (Providence, January 14), City Hall Auditorium (Portland, Maine, January 16), Jordan Hall (Boston, January 17), Maine (January 13), Central High School of Needle Trades (New York, January 25), and the Metropolitan Opera House (New York, January 26), where they performed after "Fella Figlia Dell Amore" from Verdi's *Rigoletto,* and preceding "Anvil Chorus" from Verdi's *II Trovatore* and "March" from Bizet's *Carmen.* Their repertory included "Welcome

Dance," "Haitian Play Dance," "Caribbean Congo," "Chants and Rhythms of Haiti," "Mischievous Interlude," and "Dance of Strength." Pearl was billed as "the dancing star of *Show Boat.*" The tour continued at Page Hall of the New York State College for Teachers (Albany, February 5), Gary, Indiana (February 7), and Leo Mandel Hall at the University of Chicago, sponsored by American Youth for Democracy (Chicago, February 9).

In August she participated in a performance and staged a student dance recital at the Jacob's Pillow Dance Festival, and in December appeared in *Calypso* in Boston, renamed *Caribbean Carnival* for its New York run, December 5–13. A dance in this show, "Zinge," was based on the Shango deity; "Rookoombay" was also part of the repertory. She performed in New York at the Brooklyn Academy of Music, the Central High School of Needle Trades, and the International Theatre. She also received the Page One Award from the Newspaper Guild of New York.

In this year she also performed "Santos," "The Witch Doctor," and "Shango."

1948

As part of the 92nd Street Y education program, Primus participated in a dance lab run by critic Walter Terry, "Dance as a Social Force." She continued performing extensively. On March 21, at a Dance Observer Benefit at the Y, at which Agnes DeMille served as Mistress of Ceremonies, Primus performed "Santo," with percussionist Alphonse Cimber and singer Helen Tinsley. Other participating artists included Martha Graham; Merce Cunningham with John Cage, pianist; Jane Dudley; William Bales and Sophie Maslow trio; Jean Erdman; Nina Fonaroff and Robert Emmet; Anita Zahn; Hanya Holm workshop group (Mary Anthony, Joan Kruger, Bambi Linn, Annabelle Lyon, Ray Harrison, Oliver Kostock, Alwin Nikolais, and Glen Tetley); José Limón; Iris Mabry; and Anna Sokolow.

On April 8 she performed at Smith College (Northampton, Massachusetts) with singer Helen Tinsley, dancer Lily Peace, pianist Renee Cutler, and drummer Alphonse Cimber. Joe Harvard was the stage manager. April 10 she performed at the Central High School of Needle Trades in New York. The first half of the program was her traditional "Dark Rhythms" format. Additional titles in the second half included "Primitive Pastel," danced by Primus and Company, with music by Camilla De Leon. The program note described it as a "mood piece." "Another Man Done Gone" was danced by Lily Peace, Romenia McDaniels, and Jeanne Greenidge, and "Waltz Boogie" was danced by Matt Turney, Jeanne Greenidge, and Romenia McDaniels, with music by

Mary Lou Williams. April 11 took her back to the 92nd Street Y and April 22 to the American Museum of Natural History as part of the "Around the World with Dance and Song" series. An additional title for this performance was the solo "Snatches of Calypso."

On April 28 she performed at Fisk University, where she received the Julius Rosenwald Fellowship for Research and Study in West and Central Africa. Also in April she performed at the University of Illinois, and May 23 and 25 at the Mansfield Theater with New Dance Group Artists she performed similar "Dark Rhythms" programs. Additional titles included "Tamboule" ("Stick Dance"), which was danced by Padjet Fredricks. The program note states, "The dancer challenges an imaginary foe" and informs the audience that this piece originates on the west coast of Africa. "Another Man Done Gone" was danced by Lily Peace and Padjet Fredricks, as was "Scorpio," with music, "Signs of the Zodiac," by Mary Lou Williams. The program note for "Scorpio" was "Fatal Fascination." An additional piece was "Jungle Fantasy," with music by Esy Morales. On the May 23 and May 25 programs at the Mansfield Theater, the section called "Spirituals" included "Motherless Child," "Gonna Tell God All My Troubles" (with Lillie Peace and Padjet Fredericks), and "Great Getting Up Mornin'." The pianist was Camilla de Leon, singer Helen Tinsley, drummer Norman Koker (Coker), and costumes by Charles Seebree. The "Songs of Protest" included "Another Man Done Gone." This program also included "Shouters of Sobo," (to a Trinidadian chant), "Santo" was performed on May 25 with the program note that this was "conflict between old patterns and new (Afro-Cuban)."

On July 29 the company performed "Dark Rhythms" at Howard University in Washington, D.C. Yael Woll was the narrator and lighting and stage manager for this performance.

On December 13 Primus left for Africa. "Spirituals and Shout Songs of America" was published in *Dance Encyclopedia*, New York. She was listed as the Woman of the Year on a "Scroll of Honor" of the National Council of Negro Women. Another piece introduced this year was "Play Dance of the Caribbean."

1949

Throughout this year, Primus traveled and studied in West and Central Africa, where she was adopted by leaders of tribes of the Yoruba, Mano, Gio, and Vai peoples. From December 1948 through April 1949 she was in Nigeria; from May to August 1949 in Belgian Congo (Zaire/Congo). On December 3, 1949, she was awarded the Star of Africa by the president of Liberia, William

Tubman. Also in this year she published "Primitive African Dance and Its Influence on the Churches of the South," in *The Dance Encyclopedia*. John Martin published excerpts of her letters in the *New York Times*. Margaret Lloyd's book *The Borzoi Book of Modern Dance* was published and included an extensive essay on Primus. New works included "American Folk Dance," "Fanga," "Go Down Death," "Invocation," "Chicken Hop," and "Prayer of Thanksgiving."

1950

Upon her return from Africa, Primus performed in concerts and lecture demonstrations, and continued graduate work and writing. On May 4 she gave a "Dark Rhythms" lecture demonstration at the American Museum of Natural History. The dancers included Marguerite James, Arleen Howell, and George Shipman. Alphonse Cimber and Moses Miann were the drummers, and Helen Tinsley sang. She gave a program especially for children, "The Magical Origin of Dance, Dark Rhythms," at the Henry Street Playhouse with the New York Dance Film Society, and another "Dark Rhythms" performance at Kaufmann Auditorium of the 92nd Street Y, with Pearl Buck at the event. She performed and taught at Jacob's Pillow. She continued to study at Columbia and published "In Africa" in the October issue of *Vogue* and "Earth Theatre" in the December volume of *Theater Arts*. Performances included "Benis Women's War Dance," "Dance of the Fanti Fisherman," "Everybody Loves Saturday Night," "Egbo Esakapade," "Fertility," "The Initiation," and "Hi-Life." On August 31 she married Yael Woll.

1951

A January 14 performance at the 92nd Street Y advertised, "New numbers based on travels to Africa: 'Excerpts from My African Journey.'" Part I included "Dance of the Benis People," and Part II, "Fanga, or Dance of Welcome," "Blind Beggar Woman," based upon a legend of Senegal, and "Initiation," based upon the many ceremonial initiations that she underwent during her stay in Africa. All choreography was by Primus, the drummers were Alphonse Cimber and Moses Miann; the singer was Helen Tinsley; and the dancers were Charles Blackwell, Lorraine Greenberg, Frank Killebrew, Louis Paschall, Charles Queenan, George Shipman, and Gloria Smith. The pianist was Lionel Belasco and lights were designed by Joe Harvard. Costumes were based on authentic designs and executed by Nellie Hatfield and Signey Senior. "Freedom Train" was based on an old experimental group dance.

A benefit for the New Lincoln School on February 2 at Assembly Hall, Hunter College, demonstrates the range of choreographies added after Africa as well as her dedication to themes of American origin. Part I, "Dark Rhythms," included "African Ceremonial" (performed by Primus, Charles Blackwell, George Mills, Charles Queenan), "Chants" (Ruth Reese), and "Excerpts from an African Journey," which included "Egbo-Esakapade" from Benin (Primus and Company), and "Prayer of Thanksgiving" (Primus) with the program note, "Let us walk into the fields and view the harvest, then let our voices rise with the drums to thank God." "War Dance" (the Men) followed with the program note, "The warriors challenge the God of War and destroy him. By his destruction there will be peace." Then "Fanga" was performed (Primus, Blackwell, Mills, Queenan), with the program note, "I welcome you. My hands bear no weapons. My heart brings love for you. I stretch my arms to the earth and to the sky for I alone am not strong enough to greet you." After "Fanga" came "Everybody Loves Saturday Night—A Country Dance" (Pearl Primus and Company), "Drum Talk" (Moses Miann), "Conga Interlude" (George Mills), and "Santos" (Primus). The program note for "Santos" was, "The dancer is compelled to obey the rhythms of the drums. These rhythms speak the language of the serpent. In Cuba the worship of the snake was forbidden by the Christian masters, and this led to tremendous inner conflict among the slaves."

Part II began with "Lamentation" (Primus). The program note said, "In the cry of the people there comes the memory of once joyous moments, but the tears weigh down the heart and the dancing feet are stilled." This section included "Creole Songs" (Ruth Reese), "Study in Nothing," and "Mischievous Interlude" (Primus and Queenan). "American Suite" included "Lonesome and Weary Traveler" (Blackwell) and "Hard Time Blues" (Primus), for which the program note stated, "In the South of the United States many people still live in extreme poverty. They are forever indebted to the landowners who live far away. This dance is a protest against the system which robs the people of the fruits of their labor." It also included "Folk Dance" (Queenan), and "Spirituals." The program note for "Spirituals" read, "These are the songs which carried the Negro people through their period of slavery. Embracing every known emotion, these spirituals developed as powerful songs of hope, and were used as weapons for freedom. Today they are called America's great folk music and are used to express not only the prayers of the American Negro but also the emotions and hopes of all peoples of the world." The four dances in this section were "Motherless Child" (Primus)," "Gonna Tell God All My Troubles" (the Men), "Freedom Train" (Primus and Company), and "Great Getting Up Mornin'" (Primus).

Part III included the "The Initiation." The program note read,

"Throughout the long centuries man has searched for methods of under-standing and conquering not only his environment but also himself. He has not limited this search to the physical only. He has ventured into the psychological and spiritual realms of life. In spite of all this, each individual must at one time or another pass through his own jungle. He must meet Fear. He must conquer or be conquered, for Man cannot live with Fear." In this performance the "Initiate" was performed by Pearl Primus, "First Fear" by George Mills (The Formless One), and "Third Fear" by Charles Blackwell (The Mighty One). A later program added another fear, "The Crawling One." The music was com-posed by Joseph Liebling. Then "Folk Songs" was performed by Ruth Reese and, finally, "Impinyuza." The program note read, "Let us dance the elegance of our people . . . their dignity, their beauty, and their strength!! Let our feet fly over the earth and our faces reflect our ecstasy. (Dance of the Isyaka, Batwa, Corps-de-Ballet of the King of the giant Watusi, in the Belgian Congo.)" The credits included choreography, Pearl Primus; dancers, Charles Blackwell, George Mills, Charles Queenan; master drummer, Moses Mianns; singer, Ruth Reese; pianist, Joseph Liebling; lighting and stage manager, Yael Woll; costume consultant, Charles Queenan; costumes executed by Nellie Hatfield; additional jewelry by Art Smith; and wardrobe mistress, Frances Pinkett.

Other programs from this period included: "The Beggar of Mandi-yang," performed by Queenan, with one drum and piano, and "Country Dance," Pearl Primus and Co. Program note: "This social dance is found in the large cities on the west coast of Africa. The dancers often leave their partners and dance for the sheer joy that comes with interpretation of music and suites of spirituals, including 'You Pray For Me,' and 'Tell God All My Troubles.'" Joseph Commodore was part of the company at this time and drummed with Moses Mianns. Osborne Smith was another singer. Yael Woll continued to function as lighting technician and stage manager, and Charles Queenan was the costume consultant, working with authentic designs to cre-ate costumes for "African Ceremonial," "Excerpts from an African Journey," "Impinyuza," "Country Dance" (Primus costume), and "Initiation."

On February 7 and then again on April 8, the company performed in John M. Greene Hall at Smith College, the latter concert advertised as "Dark Rhythms—Africa in Dance and Song." Between October 26 and December 26 there were performances in England at Stratford-upon-Avon, the Prince's Theatre in London, and a Royal Command Performance for King George VI in Victoria Palace.

An article entitled "Pearl Primus" appeared in the January issue of

Ebony magazine. Primus's essay, "Out of Africa" (written in 1948) was published in Walter Sorrell's book *The Dance Has Many Faces,* and "Earth Theatre of Africa" was published in *Monthly Magazine,* Brooklyn Institute of Arts & Sciences, New York. Primus collaborated with her good friend Marjorie Kinnan Rawlings, author of *The Yearling,* on the *Women of Zor,* a drama that remained unfinished but to which Pearl remained committed for the rest of her life. Primus's students performed at the Central High School of Needle Trades, and she lectured at Brooklyn Academy of Music and Hunter College. She performed again at Café Society Downtown and taught at Columbia University.

"Impinyuza" premiered during this concert season.

1952

Primus performed in England on January 4, 5, and 6 and gave a command performance on January 7 at the inaugural ceremonies of President Tubman in Liberia. This was her second trip to Liberia. The tour continued to Israel on January 8. There was a command performance for the mayor of Tel Aviv and additional performances in theaters, settlements, kibbutzim, and immigration camps. In February the company performed in France and by March they were back in the United States. On March 8 there was a performance of "Dark Rhythms" at the 92nd Street Y.

In this period Primus was under investigation by the FBI, and while performing in Los Angeles her passport was revoked. Her name does not appear on the "Red Channels" list of blacklisted artists. On October 16 she appeared with her lawyer, Herbert Levy, before the FBI with a signed document explaining her involvement with radical politics. Another new piece was "Carnival."

1953

In June Primus left with a group to study in Trinidad and the West Indies. In Trinidad she reconnected with Beryl McBurnie and met Percival Borde. She studied African-based rituals, such as Shango and Rada, and traveled to Carriacou to attend the Nation Dances. She gave a command performance for the governor of Port of Spain at the famous Little Carib Theatre. While in Trinidad she made plans to bring dancers and drummers to New York. Returning to the 92nd Street Y that year she created programs for children. She added "Kalenda" and "Limbo" to her repertory.

1954

Most important this year was Percival Borde's arrival in New York. On July 11, at the 92nd Street Y, as part of a New York City Summer Dance Festival, Borde performed with the company. The program included an introductory section with two dances, "Little Girl Lost" performed by Carol Hyman, and "The Weaver of Tales" performed by Primus. Next were "Excerpts from Carriacou," which included "Manding," "Halichord," and "Ibo," performed by Primus and Borde. The program note described Carriacou as a "tiny island in the West Indies where the old people still dance the memories of their African ancestors." Two other sections included African Venture with "Cat Dance," "African Folk Tales," "Tamboule," and "Zulu War Dance," and a South American Suite which included "Congo," "The Castilian," "Mambo," and "Cha Cha." These were all performed by Primus, Borde, and Hyman. She gave lecture demonstrations at the Museum of Modern Art and a lecture demonstration for the Gold Coast Students Cultural Association. Primus was hired to recatalogue the entire African art collection of the Newark Museum in New Jersey and as consultant for the museum's "African Exhibit." She also was the ethnologist for an exhibit "The Dancing Masks of Africa" at the Wildcliff Museum in New Rochelle, New York. "La Jablesse" was premiered.

1955

On January 19 Onwin Babajide Sebastian Primus Borde was born. However, Onwin was first named Onwin Sebastian Woll, as Primus and Woll were not yet divorced. Pearl withdrew from performance for months and in several letters refers to a nervous breakdown at this time. Between October 24 and December 10 the company toured extensively to colleges throughout New England and the South. They performed at Williams College (Massachusetts), St. Lawrence University (New York), Virginia State College, Virginia Union University, Kentucky State College, Illinois State Normal University, Monmouth College (Illinois), Temple Israel (Oklahoma), Spelman College (Georgia), Alabama A & M College, Alabama State College, Savannah State College (Georgia), Fort Valley State College (Georgia), Florida A & M University, Southern Carolina State College, West Virginia University, State Teachers College of New York, Mount Holyoke College (Massachusetts), University of New Hampshire, Bradford Junior College (Massachusetts), Jordan Hall (Massachusetts), Skidmore College (New York), and three more performances at State University Teachers College of New York and Harpur College (New York).

1956

In September, a small company sailed to France. From October to November they had Italian engagements, performing at the Quirino Theatre in Rome as part of an International Dance Festival Series. They then traveled to Liberia, where they performed in honor of President William V. S. Tubman, sponsored by Mediterranean Center of Culture and Entertainment. A trip to Israel was under discussion but did not materialize. Back in the United States, with Primus as assistant director, *Mister Johnson* had a twelve-week run at the Martin Beck Theater in New York, from March 29 to May 5. *Mister Johnson* was produced by Cheryl Crawford and Robert Lewis, written by Norman Rosten, and based on a novel by Joyce Cary dealing with British colonial days in Nigeria. The show was directed by Robert Lewis, with scene, lighting, and costume design by William and Jean Eckart. The role of Mister Johnson was played by Earle Hyman. The opening night cast included dancers and drummers Geoffrey Beddeau, Percival Borde, Alphonse Cimber, Louise Gilkes, Samuel Phills, Josephine Premice, Pearl Reynolds, and Mary Waithe, among others. Other performance engagements included the Brooklyn Academy of Music and the McMillan Theater at Columbia University, where Primus was a member of the International Students Club. In April, Primus withdrew from Columbia and transferred to New York University to continue her doctoral studies. At NYU she studied arts for children and educational TV, among other courses. She was inducted into the New York University chapter of the Alpha Kappa Delta National Honor Society.

1957

Primus continued to study, dance, and write. She studied Catalonian dance in Barcelona, and published "Dance in Africa" in the December issue of *Way Forum*, published by the World Assembly of Youth, Paris. Performances included appearances at the Carter Barron Amphitheater in Washington, D.C.

1958

Primus received her master's degree in educational sociology and anthropology from the School of Education at New York University. Her studies were supervised by Gladys Andrews, pioneer in the field of dance education. She performed at St. Marks Playhouse and the Jan Hus Auditorium in New York. "Africa" was published in the March issue of *Dance Magazine*. "African Dance" was published in *Presence Africains* (Dijon, France). New work included "Royal Ishadi and "Lema Lashina," both dances of the royal wives of the king of the Bushongo people. Other new works were "Temne," "Yoruba Court Dance," "Aztec Warrior," "Ibo," "Earth Magician," "Engagement Dance," and "Ntimi."

1959

International travel was at the forefront of Primus's work during this period. She was a United States delegate at the First National Conference of Negro

Artists and Writers in Rome, Italy, hosted by the Society on African Culture, where she presented "Cultural Dance Concert." With Percival Borde, she was appointed chairman of cultural activities and director of the African Center of Performing Arts, Konama Kende, in Monrovia, Liberia, to establish a new performing arts center and further the study and presentation of African dance in Africa. Konama Kende translates as "a new living thing." Her Liberian research trip this time spanned 1959–61.

She performed "Cultural Dance Concert" at St. Marks Playhouse in New York. She sat for PhD comprehensive exams but the degree itself was not finished for many more years. New work included "Ritual" and "Chirrup, a Nation Dance."

1960

The opening of the Konama Kende Performing Arts Center was celebrated with eighteen presentations, including a premier at Monrovia's City Hall in March and eighteen presentations between April and June. Primus herself performed in a benefit for the Performing Arts Center. In December, with Percival Borde and company, she gave a command performance for Haile Selassie, emperor of Ethiopia, when he visited Liberia. At New York University, her PhD committee agreed at first to allow her to dance her PhD thesis, but this was ultimately disallowed, causing her great distress. At the New Dance Group, she gave a lecture demonstration, "Meeting Life Crises Through the Dance," which became a staple of her lecture repertory. New dances included: "Whispers," "Story of a Chief," "Nafitombo," "Kwan," "Zo Kangai," and "Konama."

1961

Primus continued as the director of the African Performing Arts Center and from January through November gave presentations to sixty-eight government and private organizations throughout Liberia. The company included indigenous Liberian dancers, singers, and musicians. She and Borde choreographed African dances for "African Carnival," presented by the African Research Foundation of Liberia. In November 15, her divorce from Yael Woll was finalized in Juarez, Mexico, and recognized in New York on November 27. On December 15 she married Percival Borde in New York City. Borde's divorce from Joyce Borde was obtained in Florida and finalized on October 13. "The Wedding" premiered in this season.

1962

In 1962 and 1963 Primus and Borde returned to live in Liberia, and during this period they traveled throughout West Africa. The Pearl Primus Dance Tour of Africa, "New Artists in Africa," was sponsored by the Rebekah Harkness Foundation in cooperation with the U.S. Department of State. It included travel to Ghana (March), Liberia (May), Rhodesia (Zimbabwe) and Belgian Congo (DRC) (June and July), and Benin (October) as well as Cameroons, Dahomey, Guinea, Senegal, Mali, Nigeria, Rwanda-Burundi, Togoland, and Union of Central African Republic. They performed for heads of state in Cameroons, Dahomey, Ghana, Mali, Nigeria, Rhodesia, Sierra Leone, and Togo. The tour included twenty-eight concerts, in which they performed with African artists. Controversy erupted surrounding the teaching and presentation of African artists in Africa under the direction of artists from the United States. Primus called this tour "Venture into the Soul of a People." Additionally she created "The Man Who Would Not Laugh" and "To the Ancestors."

1963

Back in New York, Primus and Borde founded the Primus-Borde School of Primal Dance. They performed at the 92nd Street Y in a memorial concert for dance pianist and composer Freda Miller, and again at New York University. They continued to give lecture demonstrations and performances, including a lecture demonstration for high school students at New York University. She also performed at the Community Church of New York. Primus performed "Ti Bongo" (Your Dance) with Percival Borde at their Twenty-fourth Street studio. John Martin published *Book of the Dance*, which includes descriptions of Primus's work. "African Dance" was republished in the special edition of *Presence Africaine* under the title "Africa Seen by American Negroes." New works or productions included: "Mang Betu," "Le Bola," "Life Crisis," "Earth Theatre," and "Black Rhythms."

1964

The Primus-Borde Dance Studio reopened at 17 West Twenty-fourth Street and they founded the African-Caribbean-American Institute of Dance Arts as part of Earth Theater. At New York University Pearl was inducted into Pi Lambda Theta (Rho chapter) and Kappa Delta Pi (Beta Pi Chapter). "Dreams and the Dance" was published in September in the *Journal of the American Academy of Psychotherapists*.

1965

While continuing to perform—"Dark Rhythms" was performed at the Circle in the Square Theater in New York—Primus's work focused in this period on education.

She received a United States Office of Education Arts and Humanities Grant to develop a lecture-demonstration format for elementary schools and

prepare methodology for research and assessment. The first presentation
took place at the Little Red Schoolhouse in New York on December 2, 1965,
in coordination with New York University's School of Education, Office of
Educational Research Services. From 1965 through 1969 she studied and
prepared ethnic dance performances for public school settings. With José
Limón she served as a panel member at the National Dance Teachers Guild
First Regional Conference at the Neighborhood Playhouse in New York. As
part of the lecture demonstrations she created "Anase the Spider" and "Village
Scene."

1966

Between January and June, Primus gave lecture demonstrations in forty New
York public schools. This U.S. Office of Education project was entitled "A Pilot Study Integrating Visual Form and Anthropological Content for Teaching
Children Ages 6–11 About Cultures and Peoples of the World." The project
received additional support from the Universalist Unitarian Service Committee. Journalist Nat Hentoff described Primus's school performances and their
implications for curriculum development in the February issue of *American
Education*. Primus was invited to perform "Dance, a Lecture Demonstration"
at the McBurney Branch of Young Men's Christian Association and again
on July 20 at the National Conference on Education of the Disadvantaged,
presented by the U.S. Department of Health, Education, and Welfare's Office
of Education.

1967

Primus continued to seek academic appointments, and this year was an
artist-in-residence at Pratt Institute in Brooklyn. On July 26, 27, and 28, she
performed "Dark Rhythms" at the Library and Museum of Performing Arts
at Lincoln Center. On November 18 with Percival Borde and company they
presented "The Talking Drums" at Irvington High School.

1968

Continuing her educational projects, Primus conducted a seminar hosted by
New York City's Department of Cultural Affairs, "Pilot Workshop in the Cre-
ative Application of Movement Inspired by Authentic African Dance Forms."
In February she submitted an extensive *Final Report* to the U.S. Department
of Health, Education, and Welfare's Office of Education and Department of
Research, "A Pilot Study Integrating Visual Form and Anthropological Con-
tent for Teaching Children Ages 6 to 11 About Cultures and Peoples of the
World; Specifically, the Preparation of a Danced Presentation with Lecture
Interpreting Some of the Cultural Values in West and Central African Com-

munities," dedicated to "All the thousands of children who responded to the dance with exultation."

"Dance as Cultural Expression" was published in *The World Today in Health, Physical Education and Recreation,* edited by C. Lynn Vendien and John E. Nixon, published by Prentice Hall, Inc.

1969

Primus was hired as a professor at Hunter College, where she taught until 1974. One course she developed for Hunter was "Dances of the Afro-American Heritage."

At the invitation of the Ford Foundation's Public Education Division, she traveled to Great Britain on a study grant to investigate dance in English primary and secondary school curricula in order to assess the value of these programs in the U.S. public school system. While in England, she performed "Awareness of Self" at I.M. Marsh College of Physical Education in Liverpool. At the American Dance Therapy Association's 4th Annual Conference in Philadelphia, she lectured on "Life Crises: Dance from Birth to Death." This lecture was published in the *American Dance Therapy Association Proceedings.* In the late '60s and early '70s, she continued to direct the Primus-Borde School of Primal Dance at the West Twenty-fourth Street studio. "African Dance" was reprinted in *African Heritage, Anthology of Black African Personality and Culture,* by Collier Books. New work created: "Masangee."

1970

Primus continued to teach at Hunter College and was awarded a Centennial Medal, the President's Medal, by President Jacqueline Wexler. Borde was appointed professor of theater arts and black studies at SUNY/Binghamton. Continuing her focus on dance in public education, Primus received a commendation from the White House for her participation in a "Conference on Children and Youth," for which she choreographed a presentation titled "Creativity in Education." "African Dance" was reprinted in *Headway, a Thematic Reader,* published by Holt, Rinehart and Winston, Inc. Primus and Borde purchased a home at 225 Coligni Avenue, New Rochelle, New York. New work created: "Dance of Lights."

1971

Primus's work in education continued. With Percival Borde as well as Alphonse Cimber on drums, and chants by Amandina Lihamba, Onwin Borde, and Cheryl Borde, Miller-Brody Productions released the records *Africa in Story, Legend, Song and Thought,* which included stories, songs, rhythms, and proverbs of the villages of Central and West Africa. Primus was invited as a guest lecturer to the University of Illinois in Champaign, on February 10 presenting "The Black World: Perspectus" and "African Dance Concert." She was also honored with an Achievement Citation from the Hunter College High School faculty and a National Culture Through the Arts Award from the New York Federation of Foreign Language Teachers. In December Primus appeared on NBC's *The Today Show*, to perform and discuss "Dance and Life." It is likely that this was an appearance with Haitian dancer Jean-Leon Destine and ballerina Maria Tallchief. "Dance Among the Black People in America" was published in *Focus on Dance VI*, a journal of the American Association for Health, Physical Education and Recreation.

1972

Primus continued to teach at Hunter College and to travel between New York City, New Rochelle, and SUNY/Binghamton. The Black Academy of Arts and Letters granted her honorary membership, and she was selected as "One of Westchester's Most Admired Women."

1973

On April 28, Primus was inducted into the Hunter Hall Of Fame and on May 30 into the Hunter College Chapter of Phi Beta Kappa (Nu Chapter) of New York. At Hunter, she performed "Hymn to the Rising Sun." She was honored by the Westchester Chapter of Hunter Alumni, and she received a commendation from the Human Rights Commission in New Rochelle. She participated in the Phyllis Wheatley Poetry Festival at Jackson State College in Mississippi, dedicated to the memory of the enslaved poet Phyllis Wheatley.

1974

Primus reconstructed "Fanga" for Judith Jamison and "The Wedding" for the Alvin Ailey American Dance Theater, performing at the City Center Theater between May and June and again in July at the State Theater at Lincoln Center in New York. She was honored as the Woman of the Year by Zeta Phi Beta, an international black sorority dedicated to volunteer service and social and civic change. Primus resigned from her teaching position at Hunter College. *Dreams and the Dance* was published by the American Academy of Psychotherapists.

1975

No longer teaching at Hunter, she refocused attention on completing her PhD. In August her dissertation proposal, "Sculpture-danced," was accepted by her committee at New York University. She served on the board of directors for the Westchester Council on the Arts and the Neuberger Museum in Purchase. On February 22 in New Rochelle, she lectured and performed "Dance—A

Teaching Tool" at the Zeta Phi Beta Annual Conference. She had an Artist-in-Residence appointment to teach in the Ethnic Dance Enrichment Program at Spelman College, where on March 1 she presented the lecture "Life Crises." On June 7 Earth Theater performed at the Whitney Young Auditorium in New Rochelle. She received a Westchester Council on the Arts grant for a graduate program at Iona College.

1976

Primus received a Choreographer's Grant from Harlem Cultural Council to perform "Fanga." She served on the Harlem Cultural Council. She also received a Community Service Citation Award from the New Rochelle branch of the NAACP. Lincoln University in Pennsylvania, the first degree-granting, historically black university in the country, acknowledged her major contribution to black culture with a Meritorious Award.

1977

On February 5 Primus gave a presentation called "Roots" at the University of Pittsburgh. Primus received the Outstanding Pioneer Award from the Audience Development Committee in New York.

1978

In March, Primus received her PhD in educational sociology and anthropology from the School of Education at New York University. Her thesis was titled "An Anthropological Study of Masks as Teaching Aids in the Enculturation of Mano Children." "Earth Theater" gave a concert at Lakeside Theater in Nassau County, New York, in preparation for a concert series at the Theatre of the Riverside Church the following year. The company also performed "Celebration" at an Independence Festival in New York City. That fall the Alvin Ailey American Dance Theater presented Primus with the Dance Pioneer Award. She also incorporated the Pearl Primus Dance Language Institute "to promote the dissemination of information about the dance . . . to educate as to the arts, with emphasis upon dance, including but not limited to the teaching and appreciation of ethnic dancing to average individuals, those already trained in the dance, and physically handicapped individuals." She received a National Endowment for the Arts Choreographer's Grant to reconstruct three dances from her repertory. On July 19 Onwin legally changed his surname from Woll to Borde.

1979

Primus and Borde reunited in performance to enthusiastic reviews. On March 22, 23, and 24, the company performed at the Theatre of the Riverside Church. The dancers included: Leslie Butler, Sheila Durant, Larry Ferrell, Dianne

Garry, Morris Johnson, Jr., Leslie McGriff, Percival Borde, Andree Valentine, Mary Waithe, and Elbert Watson. Chanting and drumming were Onwin Borde, Alphonse Cimber, John ("Tunisi") Davis, Harrison Buster, Melvina Jagacki, and Earl Thorne (known now as Earl Robinson, or Ayan Layo). The program included: "Dance with Rattles" (Sierra Leone), "Fanga," "Fertility," "Impinyuza," "Invocation," "La Jablesse," and "War Dance." "Afro-American Scenes" included "Michael Row the Boat Ashore" and "Wade in the Water."

In March, April, and May, Primus conducted a residency in three East Harlem public schools, including the Harbor Junior High School for the Performing Arts, East Harlem Performing Arts School, and Boy's Harbor Performing Arts School.

Some of the students participated in the July 3 Carnegie Hall performance of "The Wedding," which was part of the New York Ethnic Dance Festival '79. The program noted that this was one of her classics based on African lore. "Amidst joyous dancing The Bride is escorted to the home of her new husband—only to be confronted by the Demon of Fear. A drama between the Power of Good and the Forces of Evil." The cast included Jaibundu/The Mother: Pearl Primus; Umusambi/Crested Crane/Honored Guest: Percival Borde; The Bride: Tahnia Owens; Big Sister: Mary Waithe; Small Sister: Christine Dhimos; Demon of Evil: Henry Daniel; Demon's Assistant: Mark Rubin. The Singer was Gessy Lewis; the Drum Spirit was Onwin Borde; and the Village People were the dancers and musicians. Members of the Pearl Primus company were Mary Waithe, Andree Valentine, Diane Gary, Lydia Payne, and Larry Ferrell. Members of the Alvin Ailey American Dance Theater were Henry Daniel, Christine Dhimos, Sebastian Ellison, Janet Jubert, Alice Krawkowski, David McCauley, Tahnia Owens, Carol Penn, Kay Pesek, George Randolph, Mark Rubin, and Jill Wender. Participating students from the Harbor Jr. High School of Performing Arts Dance were: Yolanda Cummings, Monique Highland, Laceine Owsley, Gernethia Pettiforde, Sarina Reddick, Tracey Reddick, Yvette Rodriquez, Mildred Sanchez, Leslie Tucker, Sandra Vasquez, and Crystal Vick. The musicians were Alphonse Cimber, Onwin Borde, John Davis, Earl Thorne (Earl Robinson/Ayan Layo), Harryson Buster, and Kofi Atigbi, and the singer was Gessy Lewis. Lighting design was by Sandra Ross.

On August 17 Earth Theater opened at the Perry Street Theater, New York. The program included African, Caribbean, and American dances. This concert featured "Caribbean Chirrup," "Fanga," "Invocation," "Michael Row the Boat Ashore," "The Wedding" (Larry Ferrell: Evil Spirit; Tahnia Owens:

the Bride), "Impinyuza" (Percival Borde), "Yanvaloo," and "Motherless Child" (singer: Lillias White). Dancers included Sheila Durant, Diane Gary, Andree Valentine, and Mary Waithe. Percussionists included Onwin Borde, Alphonse Cimber, and John ("Tunisi") Davis. On August 18 the program was performed at Damrosch Park as part of the Lincoln Center Out-of-Doors Festival. On August 22 Primus lectured on "The Inner Being of African Sculpture." On August 31, Borde died at the Perry Street Theater, just after performing "Impinyuza."

For these performances Primus had been awarded a National Endowment for the Arts grant to reconstruct "Fanga," which she dedicated to Dr. Ethel J. Alpenfels, and to create a new work, "Five Masks," based on her PhD dissertation.

Primus taught at the Community Action Agency in New Rochelle and at the New Dance Group. She was granted honorary membership in African American Educational Associates, and received the National Association of Media Women's Award from its Long Island chapter.

1980

After the death of Percival Borde, Primus toured briefly throughout the Midwest and California with the Earth Theater Company, performing at the University of Illinois in Champaign, the Fermi Lab, and the Masonic Temple in San Francisco. She was the recipient of a National Endowment for the Arts choreographer's grant to choreograph "Three Wonderful Creatures" and "Ntimi" (begun in 1958), works that were not completed, and to continue the investigation of cultural sources of dances created by her and Borde. She completed Borde's contract at SUNY/Binghamton.

1981

A performance at the Theatre of the Riverside Church was dedicated to Percival Borde, as was "Drum Talk," a tribute to Alphonse Cimber for which Joe Nash was the speaker. Additional honors and awards continued as Primus received another National Endowment for the Arts dance fellowship, an NAACP Meritorious Award from the Broome County, New York, chapter, and recognition by the National Council of Negro Women, Inc. She was granted membership in the Junior Black Academy of Arts and Letters.

1982

From fall 1982 through spring of 1984, Primus served as the Master of Cora P. Maloney College at the State University of New York at Buffalo. She held an appointment as associate professor of theater as well as an appointment as visiting associate professor in the Department of African and Afro-American

Studies at SUNY/Albany. She spoke in New York on a panel, "The Impact of Africa on Dance in the Americas," with Thomas Pinnock and Tina Ramirez as the other panelists and Duane Jones moderating. She was a recipient of a National Endowment for the Arts dance fellowship.

1983

Primus continued as the director of the Cora P. Maloney College, received another National Endowment for the Arts fellowship, and published two articles in a special dance edition of *Caribe Magazine,* which also featured a photographic tribute. She granted Mary Waithe permission to stage "The Wedding" with the Barbados Dance Theatre Company.

1984

In August, Primus made her first trip to Barbados. From the fall of 1984 through the spring of 1992, Primus had continuous appointments in the Five Colleges in western Massachusetts: Amherst, Hampshire, Mount Holyoke, and Smith Colleges and the University of Massachusetts Amherst. She received a National Endowment for the Arts fellowship to reconstruct "Excerpts from an African Journey" for a Five College Dance Department faculty concert in November. This performance was dedicated to Percival S. Borde, "known to us as Umusambi, the Crested Crane, Jangbanolima, Ifatola, Father and Husband." Two of the chants, adapted specifically for Pearl Primus' Productions, were "Ishe Oliwa," adapted by Nigerian composer Solomon Ilorin, and "Ukitaka Kulima," adapted by Amandina Lihamba. The traditional costumes were lent by Pearl Primus Dance Language Institute, Inc. Onwin Borde was the lighting consultant and Cheryl Byron of Pearl Primus Earth Theater was the assistant for rehearsals. Joyce Knight assisted with costumes. Primus acknowledged as guest artists Onwin Babajide S. Primus Borde and Bamidele Osumarea, music director, Art of Black Dance and Music Company, Boston, and artistic director of Bamidele Dancers and Drummers. The program included: "Dance with Rattles" (Maidens dance to show their beauty and grace; Sierra Leone) and "Kwan—Work Scenes. Rowing. Rice Fanning. Sweeping. Pounding. Washing." Primus performed "Fanga." In November, she delivered the Ethel J. Alpenfels Distinguished Lecture at the Annual Conference of American Anthropologists, in Denver.

1985

On February 26, she performed at SUNY/Albany as part of African American History Month. She received the American Anthropological Association Distinguished Service Award in Washington, D.C., and choreographed and produced "A Struggle for Memory" for a Five College Tribute to Black History Month. During a trip to Barbados, excerpts from Primus's works were presented by the Barbados Dance Theatre Company as part of the fourth New Work Festival of the African Diaspora, August 2–10. Upon her return, she initiated a Barbados Exchange Proposal and was featured in an article and on the cover of *CONTACT Magazine* of the University of Massachusetts. In May she was the commencement speaker at Hampshire College. She received a choreographer's fellowship grant from the National Endowment for the Arts.

1986

Primus received the Ernest O. Melby Award for Distinguished Alumna from New York University and initiated an exchange between the University of Massachusetts Amherst/Five College Dance Department and the Barbados Dance Theatre Company. She taught a summer intensive at the East Street Dance Studios in Hadley, Massachusetts. On December 20, 1986, Primus was awarded the key to the City of Schenectady by Mayor Karen Johnson for her contributions to the Hamilton Hill Arts and Crafts Center and the City of Schenectady. She received a choreographer's fellowship grant from the National Endowment for the Arts.

1987

Barbadian dancer Jerry Lavine performed under Primus's direction in productions at the University of Massachusetts Amherst and at Smith College. During the spring semester at the university Primus worked with Roberta Uno on a New World Theater production of Wole Soyinka's "The Lion and the Jewel," which reunited her with Gordon Heath. In May she restaged "Excerpts from 'The Wedding'" for Rebecca Nordstrom and Jerry Lavine, who performed in a Smith College graduation concert. Primus led a study group to Barbados during the summer. She lectured at the Jacob's Pillow Dance Festival and received a choreographer's fellowship grant from the National Endowment for the Arts.

1988

In June, with a grant from the Ford Foundation to reconstruct, present, and videotape for archival purposes, Primus reconstructed "The Negro Speaks of Rivers," "Strange Fruit" (Kim Bears, performer), and "Hard Time Blues" (Warren P. Miller II, performer) for the American Dance Festival Series "The Black Tradition in American Modern Dance." Spelman College awarded Primus a Doctor of Humane Letters degree, and she received a President's Award for Dance from Manhattanville College in Purchase, New York. She was hosted by Mozel Spriggs at Spelman College and Greta Levart at Manhattanville College. The 17th Annual African Street Festival in New York dedicated its activities on July 3 to Primus. Also, she was featured in a photographic exhibit, Black Women in the Arts, in the Gallery of the Harlem State Office Building New York State Division for Women. On June 4, there was a "Tribute to Pearl Primus," as part of the Festival of Osun. The Caribbean Cultural Center in New York sponsored a photography exhibit documenting Primus's career, and the Schomburg Center included Primus in its New York exhibition, "Ten Great Dance Masters." She organized an advisory committee for the Pearl Primus Dance Language Institute Inc., the last incarnation of a plan for a comprehensive school that would teach dance, music, language, and culture. She received another choreographer's fellowship grant from the National Endowment for the Arts.

1989

Primus lectured on dance and culture at Spelman College and at the North Carolina Institute of the Arts; she also gave a lecture/demonstration at Hampshire College. With a choreographer's fellowship from the National Foundations for the Arts she created a new work, "The Griot," for Linda Spriggs. Spriggs was in residence in Amherst in May for the development of this work. "The Griot" premiered in November as part of Ann Arbor Dance Works fall season.

1990

Primus was an adjunct professor of dance at the School of Education, Health, Nursing and Arts at New York University. She was honored at the Smithsonian Institute Convention by the Office of the Mayor, who proclaimed February 2 Pearl Primus Day in Washington, D.C. She was named a "Living Legend" at the National Black Arts Festival and was the queen of the first Carnival given by the Peach Street Carnival Committee, both in Atlanta, Georgia. In the spring, she was the Chancellor's Distinguished Lecturer at the University of California/Irvine and in December she restaged "Impinyuza" for the Alvin Ailey American Dance Theater. She received a choreographer's fellowship grant from the National Endowment for the Arts.

1991

On April 1–6, Primus was the Lucia Chase Fellow at the North Carolina School of the Arts. In May and June, she received honorary doctorates from the School of the Arts in Valencia, California, the Boston Conservatory, Hunter College of CUNY, New York, and the New School for Social Research. She received a two year fellowship to create a dance, "Five Heroines of Afro-American Heritage," and a National Endowment for the Arts film/video grant to preserve film of her dancing in Zaire, Africa, in 1949. On July 9 she received the National Medal of the Arts, awarded by President George H. W. Bush.

On July 30 she gave the keynote address at the Fourth Dance and the Child International Conference in Salt Lake City. At the American Dance Festival she received the first Balasaraswati/Joy Ann Dewey Beinecke Chair for Distinguished Teacher. She was honored as a "Living Legend" by the National Black Theater Festival in Winston-Salem, North Carolina, received the Distinguished Achievement Award from the Association of Black Anthropologists "in celebration of a lifetime of scholarship, creativity and public service," and, in November, the First Arts and Entertainment Award from the New Rochelle branch of the NAACP. The Boston Conservatory established the Pearl Primus Scholarship in Dance. She received a certificate of commendation from the President of Harvard University for achievement in the arts and excellence in teaching, and Harvard's Ruth Page Award.

1992

Primus traveled to Portugal in January for a residency hosted by former student Jorge Levi. September through December she was engaged in a joint residency hosted by Howard and American Universities in Washington, D.C. "Pearl Primus' 50th Anniversary Residency" was sponsored by Lila Wallace-Reader's Digest Arts Partners Program and administered by the Association of Performing Arts Presenters (APAP). It included a photo exhibit at the Anacostia Museum in Washington, D.C., funded by the Lila Wallace-Reader's Digest Fund and American University and then another photo exhibit, "Pearl Primus 1943–1992: An Historical Photo Exhibit," at the Howard University Fine Arts Gallery. The residency culminated in performances on December 3, "The Works of Pearl Primus," in Crampton Auditorium at Howard University, and on December 12 with performance of the "Works of Pearl E. Primus Earth Theatre," featuring reconstructions of "Invocation," "Prayer of Thanksgiving," "The Negro Speaks of Rivers," "The Wedding," "The Griot," "Caribbean Vignettes," and new work, "Dance to Save Lives," at the Kennedy Center. Kim Bears and Sheron Trotman assisted in this extended residency. Linda Spriggs performed "The Griot." Primus was celebrated in an exhibit, "African Diaspora Woman," at New York's Caribbean Cultural Center, under the direction of Marta Vega. She gave the Marion Chace Memorial Lecture, entitled "Cultural Bridges," at the American Dance Therapy Association.

1993

Primus taught African, Caribbean, and Primus modern techniques at the school for the Louisville, Kentucky, Ballet Company, master classes at the Dallas, Texas, performing arts magnet schools, and at the African Caribbean Cultural Dance Center in Binghamton, New York. She taught black dance history classes at the Alvin Ailey American Dance Center and at Manhattanville College in Purchase, New York. From August 15 to September 30, Howard University hosted an art exhibit "Celebrating Fifty Years of Dance/A Search for Roots: The Life and Works of Pearl E. Primus." On October 23, as part of its Guest Artist Series, the University of Michigan Department of Dance held "A Celebration of the African-American Tradition in Dance," with Primus, Onwin Borde, Kim Bears, and Linda Spriggs in "The Works of Pearl Primus." Mary Waithe restaged "The Wedding" for a performance celebrating the Barbados Dance Theatre Company's twenty-fifth anniversary. On June 19, she was interviewed by James Briggs Murray, director of the Schomburg Center for Research in Black Culture in New York, as part of an oral history project.

Primus was the keynote speaker at the Third Annual Zora Neale Hurston Festival of the Arts and Humanities in Eatonville, Florida, and the graduation speaker in White Plains, New York. She was honored by Festival founder and director Chuck Davis at DanceAfrica, at the Brooklyn Academy of Music, and received highest honors at the Black Dance Conference at Morgan State College in Baltimore. At the New Dance Group Choreographer's Celebration Kim Bears danced "The Negro Speaks of Rivers," representing Primus's choreography between 1943 and 1950. Primus was named one of Five Heroines of Heritage, a two-year National Endowment for the Arts project, and received a choreographer's fellowship grant for the creation of new work, and she continued documentation of earlier work and professional performances. Primus made her last trip to Barbados.

1994

On February 24 she lectured on "Afro Brazilian Dance and Religion" at the Claremont Graduate University, in Claremont, California, and gave a master class for the Scripps and Pomona Colleges dance programs. She also gave master classes at the University of California at Irvine and at California Institute of the Arts.

On March 2, in Claremont, she began work on the restaging of "Strange Fruit" for performance at the Los Angeles County Museum of Art, with the American Repertory Dance Company, Michele Simmons, soloist, and Bonnie Oda Homsey, rehearsal director. On April 28–30 "Strange Fruit" was performed by Michele Simmons on a program entitled "Weeping Women in Dance: Classic American Solos" at the Los Angeles County Museum of Art's Bing Theater, in conjunction with a Picasso exhibit. In the spring and fall, Primus continued to teach as an adjunct professor at New York University. A few days before she died, Primus was notified that she had received the National Endowment for the Arts Artist Teacher/Mentor Award for her lifetime achievements and contributions to the field of dance. This was the second and last time this award was given.

Pearl Primus died on October 29, 1994, at her home in New Rochelle, New York.

Appendix II: Interviews

Rashidah Ismaili AbuBakr, September 23, 2005, New York, NY, and
    October 10, 2005, Amherst, MA
Herbert Adlerberg, September 9, 2006, Telephone
Dovi Afesi, October 25, 2007, Amherst, MA
Molly Ahye, May 29, 2007, Telephone
Ethel Allen, July 6, 2006, Amherst, MA
Billie Allen Henderson, August 15, 2007, Telephone
Ahuva Anbary, January 17, 2008, Telephone
Eloise Hill Anderson, October 8, 2007, Telephone
Maya Angelou, November 30, 2007, New York, NY, and September 30,
    2010, Telephone
Fred E. Baker, July 27, 2004, Telephone
Terry Baker, November 9, 2003, New York, NY
De Ama Battle, January 15, 2008, Telephone
Kim Y. Bears-Bailey, February 13, 2004, Philadelphia, PA, and e-mail
Gloria Beckerman, December 15, 2005, Telephone
Holly Betaudier, May 28,2007, Port of Spain, Trinidad
Marjorie Boothman, May 30, 2007, Port of Spain, Trinidad
Onwin Borde, February 22, 2004, Telephone
Cheryl Borde-Johnson, October 21, 2006, New York, NY, and May 30, 2007,
    Port of Spain, Trinidad
Joan Myers Brown, February 12, 2004, Philadelphia, PA
Kwesi I. Camara, October 19, 2003, New York, NY
April Cantor, January 2, 2004, New York NY
Frances Johnson Charles, March 8, 2006, Telephone
Johnetta B. Cole, January 13, 2004, Greensboro, NC
Jill Ker Conway, July 5, 2006, e-mail
Margaret Cunningham, June 26, 2003, Telephone
Joyce Curtain, June 1, 2007, Telephone
Charles R. "Chuck" Davis, January 14, 2004, Durham, NC
John W. "Tunisi" Davis, November 9, 2003, Bridgeport, CT
Gemze de Lappe, July 28, 2004, New York, NY
Merle Derby, June 5, 2003, New York, NY
Jean-Leon Destine, November 11, 2004, Telephone
Lynn E. Frederiksen, July 11, 2001, and June 18, 2003, Amherst, MA, and e-mail

Eva Desca Garnet, October 20, 2003, Telephone

Margaret Goodfellow, December 4, 2007, Telephone

Brenda Dixon Gottschild, October 24, 2004, East Lansing, MI

William Greaves, February 27,2004, South Hadley, MA

Jacqueline Hairston Hendy, January 31, 2004, New York, NY

Ginette Havisward, November 26, 2007, Telephone

David Julian Hodges, October 17, 2003, New York, NY

Geoffrey Holder, July 24, 2007, New York, NY

Bonnie Oda Homsey, August 24, 2004, Los Angeles, CA

Nancy Jacobs, May 24, 2003, Christ Church, Barbados

Judith Jamison, May 20, 2003, New York, NY

Sherrill Berryman (Miller) Johnson, August 9, 2006, Telephone

Sophie Charles Johnson, April 8, 2006, New York, NY

Evelyn Karlin, October 15, 2003, Telephone

Theodore (Ted) and Lee Kazanoff, February 19, 2004, Telephone, and
    November 20, 2004, Boston, MA

Billie Kirpich, July 14, 2004, Saratoga Springs, NY

Margot Lehman, August 13, 2005, Saratoga Springs, NY

Jorge Levi, December 20, 2005, e-mail

Julia Levien, September 12, 2005, Telephone

Herbert Monte Levy, May 8, 2003, New York, NY

Tias Little, November 8, 2007, Telephone

Richard A. Long, August 7, 2007, Telephone

Muriel Manings, April 15, 2003, New York, NY

Michael Manswell, September 16, 2007, New York, NY, and September 23,
    2007, Telephone

Dianne McIntyre, December 10, 2008, Telephone

Donald McKayle, May 5, 2003, New York, NY

Renee Cutler Meer, September 23, 2005, Mount Vernon, NY

Claire Miller, February 8, 2007, Telephone

Ivor Miller, July 13, 2001, Telephone

Warren P. Miller II, June 25, 2006, Telephone

Torrance Mohammed, May 4, 2007, Port of Spain, Trinidad

Emmett Jefferson (Pat) Murphy, July 17, 2005, Amherst, MA

Joe Nash, October 10, 1995, December 18, 1995, May 4, 2003, and March 2005,
    New York, NY

Norbert Nathanson, September 20, 2006, Telephone

Rebecca Nordstrom, May 19, 2006, Amherst, MA

Elizabeth Fernandez O'Brien, July 11, 2001, and June 18, 2003,
  Amherst, MA
Dorothy Perron, April 10, 2003, Telephone
Naima Prevots, June 26, 2006, August 15, 2006, Telephone
Edward W. Primus III, November 6, 2005, New York, NY
Latir Primus, September 24, 2005, New York, NY
Loris P. Primus, October 26, 2005, New York, NY
Virginia Primus, January 10, 2005, White Plains, NY
Louis Ramos II, January 13, 2004, Lumberton, NC, and May 20, 2009,
  Durham, NC
Veleria Ramos, January 13, 2004, Lumberton, NC, and May 20, 2009,
  Durham, NC
Josephus "Femi" Richards, July 2, 2006, Amherst, MA
Paul Robeson, Jr., May 4, 2004, Telephone
Patricia A. Rowe, July 16, 2006, Telephone
John Ruddock, July 10, 2001, Telephone
Roger Sanders ("Montego Joe"), October 20, 2003, New York, NY
Marjorie Senechal, September 12, 2007, Northampton, MA
Donna E. Shalala, January 29, 2004, Telephone
Rina Sharett, January 24, 2008, Telephone
Stan Sherer, September 12, 2007, Northampton, MA
E. Gaynell Sherrod, October 17, 2003, New York, NY
Michele Simmons, August 24, 2004, Los Angeles, CA
Linda A. Spriggs, September 21, 2007, and September 26, 2007, Telephone
Mozel J. Spriggs, March 22, 2006, Telephone
David St. Charles, December 22, 2005, Telephone
Ekwueme Michael M. Thelwell, July 14, 2006, Amherst, MA
Emiko Tokunaga, August 3, 2004, Amherst, MA
Yasuko Tokunaga, August 3, 2004, Amherst, MA
Sheron Trotman, September 11, 2007, September 12, 2007, e-mail
Charles (Joe) Trupia, May 13, 2003, Sand Lake, NY
Roberta Uno, September 6, 2006, Telephone
Glory Van Scott, June 20, 2003, New York, NY
Dorothy Vislocky, December 20, 2005, Telephone
Mary Waithe, May 26, 2003, Christ Church, Barbados, and e-mail
Donald Washington, December 18, 1995, New York, NY
Sylvia Waters, May 18, 2004, New York, NY
Dudley Williams, May 18, 2004, New York, NY

Archbishop Granville Williams, May 28, 2003, Christ Church, Barbados
Yael R. Woll, November 20, 2004, Westchester, NY, and e-mail
Jeffrey Wright, May 6, 2007, Telephone
Eva Koonan Zirker, September 17, 2007, and e-mail

A Note on Sources and Documentation

To create this narrative of Pearl Primus's life and work, we have relied on five sources:

1. Transcripts and notes from unpublished interviews conducted by Peggy Schwartz. These materials are in the authors' possession. A list of interviews and dates is provided in Appendix II. To avoid unnecessary references, when these interviewees are quoted in the text, they are identified there and the quotations are not separately cited.

2. Unpublished writings by and about Pearl Primus. Unless otherwise noted, these materials are housed in the American Dance Festival (ADF) Pearl Primus Collection at Duke University. Materials that can be found in the ADF Collection, such as poetry, letters, reviews, and performance programs, are not cited separately, but the sources of other unpublished writings (e.g., files of Five Colleges, Inc., or the FBI files) are cited throughout the text.

3. Published interviews and documents, whether part of the ADF Collection or found elsewhere, are cited when they are mentioned or quoted in the text.

4. Books, articles, and websites are cited when quoted, summarized, or used as sources of information.

5. The authors' personal knowledge of and experience with Pearl Primus, which are identified as such in the text.

Notes

Introduction

1. Thomas DeFrantz, in "African-American Dance: A Complex History," comments on the lack of a full length biography of Primus, who "figures unequivocally among the 'pioneers' of African American concert dance." Thomas F. DeFranz, ed., *Dancing Many Drums: Excavations in African American Dance* (Madison: University of Wisconsin Press, 2002), 21.

2. John Perpener, *African-American Concert Dance: The Harlem Renaissance and Beyond* (Urbana and Chicago: University of Illinois Press, 2001), 174–75.

   Richard C. Green, in his essay on Primus in DeFrantz's book, "(Up)Staging the Primitive: Pearl Primus and 'the Negro Problem' in American Dance," writes in the language of contemporary cultural critics and historians. While he sets the discussion of her career in a critical context, his is not a language that reveals Primus to those unschooled in academic vocabularies. He writes about her "racialized" body, her need to be "recuperated" as a dancer, the "problematizing" of her assimilation into the canon of American modern dance. In his last paragraph, however, Green reveals self-doubts about this approach. He writes, "Various questions and voices haunted me from the beginning to the end: What are you writing on Primus? Did you interview her? Did you see her dance? Never having seen her perform 'live,' I have come to know Primus through the eyes and words of others" (133).

3. The title comes from Pearl's interview with James Murray, Schomburg Center for Research in Black Culture, New York Public Library, June 19, 1993.

4. A list of interviews is in Appendix I. A comparison with Katherine Dunham arose in many of the interviews, questioning why Dunham is remembered and celebrated and Primus is less known, why there seems to be room for only one black diva. Those devoted to securing the rightful legacy of Pearl Primus in the cultural history of black arts in America are not looking to do so at the expense of Dunham's major contribution, but to open up an important discussion, one that has to do with the body itself and that perhaps sheds light on culture. Pearl was small, compact, muscular, and very dark-skinned, Dunham a tall, fair-skinned woman, whose beauty reflected "white" concepts. In *The Black Dancing Body: A Geography from Coon to Cool* (New York: Palgrave Macmillan, 2003), Brenda Dixon Gottschild brilliantly analyzes skin and color, as well as feet and hair and other body parts, but does not specifically note the difference between

these contrasting figures. In interviews, however, the issue of color came up again and again. This book in no way intends to diminish the importance of Dunham's struggle and her contributions to the cultural landscape of dance in America. Rather we hope to show the value of Pearl's contributions in their own dimensions. Pointing to the different overall directions of their works, filmmaker Norbert Nathanson said, "Dunham took it [the African dance] to Broadway and Pearl took it to its roots."

James Murray related a story that helps explain a source of a competitive tension between these two great divas of black dance. He had invited both Pearl and Katherine Dunham to participate on a panel titled "An African American Dance Forum." He wrote:

> Talley [Beatty]informed me that having Dunham and Primus on the same panel at the same time was unheard of and inquired as to how I managed such a feat. I told Talley that I had a friendship with them both and it would never have occurred to me not to ask them both. This story has its roots in my having been informed by Pearl Primus that Katherine Dunham had invited Pearl to join the Dunham Company early in Pearl's career. According to Pearl she declined indicating to Ms. Dunham that she had her own artistic ideas that she felt obliged to pursue. Supposedly, as virtually no one would ever decline such an invitation, the two were never friendly thereafter. [Personal correspondence, October 20, 2009]

Indeed, when, on May 5, 2002, Peggy personally approached Dunham in New York to ask her about her assessment of Pearl's place in the history of black dance in America, she responded enigmatically, "I did not know Ms. Primus."

5. Personal communication, October 24, 2004.

ONE Laventille to Camp Wo-Chi-Ca

1. In a June 19, 1993, interview with James Murray, Pearl says, "I was born in Trinidad and have many birthdates, but the one that is probably most accurate is November 29, 1919." Schomburg Center for Research in Black Culture, New York Public Library. The authors were told in Port of Spain, Trinidad, that the municipal records for this period were lost in a fire.
2. Interview with James Murray, Schomburg Center.
3. Naima Prevots interview. Pearl also gave a family mezuzah to Marjorie Senechal and Stan Sherer.

4. Quoted in Richard C. Green, "(Up)Staging the Primitive: Pearl Primus and 'the Negro Problem,'" in American Dance," in *Dancing Many Drums: Excavations in African American Dance,* ed. Thomas F. DeFrantz (Madison, Wisconsin: University of Wisconsin Press, 2002), 110.
5. Interview with James Murray, Schomburg Center.
6. Quoted in Philip Kasinitz, *Caribbean New York: Black Immigrants and the Politics of Race* (Ithaca, NY: Cornell University Press, 1992), 47.
7. John Perpener, *African-American Concert Dance: The Harlem Renaissance and Beyond* (Urbana and Chicago: University of Illinois Press, 2001), 162.
8. Kasinitz, *Caribbean New York,* 8.
9. Kasinitz, *Caribbean New York,* 53.
10. Hampshire Commencement, 1985, unpublished transcript.
11. Dana Gioia, "An Interview with Cynthia Ozick," *The Writer's Chronicle* 41, no. 6 (May 2009), 10. A remarkable number of women who graduated from Hunter High went on to distinguished careers, including Lucy Davidowitz (1932), Ruby Dee (1939), Hortense Calisher (1928), Florence Howe (1946), and Cynthia Ozick (1946). Ozick remarked, "When I entered Hunter High in 1942 Pearl Primus was already a Hunter legend; the teachers spoke of her proudly, and once she came to perform for us in our weekly assembly" (e-mail communication, July 9, 2009).
12. Lily Mage taught at Hunter College for an extended period beginning in 1930. A Mage Award was created in honor of her devotion to Latin American and Caribbean history. She and Pearl shared cultural events and nature excursions.
13. Interview with Billie Kirpich, July 14, 2004.
14. Interview with James Murray, Schomburg Center, June 19, 1993.
15. Ibid.
16. Pearl Primus, "Personal Statement," *Dance Magazine,* 1968.
17. Quoted in June Levine and Gene Gordon, *Tales of Wo-Chi-Ca: Blacks, Whites and Reds at Camp* (San Rafael, CA: Avon Springs Press, 2002), 8.
18. Levine and Gordon, *Tales of Wo-Chi-Ca,* xi.
19. Wo-Chi-Ca Camp Brochure, 1947, private collection of Renee Cutler Meer.
20. Levine and Gordon, *Tales of Wo-Chi-Ca,* 52.
21. Ibid., 23.

TWO   A Life in Dance

1. William Korff, "History of the New Dance Group from the 1930s to the 1970s," in *The New Dance Group Gala Concert Retrospective* (New York: American Dance Guild Publications, 1993), 3.

2. Korff, *New Dance Group,* 3.

3. MaryAnne Santos, in *Dancing Rebels* (Providence, R.I.: American Dance Legacy Institute, 2002), 8.

4. Margaret Lloyd, *The Borzoi Book of Modern Dance* (1949; rpt. Princeton, N.J.: Dance Horizons, 1987), 269.

5. Ibid.

6. "Black Visions '89, Movements of Ten Dance Masters." Interview with James Briggs Murray. Catalogue for exhibit. Tweed Gallery at City Hall Park, 52 Chambers Street, New York City, 27.

7. http://jwa.org/encyclopedia/article/hadassah-spira-epstein, January 2, 2010.

8. Meeropol is also known for having adopted the two young sons of Ethel and Julius Rosenberg, who were convicted of spying for the Russian government and put to death in the electric chair. Additionally, he was Donald McKayle's high school English teacher.

9. Bonnie Oda Homsey, unpublished material. Courtesy of the author.

10. *Borzoi Book of Modern Dance,* 271. Pearl never taught this work to a woman, as she never believed there was another woman who had the strength to perform it in the way it was intended. Warren Miller was the only dancer to receive this work from Pearl in a reconstruction for the American Dance Festival in 1988.

11. *Lewiston Evening Journal,* Lewiston, Maine, November 5, 1943.

12. Donald McKayle, *Transcending Boundaries: My Life in Dance* (London and New York: Routledge Harwood, 2002), 22.

13. John Martin, *New York Times,* February 21, 1943.

14. A distinguished professor at the University of California at Irvine's Claire Trevor School of the Arts, McKayle currently serves as artistic adviser for the José Limón Dance Company.

15. *Dust Off Your Dreams. The Story of American Youth for Democracy* (New York, 1945), 11.

16. *Dust Off Your Dreams,* 2.

17. Langston Hughes, "Here to Yonder," *Chicago Defender,* July 3, 1943.

18. *Borzoi Book of Modern Dance,* 273.

19. Quotes are from Martin Duberman, *Paul Robeson: A Biography* (New York: The New Press, 1989), 284.

20. John Martin, *New York Times,* June 13, 1943.

21. Richard Dier, "Interview with La Primus," *Afro-American,* October 21, 1944.

22. Dier interview.

23. Unknown newspaper, dated January 1, 1947. Collection of Jacqueline Hairston Hendy.

24. Ralph Lewando, *Pittsburgh Press,* November 14, 1946.
25. J. Dorsey Callaghan, *Detroit Free Press,* January 16, 1947.
26. Unidentified review of North Carolina performance.
27. *Charleston Gazette,* November 18, 1946.
28. *Detroit Times,* undated review. Collection of Jacqueline Hairston Hendy.
29. Unidentified review. Collection of Jacqueline Hairston Hendy.
30. Program Notes, 1945-46 Concert, YMHA.
31. *The Borzoi Book of Modern Dance,* 273.
32. Ibid.
33. *Evening Bulletin,* October 21, 1947.
34. Warren Storey Smith, *Boston Post,* January 16, 1947.
35. Unidentified newspaper, November 4, 1947. Collection of Jacqueline Hairston Hendy.
36. NC Standifer Archive of Oral Interviews, University of Michigan African-American Music Collection, VHS Tape 051-16-4, February 16, 1989.
37. The unpublished FBI file was obtained through the Freedom of Information Act and is in the authors' possession. All quotations are from the file.

THREE   African Transformations

1. Peter Ascoli, *Julius Rosenwald: The Man Who Built Sears, Roebuck and Advanced the Cause of Black Education in the American South* (Bloomington: Indiana University Press, 2006), 395.
2. "Pearl Primus to the Land of Drum Throb and Dance," *Sunday Star,* December 17, 1948.
3. *Observer,* September 28, 1949.
4. *New York Herald Tribune,* January 15, 1950.
5. Walter Sorrell, *Looking Back in Wonder: Diary of a Dance Critic* (New York: Columbia University Press, 1986), 173.
6. Marcia Heard, "African Concert Dance Traditions in American Concert Dance," PhD diss., New York University School of Education, 1999, 183.
7. *Sing Out* 48, no. 2 (Summer 2004).
8. Eric Charry, "Introduction," in *The Beat of My Drum: An Autobiography* (Philadelphia: Temple University Press, 2005), 11. Pearl was distressed by Olatunji's use of her material, but years later, in the mid-1980s, Pearl brought Olatunji to our home in Amherst for a dinner. By then, these distinguished elders were reconciled, each having created a path to their own success.
9. "Introduction," *The Beat of My Drum,* 11 and 12.

10. The authors were part of this class.
11. *New York Times,* May 24, 1948.
12. *Ebony* 16, no. 3 (January 1951), 55–58.

FOUR   Teaching, Traveling, and the FBI

1. *Theater Arts,* December 1950, in the ADF Collection.
2. Review by Norman Holbrook, December 4, 1951. ADF Collection.
3. Quotations are from an unidentified London newspaper, November 24, 1951. ADF Collection.
4. *The Afro-American,* February 9, 1952.
5. Publicity material put forward by Consolidated Concerts Corp. after her tour states that "Dancer Finds No Bias in Israel." "Pearl Primus, the American dancer who has just completed a series of 30 concerts in Israel, declares that she sensed neither racial antagonism or color prejudice in the new nation during her stay there."
6. Edward Eugene Cox, Democratic congressman from Georgia (1925–51).
7. *New York Times,* December 23, 1952. ADF Collection.

FIVE   Trinidad Communities

1. Interview with James Murray in *Black Visions '89: Movements of Ten Dance Masters, exhibit at the Tweed Gallery, New York, January 30–February 24, 1989.* Schomburg Center for Research in Black Culture.
2. Lorna Burdsall, *More Than Just a Footnote: Dancing from Connecticut to Revolutionary Cuba* (Quebec, Canada, 2001). Self published, printed by AGMV, 35.
3. Ibid., 35.
4. Ibid., 35–36.
5. Ibid., 37.
6. Ibid., 37.
7. Ibid., 38–39.
8. Ibid., 39.
9. Ibid., 38–39.
10. Subsequent conversations with Woll led us to believe that throughout Pearl's pregnancy there was some uncertainty about the child's father. This tension may help explain Pearl's references to a breakdown after she gave birth.
11. "The Negro on Broadway, 1955–56: Pits and Peaks in an Active Season," *Phylon* (1940–56) 17, no. 2 (1956): 231–32. Published by Clark Atlanta University.

SIX   Return to Africa

1. *New York Times,* July 31, 1960.
2. Yvonne Daniel, *Rhumba: Dance and Social Change in Contemporary Cuba* (Bloomington: Indiana University Press, 1995).
3. John Martin, *New York Times,* July 31, 1960.
4. Ibid.
5. *Herald Tribune,* July 31, 1960.
6. Ibid.
7. *New York Times,* August 9, 1960
8. Joseph Wershba, *New York Post,* August 9, 1960.
9. Peter Pan, *Daily Times* (Lagos), June 23, 1962.
10. Sam Akua, *Daily Times* (Lagos), June 19, 1962.
11. F. I. Okonkwo, *African Pilot,* July 13, 1962.

SEVEN   The PhD

1. Pearl Primus, "An Anthropological Study of Masks as Teaching Aids in the Enculturation of Mano Children," PhD diss., New York University, 1977, 41.
2. Ibid., iii.
3. Ibid., v.
4. Ibid., ix–xi.
5. Ibid., 2.
6. Ibid., 26.
7. Ibid., 34.
8. Ibid., 83.
9. Ibid., 61–62.
10. Ibid., 65–66.
11. Ibid., 69.
12. Ibid., 73 and 78.
13. Ibid., 106.
14. Ibid., 109.
15. Ibid., 110.
16. Ibid., 115–17.
17. Ibid., 119–20.
18. Ibid., 17.

EIGHT The Turn to Teaching and Return to the Stage

1. Natt Hentoff, "An Inheritance Comes to P. S. 183," United States Department of Health, Education and Welfare, Office of Education, February 1966, 175.
2. Ibid., 177.
3. Ibid., 180–81.
4. Ibid., 181.
5. Ibid., 182.
6. *Pearl Primus' Africa—In Story, Legend, Song and Thought,* Miller-Brody Productions, New York, P 601–3, 1971, 33⅓ rpm (jacket notes).
7. Frances Herridge, *New York Post,* May 23, 1974.
8. Robert J. Pierce, *Village Voice,* May 23, 1974.
9. Anna Kisselgoff, *New York Times,* May 15, 1974.
10. Anna Kisselgoff, *New York Times,* December 15, 1990.
11. Clive Barnes, *New York Post,* May 3, 1979.
12. Don McDonagh, *New York Times,* August 17, 1974.
13. Anna Kisselgoff, *New York Times,* March 24, 1979.
14. Jean Nuchtern, *Soho Weekly News,* March 29, 1979.
15. Jennifer Dunning, *New York Times,* August 17, 1979.

NINE Academic Trials and Triumphs

1. Interview with Zita Allen, *New York Amsterdam News,* June 21, 1980.
2. *Challenger,* December 8, 1982.
3. *Reporter* (SUNY/Buffalo), January 27, 1983.
4. Ibid.
5. *Challenger,* February 2, 1983.
6. *Daily Hampshire Gazette* (Northampton, Massachusetts), February 8, 1951.
7. Letter from Pat Murphy to Murray Schwartz, January 13, 1984.
8. Minutes of Deans and Deputies Meeting, Five Colleges, Inc., June 4, 1987.
9. Letter from Pat Murphy, June 4, 1987.
10. Memo from Pat Murphy, April 15, 1987.
11. Ekwueme Michael Thelwell, Afterword, in Gordon Heath, *Deep Are the Roots: Memoirs of an Expatriate* (Amherst: University of Massachusetts Press, 1992), 173 and 188.
12. Richard Trousdell, Epilogue, in Heath, *Deep Are the Roots,* 172.
13. Steven Ruhl, *Amherst Bulletin,* February 26, 1986.
14. Ibid.

TEN Transmitting the Work

1. Program Brochure.
2. *Capital Spotlight,* October 22, 1992.
3. David Gere, *Los Angeles Times,* April 26, 1994.

ELEVEN Barbados: Return to the Sea

1. Omowale Elson, ed., *The Revelations of the Spiritual Baptists in Barbados* (30th Anniversary) (Barbados: Nation Publishing, 1987), 3.
2. Richard Long, *The Black Tradition in American Dance* (New York: Rizzoli International, 1989).

Works Cited

Akua, Sam. "Primus Dances—To a Degree." *Lagos Daily Times,* June 19, 1962.

Allen, Zita. "An Interview with Pearl Primus." *New York Amsterdam News,* June 21, 1980.

American Dance Festival Archives: Extensive collection of Dr. Pearl Primus's personal and professional correspondence, essays, lectures, articles, personal journals, and national and international newspaper articles and reviews spanning her career, from 1943 to 1994.

"Anacostia Museum Presents Pearl Primus." *Capital Spotlight,* Washington, D.C., October 22, 1992.

Ascoli, Peter M. *Julius Rosenwald: The Man Who Built Sears, Roebuck and Advanced the Cause of Black Education in the American South.* Bloomington, Ind.: Indiana University Press, 2006.

Barber, Beverly. "Pearl Primus, In Search of Her Roots 1943–1970." PhD thesis. Florida State University, 1984.

Barnes, Clive. "Ailey Dance Opens with a Gala." *New York Post,* May 3, 1979.

Boyle, Sheila Tully, and Andrew Bunie. *Paul Robeson. The Years of Promise and Achievement.* Amherst and Boston: University of Massachusetts Press, 2001.

Berryman-Miller, Sherrill. "A Legacy of Pride, The Significance and Contributions of Dr. Pearl E. Primus." *Talking Drums! The Journal of Black Dance* (January 5, 1995): 4–8.

Burdsall, Lorna. *More Than Just a Footnote: Dancing from Connecticut to Revolutionary Cuba.* Quebec: Self-published, 2001.

Callahan, J. Dorsey. "African Dance Culture Gets Serious Portrayal." *Detroit Free Press,* January 16, 1947.

Charry, Eric. "Introduction." In Olatunji, Babatunde, *The Beat of My Drum: An Autobiography.* Philadelphia: Temple University Press, 1–26.

Cherry, Gwendolyn, Ruby Thomas, and Pauline Willis. *Portraits in Color. The Lives of Colorful Negro Women.* New York: Pageant Press, 1962.

Daily Worker, September 28, 1944, quoted in FBI file, p. 50.

Daniel, Yvonne. *Rhumba: Dance and Social Change in Contemporary Cuba.* Bloomington, Ind.: Indiana University Press, 1995.

DeFrantz, Thomas F., ed. *Dancing Many Drums: Excavations in African American Dance.* Madison: University of Wisconsin Press, 2002.

Dier, Richard. "Interview with La Primus: Story of a Great Dancer Who Has Been Graduated from Café Society into Big Time." *Baltimore Afro-American,* October 21, 1944.

Duberman, Martin. *Paul Robeson: A Biography.* New York: The New Press, 1989.

Dunning, Jennifer. "Pearl Primus Dancing Indoors and Out." *New York Times,* August 17, 1979.

Dust Off Your Dreams. The Story of American Youth for Democracy. New York: December 1945.

"Education Coup. Star Studded Black History Month in Buffalo." *Challenger,* February 2, 1983.

Elson, Omowale, ed. *The Revelations of the Spiritual Baptists in Barbados, 30th Anniversary.* Barbados: Nation Publishing Company, Ltd., 1987.

Ennis, Bayard F. "Highly Talented Dance Concert Given by Pearl Primus Group." *Charleston Gazette,* November 18, 1946.

FBI File. Unpublished (obtained via Freedom of Information Act).

"Five Dancers Appear in 6th Series Event." *"Y" Bulletin,* February 12, 1943.

Foulkes, Julia L. *Modern Bodies: Dance and American Modernism from Martha Graham to Alvin Ailey.* Chapel Hill and London: University of North Carolina Press, 2002.

Fulton, William. "Reds Get Cash in Fund Set Up by Guggenheim." *Chicago Daily Tribune,* October 19, 1951.

Friedes, Deborah, Mary Anne Santos Newhall, and Kyle Shepard. *Dancing Rebels.* Providence, R.I.: American Dance Legacy Institute, 2005.

Gere, David. "Dances of Sorrow, Dance of Hope." *Los Angeles Times,* April 24, 1994.

Gioia, Dana. "An Interview with Cynthia Ozick." *Writers Chronicle,* vol. 41 (May 2009): 8–14.

G.L.N. "Pearl Primus Is Wonderful in Her Dance Program Here." *Hampshire Gazette,* February 8, 1951.

Glover, Jean Ruth. "Pearl Primus: Cross-Cultural Pioneer of American Dance." MA thesis. The American University, Washington, D.C., 1989.

Gottschild, Brenda Dixon. *Digging the Africanist Presence in American Performance: Dance and Other Contexts.* Westport, Conn., and London: Praeger, 1996.

———. *The Black Dancing Body: A Geography from Coon to Cool.* New York and England: Palgrave Macmillan, 2003.

Graff, Ellen. *Stepping Left: Dance and Politics in New York City, 1928–1942.* Durham, N.C., and London: Duke University Press, 1997.

Green, Richard C. "(Up)Staging the Primitive: Pearl Primus and 'the Negro Problem' in American Dance." In *Dancing Many Drums: Excavations in African American Dance.* Edited by Thomas F. DeFrantz. Madison: University of Wisconsin Press, 2002, 105–39.

Heard, Marcia. "Asadata Dafora: African Concert Dance: Traditions in American Concert Dance." PhD thesis. School of Education, New York University, 1999.

Heath, Gordon. *Deep Are the Roots. Memoirs of a Black Expatriate.* Amherst, Mass.: University of Massachusetts Press, 1992.

Herridge, Frances. "The Dance Column. Pearl Primus with Alvin Ailey." *New York Post,* May 23, 1974.

Hentoff, Nat. "An Inheritance Comes to P.S. 183." United States Department of Health Education and Welfare, Office of Education. Washington, D.C. 1966. Reprinted in Pearl Primus dissertation.

Holbrook, Norman. *Birmingham Evening Dispatch,* December 4, 1951.

H. T. "Pearl Primus Scores at Music Hall." *Detroit Times,* private collection of Jacqueline Hairston, 1946–47 tour, undated article.

Hughes, Elinor. "The Dance. Jordan Hall Pearl Primus." *Boston Herald,* January 18, 1947.

Hughes, Langston. "On Leaping and Shouting." *Chicago Defender,* July 3, 1943.

Jackson, Naomi M. *Converging Movements: Modern Dance and Jewish Culture at the 92nd Street Y.* Hanover, N.H., and London: Wesleyan University Press, University Press of New England, 2000.

Jefferson, Miles. "The Negro on Broadway, 1955–56: Pits and Peaks in an Active Season." *Phylon* (1940–56) 17, no. 2 (1956): 227–37.

Kasinitz, Philip. *Caribbean New York. Black Immigrants and the Politics of Race.* Ithaca, N.Y.: Cornell University Press, 1992.

Kerr, Adelaide. *Lewiston Evening Journal* (Lewiston, Me.), November 5, 1943.

Kisselgoff, Anna. "African Echoes Unite Two New Ailey Works." *New York Times,* December 15, 1990.

———. "Collins and Primus in Ailey Spotlight." *New York Times,* May 15, 1974.

———. "Pearl Primus Offering Program of Dance Called 'Earth Theater.'" *New York Times,* March 24, 1979.

Koblenz, Eleanor. "Pearl Primus Is Ageless Dancer, Choreographer." *Schenectady Gazette,* December 9, 1983.

Korff, William. "History of the New Dance Group from the 1930s to the 1970s." In *The New Dance Group Gala Concert Retrospective.* New York: American Dance Guild Publications, 1993.

Kunz, Mary. "Primus—Noted Dancer Has Plans for 'Cora P.'" *Reporter,* State University of New York/Buffalo, January 27, 1983.

Levine, June, and Gene Gordon. *Tales of Wo-Chi-Ca. Blacks, Whites and Reds at Camp.* California: Avon Springs Press, 2002.

Lewando, Ralph. "Pearl Primus—Dance Recital Wins Acclaim at Settlement. *Pittsburgh Press,* November 14, 1946.

Lloyd, Margaret. *The Borzoi Book of Modern Dance.* 1949. Reprinted Princeton, N.J.: Dance Horizons, 1987.

Long, Richard. *The Black Tradition in American Dance.* New York: Rizzoli, 1989.

Lourie, Nadia. "Scores Brilliant Success in Israel. Pearl Primus Wins Hearts of Husband's People." *Color,* May 1952. Reprinted with permission of "Israel Speaks."

Manning, Susan. *Modern Dance Negro Dance: Race in Motion.* Minneapolis: University of Minnesota Press, 2004.

Martin, John. *John Martin's Book of the Dance.* New York: Tudor Publishing Company, 1963.

———."New Dance Group in Unique Offering." *New York Times,* May 24, 1948.

———. "The Dance: Allies in the Arts." *New York Times,* June 13, 1943.

———. "The Dance: Five Artists." *New York Times,* February 21, 1943.

———. "The Dance in Liberia Pearl Primus Directs First African Center." *New York Times,* July 31, 1960.

———. "The Dance Laurels—Award #2." *New York Times,* August 1, 1943.

McDonagh, Don. "Primus 'Fanga' Enchants." *New York Times,* August 19, 1974.

———. "Primus 'Wedding' a Pulsating Dance by Ailey Company." *New York Times,* August 17, 1974.

McKayle, Donald. *Transcending Boundaries: My Dancing Life.* London and New York: Routledge Harwood, 2002.

Morris, John. "House Unit to Hear Dulles on Hiss Tie." *New York Times,* December 24, 1952.

Murray, James Briggs. "Interview with Pearl Primus." Schomburg Center for Research in Black Culture, New York Public Library, June 19, 1993.

———. Interview with Pearl Primus. *Black Visions '89, Movements of Ten Dance Masters.* Catalogue for Exhibit. Tweed Gallery at City Hall Park, 52 Chambers Street, New York, N.Y.

Myers, Gerald E., ed. *African American Genius in Modern Dance.* Durham, N.C.: American Dance Festival, 1993.

———. *The Black Tradition in American Modern Dance.* Durham, N.C.: American Dance Festival, 1993.

NC Standifer Archive of Oral Interviews, University of Michigan African-American Music Collection, VHS Tape 051-16-4. February 16, 1989.

"The New Dance Group Gala Concert." Videotape. American Dance Guild, New York, 1993.

Nuchtern, Jean. "Back to Africa." *Soho Weekly News,* March 29, 1979.

Okonkwo, F. I. "This Is Unfair to Pearl Primus." *African Pilot,* July 10, 1962.

Olatunji, Babatunde, and Robert Atkinson. *The Beat of My Drum: An Autobiography.* Philadelphia, Pa.: Temple University Press, 2005.

Pan, Peter. "Sham! Shame." *Lagos Daily Times,* June 23, 1962.

Patrick, K. C., and Gary Parks, eds. "Reviews of the Century." *Dance Magazine,* April 1999.

"Pearl Primus Foremost Dancer to Unveil New Exciting Work Based on Year Long Study of African Peoples." *Ebony,* January 1951.

"Pearl Primus to the Land of Drum Throb and Dance." *Sunday Star,* December 17, 1948.

Perpener, John O., III. *African-American Concert Dance: The Harlem Renaissance and Beyond.* Urbana and Chicago: University of Illinois Press, 2001.

Pierce, Robert. "Changing Shoes and Just Changing." *Village Voice,* May 23, 1974.

Potts, Monica. "Ernest Critchlow, 91, Lyrical Painter." *New York Times,* November 14, 2005.

Primus, Pearl. "AFRICA—In Story—Legend—Song—and Thought." Miller-Brody Productions, New York, 1971.

———. "Africa Dances." *Dance Observer* 16, no. 9 (November 1949).

———. "Africa—Forward." Pearl Primus Collection, America Dance Festival Archives, August 11, 1954.

———. "African Dance." *PRESENCE AFRICAINE Africa Seen by American Negro Scholars.* American Society of African Culture, December 1963.

———. "African Dance." In *African Dance: An Artistic, Historical and Philosophical Inquiry.* Edited by Kariamu Welsh Asante. Trenton: Africa World Press, Inc., 1996.

———. *An Anthropological Study of Masks as Teaching Aids in the Enculturation of Mano Children.* PhD thesis. New York University School of Education, Health, Nursing, and the Arts Professions, 1978.

———. Commencement Address. Hampshire College, Amherst, Mass., 1985.

———. "Cultural Bridges." Marian Chace Annual Lecture. *American Journal of Dance Therapy* 15, no. 1 (1993).

———. "Earth Theatre: The Voice of the Earth." *Theater Arts Journal,* December 1950.

———. "In Africa." *Vogue,* October 15, 1950.

———. "Life Crises: Dance from Birth to Death." In *A Collection of Early Writings: Toward a Body of Knowledge.* American Dance Therapy Association, vol. 1, 1989.

———. "Living Dance of Africa: Tom-toms, Jungle Rhythms and the Advanced Art of a 'Primitive' People. *Dance Magazine,* June 1946.

———. "Statement." *Dance Magazine,* 1968.

Ruhl, Steve. "Celebrating 'the Wordless Joy of Freedom.'" *Amherst Bulletin,* February 26, 1986.

Sensenderfer, R. E. P. "Living Theater." *Philadelphia Evening Bulletin,* October 21, 1947.

Simmons, Michele. "Experiencing and Performing the Choreography of Mna Pearl Primus—'Strange Fruit.'" *Talking Drums! The Journal of Black Dance,* vol. 5 (1995): 8–10.

Smith, Warren Storey. *Boston Post,* January 16, 1947.

Sorrell, Walter. *Looking Back in Wonder: Diary of a Dance Critic.* New York: Columbia University Press, 1986.

"Star Studded Black History Month in Buffalo." *Challenger,* February 2, 1983.

Terry, Walter. "OMOWALE, Meaning 'Child Has Returned Home.'" Consolidated Concerts Corp., January 15, 1950. Courtesy of Pearl Primus. Authors' private collection.

———. "The Dance World: Liberia's New Thing Alive." *New York Herald Tribune,* July 31, 1960.

———. *New York Herald Tribune,* January 20, 1945.

Watts, Phyllis. "The Dance. Jordan Hall Pearl Primus." *Boston Globe,* January 18, 1947.

Wenig, Adele R. *Pearl Primus: An Annotated Bibliography of Sources from 1943–1975.* Oakland: Wenadance Unlimited, 1983.

Wershba, Joseph. "The Gift of Healing Is Not Always a Medical Matter." *New York Post,* August 9, 1960.

Wilson, Greg Sule. "The Story of Fanga." In *Sing Out!* Bethlehem, Pa., January 26, 2006. Copy courtesy of the author.

"Wo-Chi-Ca Camp Brochure." 1947. Private collection of Renee Cutler Meer.

Wright, Patricia. "The Prime of Miss Pearl Primus." *Contact, A Publication of the University of Massachusetts at Amherst,* vol. 10 (1985): 13–16.

Index

Ferrell, Larry, 194, 274, 275
fertility rites, 37
Fields, Lorraine, 235
Film Institute, New York City, 60
Fink, Richard, 213
Finland, 109
Fire Next Time, The (Baldwin), 207
First African Dance Theater, 142, 143
First African Performing Arts Center, 144
First International Conference of Negro
    Artists and Writers, Rome, 143
First National Conference of Negro Artists
    and Writers, 268–69
First Negro Freedom Rally, 39, 40
"First Shine" New Dance Group (NDG)
    program, 253
Fishman, Sylvia, 178
Fisk University, 69, 71–72
Fitzgerald, Ella, 254
Five Colleges, Amherst, Massachusetts,
    182, 201–2, 203, 204–5, 206, 207–9, 216–
    17, 228, 241, 277–78; concert *(1984)*, 219;
    Dance Department, 10, 205, 207, 212,
    240–42; Primus's teaching post at, 218,
    236, 277
"Five Heroines of Afro-American Heri-
    tage," 279
Flanagan, Hallie, 33
Flouton, Edna, 16
folk music, 97
"Folksay" (Maslow), 53
folk songs, 52
Folkways African Rhythm records, 27
Fonaroff, Nina, 261
Foote, Horton, 254
Ford Foundation, 176–77, 221, 278
Forrest, Alma, 257
Fort, Syvilla, 57
France, 137, 266, 267
Franklin, Joe, 104
Frederiksen, Lynn, 88, 91, 219

Fredricks, Padjet, 262
"Free to Dance" film, 223
French, LaVerne, 259
Friedes, Deborah, 29
"Fugule" dance by Dafora, 88
Fulton, William, 108

Garry, Dianne, 194, 274–75, 276
Geiskopf, Betty Jane, 259
Gentry, Eve, 253
Gere, David, 233–34
Ghana (Gold Coast), 11, 72, 142, 143, 149,
    213, 218, 270
Ghana National Cultural Society, 142
Gilfond, Edythe, 256
Gilkes, Louise, 137
Gio people of Liberia, 161, 262
Gluck, Rena, 26
Gola people of Liberia, 161
Gold, Milton, 178
Gold Coast Students Cultural Association,
    267
Gone with the Wind (Mitchell), 18–19
Goodfellow, Margaret, 246–47
Gordon, Gene, 24
Gow, James, 2
Graham, Martha, 3, 26, 30, 34, 43, 44, 45,
    57, 106, 107, 108, 125, 138, 171, 235, 253,
    261; "Lamentation" dance, 230; tech-
    nique, 34. *See also* Martha Graham
    Company/School
Great Depression, 29
Greaves, William, 42
Grebo people of Liberia, 161
Greenberg, Joseph, 259
Greenberg, Lorraine, 263
Greenidge, Jenne, 261
Griffith, Dr. Ezra, 243
griot (African storyteller), 3, 7, 78, 183, 215,
    225, 226
Guggenheim Fellowship, 81

Lincoln University, Pennsylvania, 274
Linton, Ralph, 258
Little Caribe Theatre, 119, 127, 266
Lloyd, Margaret, 12, 36, 44, 73, 263
Locke, Dr. Alain, 27
London, 105
London Festival Ballet, 138
Long, Richard, 8, 53
Los Angeles County Museum of Art, 281
Los Angeles Times, 233-34
Louis, Joe, 27
Lourie, Nadia, 106
Lucky Millinder's Orchestra, 37, 254, 256
Lunick, Olga, 259

Mabry, Iris, 254, 261
Madison Square Garden, 41, 65, 67, 256
Mage, Lily, 17, 18
Malament, Sarah, 45, 256
Mali, 270
Manings, Muriel, 31, 53
Mann, Herbie, 149
Mann, Lili, 258
Manning, Samuel, 53
Manning St. Charles, Deborah, 188
Mano people of Liberia, 157, 158, 161-62, 166, 167, 168, 262, 274
Manswell, Michael, 236, 243-44
Maples Dunn, Mary, 208
Marchant, Claude, 259
Marchant, Paul, 53, 56
Martha Graham Company/School, 26, 107
Martin, John, 38, 42, 46, 50, 93, 146-47, 149, 254, 263, 270
Marxist theory, 29
masks, 125, 157, 158, 161, 167-68, 174, 186, 195, 267, 274, 276; African, 77; ancestral, 162-63; in dances, 162, 163, 164; for education, 168; psychological, 168; spirit, 163

Maslow, Sophie, 25, 30, 34, 53, 253, 258, 261
Matija Gubec Choral Society, 256
Mayher, John S., 158, 160
Mayo, Margo, 253
McBurnie, Beryl (La Belle Rosette), 3, 31, 34, 35, 52, 116, 118, 119-20, 127, 133, 253, 254, 266
McBurnie-Artman, Frieda, 118
McCarthy, Joseph, 64, 87
McCauley, David, 275
McDaniels, Romenia, 261
McDonagh, Don, 190
McGriff, Leslie, 275
McGuiness, Joyce, 158
McKayle, Donald, 8, 9, 15, 38-39, 221, 230, 235
McLeod Bethune, Dr. Mary, 27
Mead, Margaret, 64, 159, 258
Meer, Renee Cutler. *See* Cutler Meer, Renee
Meeropol, Abel, 35
Mende people of Sierra Leone, 161
Mensah, Kofi, 142
Meringue dance, 254
Metropolitan Opera House, 47
Mianns, Moses, 89, 90, 91, 96, 105, 263, 264; as drummer for Primus, 263, 265; as singer, 265
Middlebury College, 59
Miller, Claire, 177
Miller, Frieda, 270
Miller, Ivor, 219-20
Miller, Warren P. II, 222, 223, 278
Miller, William, 259
Miller-Brody Productions, 177
Mills, Charles, 97
Mills, George, 102, 264, 265
Mister Johnson play, 136-37, 268
Mitchell, Lofton, 170, 200
Mohawk Indians, 161
Monrovia, Liberia, 143, 145, 146-47, 148

Roosevelt, Eleanor, 31, 255
Rosenthal, Jane, 257
Rosenwald, Julius, 69
Rosenwald Fund, 108, 109, 156
Ross, John, 239
Ross, Sandra, 275
Rossberg, Robert, 202
Rowe, Patricia, 159, 245, 259
Roxie Theater, 42
Royal Dutch Opera, 138
Rubin, Mark, 275
Rubin Academy of Music and Dance
    (Israel), 107
"Rush Hour" dance (Robert Battle), 94
Rwanda, 190

Salk, Dr. Jonas, 215
Sanchez, Sonia, 203
Sande female cult, Africa, 76
Sande Society, 167
Santamaria, Mongo, 32
Saunders, Garry, 105–6
Savage, Augusta, 25
Savo, Jimmy, 45
Schurman, Nona, 253, 254
Schwartz, Murray, 201–2, 203, 205, 240–
    42
Schwartz, Peggy, 222, 244, 245, 246
"Scorpio," 262
Scott, Hazel, 45, 254
Scriabin, Alexander, 34, 43
sea imagery, 20, 21
Sears, William, 258
Seebree, Charles, 260, 262
Seeger, Pete, 38, 52
Segal, Edith, 67, 125
Selassie, Haile, 143, 269
Senechal, Marjorie, 205, 206, 207, 212–13,
    241, 242
Senegal, 79, 149, 270
Senior, Segney, 263

Senufo people of the Ivory Coast, 161
Shahn, Ben, 25
Shalala, Donna, 8, 177, 179
"Shango" (Dunham), 57
Shango, god of thunder, 224, 225–26, 261
Shango dance, 121, 122, 123, 126, 132, 254;
    in Africa, 118, 119; in Trinidad, 9
Shango deity, 261
Shango Festival, 123
Shango ritual, 266
Shapiro, Harry, 259
Sharett, Moshe, 108
Sharett, Rina, 102, 108, 135, 138
Sharrer, Honore, 67
Shawn, Ted, 43
Shepherd, Kyle, 29
Sherer, Stan, 207, 212–13, 238, 242–43
Sherrod, Dr. Elgie Gaynell, 216
Shipman, George, 97, 102, 263
Shorty, Hassard, 259
shouters, 40
"Shouters," 239
shout songs, 144, 262
Show Boat, 48, 113, 119, 259, 261
Shubert Theater, Boston, 54
Sierra Leone, 88, 218, 260, 270, 277
"Signs of the Zodiac," 262
Silla, Tante, 129, 131
Simmons, Michelle, 230–35, 281
Simmons, Stanley, 259
Simms, Harry, 29
Simone, Nina, 125
Sinatra, Frank, 27
slavery, 96, 97, 110, 162, 191, 192, 257, 258,
    264
Smit, Leo, 34
Smith, Art, 265
Smith, Ferdinand, 27
Smith, Gloria, 263
Smith, Marion, 259
Smith, Osborne, 265

Trotman, Sheron, 228–29, 230, 239, 280
Trousdell, Richard, 210, 211
Trowbridge, Charlotte, 255, 260
Trupia, Joe, 173–74
Tubman, William, president of Liberia, 75,
    92, 106, 138, 142, 262–63, 266, 267–68
Turney, Matt, 58, 261
Tuskegee University, 67
Twenty-fourth Street studio, 103

United Nations, 39
University of California, Irvine, 281
University of Chicago, 48
University of Illinois, 58
University of Massachusetts Amherst, 203,
    204, 205, 206, 209, 241, 242, 245, 277,
    278
University of Michigan, 59
University of Wisconsin, 59
University Settlement House, 19
Uno, Roberta, 209–13, 278
Urban Bush Women, 10, 84
USO shows, 67, 257

Vai people of Liberia, 161, 262
Valentine, Andree, 194, 275, 276
Van Scott, Glory, 7, 170–71
vaudeville, 53, 54
Vega, Marta, 280
Vendien, Lynn, 213
"Venture into the Soul of a People"
    program, 149–50, 155, 270
Verlaine, Paul, 16
Village Voice, 185
Vislocky, Dorothy, 177–78
Vogue, 104
von Grona, Eugene, 3
voodoo beliefs, 12, 32, 254; rituals, 255

Wagley, Charles, 259
Waithe, Mary, 6, 7, 14, 32, 90, 100, 102, 137,

    139, 192–95, 198, 236–37, 238, 275, 276;
    dances in "The Wedding," 275; restages
    "The Wedding," 277, 281
"Walking with Pearl" dance cycle, 10
Walkov Newman, Sheila, 25–26
"Waltz Boogie," 261
Washington, Donald, 186–87, 192, 196,
    197–99, 245–46
Waters, Sylvia, 188
Watson, Dawn Marie, 223
Watson, Elbert, 193, 275
Watts, Phyllis, 51
Watusi people of Rwanda, 3, 49, 81, 97, 98,
    100, 128, 167, 189; dances of, 187, 198
Weavers, The, 53
Weber, William, 259
"Wedding, The," dance of Judith Jamison,
    184, 185
Weidman, Charles, 253, 258
Weiner, Ann, 34
Welsh, Dr. Raymond, 178
Weltfish, Gener, 259
Wender, Jill, 275
Wershba, Joseph, 148, 149
Wessel, Henry, 259
West Africa, 4, 6, 75, 77, 78, 149–50
West Congo, 35
West Indies, 2, 5, 13–14, 35, 116, 133, 162,
    236, 239, 245; communities of emigrants
    in New York City, 15; cultures, 253–54;
    dance forms, 31; emigration from, 12–13;
    Primus's study in, 266
Weston, M. Moran, 39–40
Wexler, Jacqueline, 178, 272
Wheatley, Phyllis, 273
White, Charles, 25, 26
White, Josh, 34, 36, 40, 45, 254, 258
White, Lillias, 276
Whitman, Walt, 45
Wicker, Tom, 205
Wideman, John Edgar, 204